UNDERSTANDING

EARLY CHILDHOOD EDUCATION & CARE

IN AUSTRALIA

A note about the cover artwork

This screen-printing was done by three- to four-year-old children from Bangalow Community Children's Centre:

'Our *Peter and the Wolf* fabric screen-print wall-hanging was initiated by the children's interest in the orchestral piece *Peter and the Wolf* by Sergei Prokofiev. Educators narrated the story and the children soon learned to decipher what was happening in the musical piece by recognising changes in tempo, volume, as well as identifying the instrument played. The children's interest grew and became a regular part of our day as an accompaniment to the children's free play that allowed for dramatization of the story, as imaginative play and in their pre-literacy interpretation of the story through their artworks.

The wall-hanging is a collection of all the Bangalow Community Children's Centre Middle Room (three- to four-year-olds) children's drawings of the characters in this musical story. Their individual drawings were cut out and screen-printed onto calico cushions as well as fabric squares (the latter of which became the final product). A special thanks goes to Ms Susan Byrne (Bachelor of Early Childhood Education) for all of her time and work in the assembly and displaying of the artworks.'

UNDERSTANDING EARLY CHILDHOOD EDUCATION & CARE IN AUSTRALIA

Practices and Perspectives

Edited by:
Joanne Ailwood
Wendy Boyd
Maryanne Theobald

LONDON AND NEW YORK

First published 2016 by Allen & Unwin

Published 2020 by Routledge
2 Park Square, Milton Park, Abingdon, Oxon OX14 4RN
605 Third Avenue, New York, NY 10017

First issued in hardback 2021

Copyright © Joanne Ailwood, Wendy Boyd and Maryanne Theobald 2016

Routledge is an imprint of the Taylor & Francis Group, an informa business

All rights reserved. No part of this book may be reprinted or reproduced or utilised
in any form or by any electronic, mechanical, or other means, now known or
hereafter invented, including photocopying and recording, or in any information
storage or retrieval system, without permission in writing from the publishers.

Notice:
Product or corporate names may be trademarks or registered trademarks, and are
used only for identification and explanation without intent to infringe.

Publisher's Note
The publisher has gone to great lengths to ensure the quality of this reprint but points
out that some imperfections in the original copies may be apparent.

Cataloguing-in-Publication details are available from the National Library of Australia
www.trove.nla.gov.au

Internal design by Julia Eim
Index by Puddingburn
Set in 11/15 pt Minion by Post Pre-press Group, Australia

ISBN 13: 978-0-367-72000-1 (hbk)
ISBN 13: 978-1-74331-860-7 (pbk)

Contents

List of tables and figures	vi
Contributors	ix
Introduction	1

Part 1: Historical, theoretical and philosophical perspectives of ECEC

1 The development of early childhood education and care in
Australia *Sandie Wong and Frances Press* — 13

2 Historical perspectives on children and childhood
Joanne Ailwood — 34

3 Theoretical perspectives on early childhood *Mindy Blaise* — 51

4 Practical approaches and philosophies in early childhood
education and care *Linda Henderson and Susan Edwards* — 72

Part 2: Perspectives and practices in ECEC policy and provision

5 Key ideas, research and challenges in early childhood education
and care *Maryanne Theobald and Gillian Busch* — 95

6 Contexts, policy and frameworks of early childhood education
and care *Megan Gibson* — 121

7 Cultural safety for Indigenous children in early childhood
education and care *Margot Ford* — 141

8 Diversity and inclusion in early childhood education and care
Melinda G. Miller — 164

9 Ethical responsibilities in early childhood education and care
Ann Farrell — 187

Part 3: Perspectives and practices in teaching and leadership

10 Planning for children's learning: curriculum, pedagogy
and assessment *Sandra Cheeseman* — 211

11 Relationships between staff, children and families
Karen Hawkins — 231

12 Understanding babies: promoting young children's learning and
development *Wendy Boyd* — 252

13 Flexible and sustainable learning environments
 Joy Goodfellow 271
14 Professionalism for early childhood educators
 Louise Mary Thomas 294

Acknowledgements 312
Index 313

List of tables and figures

Tables

1.1	Passing of Education/Instruction Acts and establishment of early childhood organisations in Australia	17
6.1	Australian ECEC contexts at a glance	124
6.2	Layers of policy	132
6.3	ECEC contexts and associated curricula, regulatory authorities and policies	133
7.1	The percentage point difference between Indigenous and non-Indigenous students in reading and numeracy in New South Wales and the Northern Territory between 2009 and 2014	148
8.1	Shifts in understandings of diversity and inclusion in Australia	167
9.1	A sample of Codes of Ethics related to professional practice in ECEC	192
10.1	Components of the Early Years Learning Framework and My Time, Our Place Framework	217
10.2	Components of the Australian Curriculum: foundation to Year 10	218

Figures

1.1	Woolloomooloo Day Nursery, 1906	16
1.2	Children at Lady Gowrie Child Centre, South Australia, c. 1940–50	18
5.1	Acting as members of a community: boys comfort a peer	103
5.2	A child's representation of the balls moving	105
5.3	A child's representation of the ball run	106
7.1	Population structure (a) by age in 2011 between Aboriginal and Torres Strait Islander and non-Indigenous people	143
7.2	Reading at Years 3, 5 and 9 in New South Wales, Victoria, Western Australia and the Northern Territory and the national average for Indigenous and non-Indigenous students	147

List of tables and figures

7.3	Eight Aboriginal Ways of Learning	154
13.1	A newly created shaded outdoor area at Beranga that uses natural timbers and soft furnishings to create a quiet space to be shared by adults and children	277
13.2	A shaded outdoor area with designated spaces that offer opportunities for particular kinds of activities	278
13.3	Children exploring the textures and natural elements within a mud patch	281
13.4	Children connecting with their community environment by viewing through windows in a fence that screens the noise of passing trains from the play area	284

Contributors

Joanne Ailwood is Senior Lecturer in Early Childhood Education and Care at the University of Newcastle. Joanne's research interests have analysed relationships of power in early childhood education, including how relationships are produced and managed in early years settings—between children and children, staff and children and parents and staff. She has also undertaken policy analysis research on preschool education and on the historical place of women/mothers in early childhood education. Overall Joanne is interested in questions about relationships of power and of care, and how women and children constitute their daily lives and relationships as mothers, early childhood practitioners and children in early years settings.

Mindy Blaise is Professor of Early Childhood Education at Victoria University, Melbourne, and brings postfoundational perspectives (feminism, posthumanism, postcolonialism, new materialism, etc.) to her work. She is a founding member and principal researcher of the Common Worlds Childhood Research Collective (www.commonworlds.net), founding member of the underground and subversive feminist academic collective, *Femdemics*, and part of the Revolutionary Planning Group. Some of her recent publications include *The Sage Handbook of Play and Learning in Early Childhood* (co-edited with Liz Brooker and Susan Edwards) and *Teaching in the Early Years Classroom* (with Joce Nuttall). Mindy is author of *Uncovering Gender Discourses in an Early Childhood Classroom*, based on an ethnography that brings queer theory and gender studies to early childhood education.

Contributors

Wendy Boyd is Senior Lecturer in Early Childhood Education and Care at Southern Cross University in a teaching and research position. Prior to entering academia Wendy had 25 years early childhood education experience working with children, aged from birth to five years, their families and other key stakeholders. She has a strong understanding of major workforce issues and the needs of early childhood students in their university programs. Her research focuses on the provision of quality early childhood education, particularly the qualities of early childhood teachers and their work.

Gillian Busch is Senior Lecturer in Education at Central Queensland University. Her research interests include children's talk-in-interaction in disputes and family mealtimes, and children's interactions with grandparents using Skype or FaceTime. Gillian has methodological expertise in qualitative approaches, including ethnomethodology and conversation analysis. Gillian's PhD (The Social Orders of Family Mealtime) was awarded the Early Childhood Australia Doctoral Thesis Award (2012). Gillian is currently involved in a research project examining young children and celebrations.

Sandra Cheeseman is a Lecturer in Curriculum and Professional Experience at the Institute of Early Childhood, Macquarie University. She brings to this role extensive experience as an early childhood teacher, director and senior manager. Sandra was a member of the consortium that developed Belonging, Being and Becoming: The Early Years Learning Framework (EYLF) for Australia and has since worked as a consultant on a number of related research and professional projects, including the Department of Education, Employment and Workplace Relations (DEEWR) Professional Learning Projects (PLPs) supporting the introduction of both the EYLF and National Quality Standard (NQS) to the sector. Currently undertaking doctoral studies, Sandra is investigating the notion of curriculum as it relates to the lives and experiences of children under two years.

Susan Edwards is Associate Professor in the Faculty of Education and Arts at Australian Catholic University. Susan is a member of the Early Childhood Futures research program, which focuses on researching issues associated with professional learning and engagement in early childhood education, including young children's play, inter-agency work, digital technologies and digital media and sustainability. Susan has recently completed work as a lead Chief Investigator on an Australian Research Council Discovery Grant (2009–12) titled 'Examining play-based approaches to teaching and learning in early childhood education and care'. She is currently working as a Chief Investigator on two new Australian Research Council Discovery Grants investigating the role of play-based pedagogies in the provision of obesity and sustainability education in early childhood, and in the use of digital technologies in the early years.

Ann Farrell is Professor of Early Childhood and Head of the School of Early Childhood, Queensland University of Technology. Earning a PhD from the University of Queensland in 2006, she received an Honorary Doctorate from Gothenburg University (Sweden) in 2012. Her research expertise is in cross-jurisdictional childhood studies, research ethics, and young children's rights to participation and protection. She served in the *Review of Ethical Practice in Global Pediatric Trials*, Eunice Kennedy Shriver National Institute of Child Health, Office of Pediatric Therapeutics, United States Food and Drug Administration, Washington DC (2009). Ann is an Australian Research Council (ARC) International Reader (IntReader) assessing ARC grants and collaborative bids between the ARC and the United Kingdom's Economic and Social Research Council; and External Assessor for Australia's National Health and Medical Research Council, the Social Sciences and Humanities Research Council of Canada and the National Research Foundation, Reviews and Evaluation Directorate, South Africa.

Margot Ford is Senior Lecturer in the School of Education at the University of Newcastle. Margot has worked in the field of sociology and education for more than 25 years, receiving a doctorate in sociology, which was published in 2009 as *In Your Face: A case study in post multicultural Australia* by Charles Darwin University Press. The focus of this book is the social dynamics of inclusion and exclusion, examining race and racism in the highly culturally diverse city of Darwin, Northern Territory. Prior to coming to the University of Newcastle, Margot worked as a lecturer in teacher education at Charles Darwin University, and before that at Bachelor Institute of Indigenous Tertiary Education. Margot has published in the areas of Indigenous education, classroom management and early childhood education. More recently she has become interested in national testing regimes and what they tell us about inequality of educational achievement.

Megan Gibson is a Lecturer in the School of Early Childhood, Faculty of Education at Queensland University of Technology. Megan's award-winning doctoral research examined early childhood teachers' professional identities. Her research focus includes professional identities, early childhood workforce, pre-service teacher education, leadership, policy and sustainability. Megan has responsibility for pre-service teacher units on leadership and management, health and wellbeing and the professional work of early childhood teachers, and has coordinated child care field studies with a focus on children birth to three years. Prior to taking up the position of Lecturer, her experience as an early childhood educator included work across a range of contexts, including child care, kindergarten/preschool and lower primary school. Most notably, Megan was Director of an internationally recognised child care centre, and led the centre's evolution in areas of sustainability, the arts and pedagogy.

Joy Goodfellow is a researcher, teacher educator and early childhood practitioner who has many years experience in the early childhood field. Her particular interests are in educators' practical professional knowledge and their role in enhancing the development of very young children. Joy was a member of the team that developed the EYLF. Her recent research has focused on gaining an understanding of the strategies infants and toddlers use when interacting within their social and physical environments.

Karen Hawkins is Lecturer in Early Childhood Education at Southern Cross University (Gold Coast campus). Her teaching interests include play and pedagogies in the early years; early childhood matters; leadership and advocacy in early childhood education; and children, families and communities. Karen's PhD thesis examined strategies to promote and support teaching for social justice in prior-to-school settings. Karen also holds a Graduate Diploma in Special Needs Education and a Masters of Education. She has held various positions, including preschool director, special needs coordinator, and university lecturer. Karen's research interests gravitate towards early childhood education, relationship building in early childhood settings, learning through play, and teaching for social justice. She has a deep respect for and interest in collaborative research methods as socially just modes of inquiry that uphold and value participant knowledge, history and expertise, particularly participatory action research.

Linda Henderson is Senior Lecturer in Early Childhood Education at Monash University. Her teaching focuses on curriculum and pedagogical leadership across both undergraduate and post-graduate courses. Linda's research interests are focused on the professional learning of early childhood teachers, including the nexus between institutional cultures and the work of early childhood teachers, the impact of reform measures on both teachers and pre-service teachers, and policy implementation by early childhood teachers. She has completed research work with Independent Schools, Victoria examining pedagogical leadership in the early years.

Melinda Miller is Lecturer in the School of Early Childhood at Queensland University of Technology. Her teaching and research interests include cultural studies, diversity and inclusion. Melinda's doctoral research focused on embedding Aboriginal and Torres Strait Islander perspectives in non-Indigenous early years contexts. The findings of her research contribute knowledge about anti-racist practices and a need to recognise how racialising practices are always present in embedding processes, even when educators' efforts are seen to be inclusive and high quality. Melinda is a regular facilitator of long-term action research projects with educators working in family day care, long day care, kindergarten, and outside school hours care, on topics including culture and diversity, education for sustainability, play and child development.

Frances Press is Associate Professor in Early Childhood Education at Charles Sturt University. She teaches and researches in early childhood education and has a long-standing interest in early childhood policy frameworks and their impacts upon practices and pedagogy. She is especially interested in how government policy can better support high-quality early childhood programs for all children and families. She is also a lover of history. In 2013, Frances co-authored, with Dr Sandie Wong, a short history of Early Childhood Australia, a seminal Australian early childhood advocacy body.

Contributors

Maryanne Theobald is Senior Lecturer in the School of Early Childhood at Queensland University of Technology. Her research interests include children's participation in the early years, and children's talk-in-interaction in disputes and friendships in the home, school and playground, with digital technologies and in multilingual contexts. Maryanne's methodological expertise is in qualitative approaches, including ethnomethodology and conversation analysis, and participatory research using video-stimulated interactions. Maryanne is on the editorial board of *Research on Children and Social Interaction* (RoSCI), Equinox. With over 25 years in early childhood education, Maryanne has experience teaching early years in Queensland preschools and facilitating professional development for educators.

Louise Mary Thomas is Senior Lecturer in the Faculty of Education and Arts at Australian Catholic University, where she is Director, Accreditation, and a member of the Faculty of Education and Arts Research Institute, Learning Sciences Institute Australia. She has previously held the positions of National Director of Early Childhood Education, Deputy Head (Learning and Teaching) and Course/Program Coordinator for BEd (EC&P) on the Brisbane campus. Her research focuses on professional identity constructions, ethics, intentional teaching and educational leadership in early childhood education and care. Louise has involvement in national and international research and publication projects. She has sole publications and has jointly published with both Australian and international colleagues. Louise has over 30 years experience working in the early childhood sector. She has worked as an early childhood teacher, consultant, professional development coordinator, senior policy advisor and as an academic and researcher.

Sandie Wong is Senior Lecturer in the School of Education at Charles Sturt University. Sandie's PhD examined the early history of early childhood education and care in New South Wales and she has an ongoing interest in exploring contemporary issues through historical methods. In 2013, she co-authored, with Associate Professor Frances Press, a short history of Early Childhood Australia (ECA), a seminal Australian early childhood advocacy body.

Introduction

Joanne Ailwood, Wendy Boyd and Maryanne Theobald

Australian perspectives and practices within early childhood education and care (ECEC) are underpinned by understandings of children, especially how they learn, their emotional and physical needs and their connectedness to family and their communities. There is strong international research evidence supporting the value of providing high-quality and accessible ECEC, and this evidence base continues to grow. Drawing on international and Australian research, this book provides an introduction to this complex and multifaceted field.

Because of the tight links between the provision of child care, women's paid work and the economy, ECEC is something of a political hot potato in Australia. In recent years the provision of ECEC has become a key policy platform for Australian governments. In 2009 the Coalition of Australian Governments (COAG) signed an historic agreement for a National Quality Agenda for the early years. This policy focus resulted in significant reform, including the development of the first Australian curriculum framework for children birth to five years, Belonging, Being and Becoming: The Early Years Learning Framework (EYLF) for Australia (Department of Education, Employment and Workplace Relations [DEEWR], 2009), the introduction of a new National Quality Framework (NQF), and the training of the early childhood workforce. Fundamental to this new policy platform was the combination of increased government funding for universal access to fifteen hours of preschool for all children in the year prior to commencing primary school, delivered by a university trained early childhood teacher; and the requirement that ECEC settings employ qualified staff.

Introduction

Federal governments have diverse views towards the governance of ECEC. With the change of federal government in 2013 came changes to the way the National Quality Agenda was delivered. Then in February 2015 ECEC was moved into the Social Services portfolio. This approach tends to emphasise the 'care' aspects of ECEC, sidelining the educational aspects. Discussions and debates regarding 'education' and/or 'care' aspects of ECEC are ongoing in Australia. With a change of prime minister in September 2015, and consequent ministry changes, ECEC was moved into the Education portfolio. There is little agreement in Australian society about what early childhood education is 'for', and what the priorities should be. The pendulum of debate tends to swing back and forth between attention to children's early education and an emphasis on the needs of adults, especially mothers returning to paid work. A key question that should be addressed here is why, politically, it seems to focus on one or the other; why should not all children and families be well provided for? Early in 2015 the CEO of Early Childhood Australia (ECA), Samantha Page, acknowledged that parents have the greatest impact upon their child's learning and development, suggesting that support for families also indirectly supports children's wellbeing. However, she goes on to note that it is essential to continue to ensure that there is a strong emphasis on quality education programs delivered by qualified staff (ECA, 2015).

The ways in which children are capable and competent have increasingly been recognised in early childhood policy, research and education. This book seeks to show how educators' work attends to the competence of young children through participatory agendas, such as including children in leading their own learning. Approaches to teaching and learning acknowledging the capacities and competency of children is internationally recognised through the United Nations (UN) Convention on the Rights of the Child (UN, 1989). In Australia, it is recognised in the EYLF (DEEWR, 2009).

Early childhood education and care is generally accepted as encompassing the ages birth to eight years. This means that our work as early childhood educators extends into the first years of compulsory schooling. This adds another layer of complexity to our field. Not only are we engaging in issues of prior-to-school education and care for children, we are also engaging in issues of formal, compulsory schooling. This complexity is explored throughout the book, by authors engaged across the birth to eight years age span.

OVERVIEW OF THE BOOK

This book introduces readers to some of the historical and theoretical background for the provision of ECEC in Australia across the birth to eight years age span. It also covers a range of issues, concepts and debates current in Australian ECEC. While much of the research and many of the debates and issues have international scope, the ways they are taken up in the Australian context reflect the specific characteristics of Australia's historical, social and political environment. The chapters in this book reflect upon international research and debates as they play out in the Australian context. Reflecting the complexity in the field, the chapters range across history, philosophy, theory, practice, policy and more. To organise the diverse contributions to this book, it is presented in three parts:

1. historical, theoretical and philosophical perspectives of ECEC
2. perspectives and practices in ECEC policy and provision
3. perspectives and practices in teaching and leadership.

Historical, theoretical and philosophical perspectives

The first part of the book sets the scene for the provision of ECEC in Australia. It is guided by the question of where ECEC in Australia has come from and how we think about children, families and ECEC. In Chapter 1, Sandie Wong and Frances Press begin with an overview of *The development of early childhood education and care in Australia*. In this chapter the emergence of early childhood education in Australia for children birth to 8 years is investigated. Wong and Press explore some of the historical complexities of the field, reflecting on the links between this past provision and our current experiences of what is a complex and multilayered professional field. The discussion in this chapter includes a brief introduction to the commencement of formal schooling in Australia, the development of provision for children birth to five years, initially from a care perspective, and the establishment of early childhood education as a specific field of professional endeavour.

Following on from this historical overview of education in Australia, in Chapter 2 Joanne Ailwood raises some historical perspectives on children and childhood. How children are thought about has changed. This chapter provides an overview of some important historical perspectives on how children and childhood have been understood, including children's work, the

Introduction

introduction of mass schooling, the child as a social being and the United Nations Convention on the Rights of the Child and how this plays out in contemporary children's lives.

In Chapter 3, *Theoretical perspectives on early childhood*, Mindy Blaise introduces four broad theoretical frameworks that have influenced our understanding of ECEC. Within each of these theories Blaise notes key concepts and thinkers and provides examples of how they impact the provision of ECEC in Australia. She ends this chapter by reminding us of the importance of the grass-roots, or 'bottom-up', theories that early childhood educators build as they reflect upon, challenge and revise their own practices. Each of the chapters in this book has theoretical underpinnings; as educators, it is our theories about who we think children are and families are that informs the kind of education and provision we provide.

The final chapter in this section is *Practical approaches and philosophies in early childhood education and care*. In this chapter Linda Henderson and Susan Edwards build on the previous chapter, presenting an introduction to the key approaches to early childhood education, including cultural historical, Reggio Emilia, Forest Schools, Multiple Intelligences, HighScope and Montessori. Case study examples of each of these approaches are discussed and links to their theoretical and historical locations are made.

Perspectives and practices in policy and provision

The second part of the book considers the policies and provision for ECEC in Australia. The guiding question for this second section is, of course, the question of how we provide ECEC in Australia. Building on the background provided in the first section, the chapters in this section explore current policies, perspectives and practices in the provision of Australian ECEC.

The section begins with Chapter 5, *Key ideas, research and challenges in early childhood education and care*, in which Maryanne Theobald and Gillian Busch showcase key ideas, international developments and contemporary research in ECEC policy and provision that inform how ECEC is shaped and provided for in Australia. This chapter begins with an overview of the ways young children learn in early childhood education, highlighting play-based learning as a pedagogical response to our understandings about children. International educational models, research from neuroscience, studies of young children,

4

economic research, and social justice principles that have influenced ECEC are discussed. Drawing on the reflections of educators working in various ECEC contexts, the chapter highlights four topics encountered by educators as part of their everyday work with diverse communities. These topics include

- the educational program for children in the early years
- relationships and partnerships with diverse families
- professional accountabilities, and
- changing constructions of childhood.

Next, Megan Gibson explores *Contexts, policy and frameworks of early childhood education and care* in Chapter 6. This chapter provides insights into ECEC provision in Australia through an examination of a range of different early childhood contexts, policy and regulatory frameworks for children from birth to eight years. Consideration of this diverse range of contexts provides insights into the ways in which the states and territories provide ECEC. Attention is given to the contemporary policy context, both in Australia and internationally, and how this shapes the field.

Specific to Australia is the need to engage in culturally safe and sensitive practices for Indigenous children and families, while also encouraging non-Indigenous children to build safe and positive relationships. In Chapter 7 Margot Ford considers *Cultural safety for Indigenous children in early childhood education and care*. This chapter provides insights into the importance of Aboriginal and Torres Strait Islander cultural understandings in the provision of ECEC across Australia. It discusses specific Indigenous approaches to the care and education of young children with examples and principles for practice. The chapter also makes links to the early childhood curriculum framework and the need for culturally competent early childhood educators.

In Chapter 8, Melinda Miller examines *Diversity and inclusion in early childhood education and care*. Miller's chapter reviews the current policy and provision for diversity and inclusion, including dis/ability, growing up in poverty, Aboriginal experiences, various family structures and cultural knowledges. Socially inclusive practices for valuing diversity in ECEC in Australia with case studies are illustrated. The implications of socially just policy and provision to ensure quality and successful outcomes for children are discussed.

Introduction

Part 2 concludes with Ann Farrell's discussion of *Ethical responsibilities in early childhood education and care*. This chapter highlights our ethical responsibilities as educators in the field of ECEC, including codes of conduct and legal issues. Scenarios of ethical dilemmas that educators may encounter in their daily work are presented and discussed with regards to three aspects of professional ethics in ECEC: ethics of participation, power and partnerships.

Perspectives and practices in teaching and leadership

Part 3 explores the ways in which the historical, theoretical, political and policy contexts discussed in the previous sections play out in our work as early childhood educators. The question of what it means to work in Australian ECEC guides the chapters in this section.

Sandra Cheeseman begins this section with Chapter 10, *Planning for children's learning: curriculum, pedagogy and assessment*. This chapter introduces students to the important trilogy of curriculum, pedagogy and assessment in early childhood settings. It makes direct links to a range of curriculum, pedagogy and assessment documents early childhood educators will encounter (for example, the EYLF, the Australian Curriculum and the NQF). The chapter introduces pedagogical practices that optimise young children's learning and development and examines how various types of assessment support children's learning and development.

In Chapter 11, *Relationships between staff, children and families*, Karen Hawkins explores the practice of relationships in early childhood settings, identifying why relationships are so important for children's learning and development. Research informs us that responsive relationships support children's learning and development. The quality and responsiveness of relationships between staff and children, between staff and staff and between staff and families is central to children's learning and development.

Wendy Boyd follows on from this discussion of relationships through an exploration of *Understanding babies: promoting young children's learning and development* in Chapter 12. This chapter provides an introduction to the importance of the first two years of life, highlighting the competence and skills of infants for implementing daily routines to support children's learning and development. While children are viewed as capable and competent, it is important to remember that young children may also be vulnerable. Given this, the capabilities and characteristics of the educator are important for quality ECEC provision for babies.

The environment is sometimes known as the 'third teacher' (Reggio Children, 1998) and in Chapter 13 Joy Goodfellow introduces the importance of *Flexible and sustainable learning environments*. This chapter explores what needs to be considered when organising the environment, what the environment says about our philosophy both of teaching and of the way children learn. The chapter discusses the physical elements of the environment—such as spaces (indoor and outdoor), materials and resources—and how these interrelate with relationships, time and the practices of sustainability. The issue of sustainability is linked closely to the quality of life for children and their rights as citizens.

In the final chapter of this book, Louise Mary Thomas explores the importance of our role as leaders in the ECEC field. Chapter 14, *Professionalism for early childhood educators*, invites us to reflect upon our profession of early childhood educators and how we view ourselves. In a country where early childhood educators suffer low status, and have working conditions below that of their primary school trained counterparts, what does it take to be an effective leader and advocate for young children?

TERMINOLOGY IN THIS BOOK AS A POINT FOR DISCUSSION

As established earlier in this Introduction, ECEC in Australia is a complex and often fraught field. A result of this complexity is the ongoing lack of agreement upon a consistent terminology. In collating this book it was necessary to ensure a consistency of terminology across the chapters. However, some in the field will disagree with the decisions made. We view this as an ongoing debate and to encourage further discussion we provide here several notes and questions about some terminology used in this book.

Teachers or educators?

Since the introduction of the National Quality Agenda all people who work in ECEC settings are to be called 'educators'. While this book has followed that trend there is a strong argument developing in Australia that a person who studies for four years at university should not be termed an 'educator' but rather a 'teacher'. This is not only to bring the discourse of the field in line with the more

Introduction

privileged schooling sector, but also because a staff member with a Certificate Three in Children's Services (a six-month Further Education qualification) is also termed an 'educator'. Which approach do you favour and why?

Education or care?

There is ongoing discussion about whether the work of an early childhood educator is education, care or a mixture of both. And at what age does early childhood finish—is it when children begin formal schooling or is it at eight years of age? Should this be called the Early Years or Early Childhood Education and Care? The term 'education and care' is more commonly used in early years fields. This is to recognise the connection between teaching and caring for children. As well as the obvious focus on teaching and learning, the role of educators is to attend to the wellbeing of children and young people. With up to 9 per cent of Australian children and adolescents being diagnosed with problems such as mental illness (including anxiety and depression) lasting longer than six months (AIHW, 2012), it is important that educators attend to the caring aspect of their role. Educators are in an ideal position to support and help build the resilience of children and families. So are we 'educators', 'carers' or both?

Preschool, kindergarten, reception, or a preparatory year?

The terminology used for providing ECEC across Australia varies significantly. For example, in New South Wales kindergarten is the first year of formal school, whereas in Queensland and Victoria kindergarten is the year before formal school. More recently, the foundation year has been added to the list of nomenclature as the first year of the Australian Curriculum. It is important to be aware of these terminology differences. What terminology is appropriate for your context? Why and how does it fit into the overall provision of ECEC in your local area?

CONCLUSION

Across Australia and internationally, the perspectives, practices and provision of ECEC continue to be discussed and researched. This book provides a contemporary view of Australian ECEC following significant upheavals in the way ECEC is viewed. The book has been produced to provide a broad and holistic view of the perspectives and practices currently at play in Australia. We hope that this contribution will continue to support the education and professional development of educators, both in training and in practice.

REFERENCES

Australian Institute of Health and Welfare (AIHW) (2012). Australia's Health 2012. The 13th Biennial Report of the AIHW. Retrieved 5 March 2015 <www.ahhw.gov.au/publication-detail/?id=10737422172>

Department of Education, Employment and Workplace Relations (DEEWR) (2009). Belonging, Being and Becoming: The early years learning framework for Australia. Canberra: DEEWR for COAG. Retrieved March 2015, <www.coag.gov.au/sites/default/files/early_years_learning_framework.pdf>.

Early Childhood Australia (ECA) (2015). Australia Needs a Vision for Early Learning. Retrieved 20 February 2015. <www.earlychildhoodaustralia.org.au>. Canberra: ECA.

Reggio Children (1998). *Children, Spaces, Relations: Meta-project for an environment for young children*. Retrieved March 2015, <www.reggioaustralia.org.au>.

United Nations (1989). United Nations Convention on the Rights of the Child (UNCRC). Geneva: United Nations.

PART ONE

Historical, theoretical and philosophical perspectives of ECEC

Chapter 1

The development of early childhood education and care in Australia

Sandie Wong and Frances Press

In this chapter you will find an outline of:
- the history of compulsory education in Australia
- how early childhood education and care emerged
- the role of the government in supporting child care
- the move towards accreditation of child care facilities.

Contemporary provision of early childhood education and care (ECEC) for children aged birth to eight years in Australia is complex. It is currently made up of a number of different service types that are funded, legislated and regulated by two different levels of government (state and federal) and are operated by a diverse range of providers. In some states, local government also plays an important role. While recognising that education, in its broadest sense, existed for Aboriginal and Torres Strait Islander peoples for tens of thousands of years prior to colonisation, this chapter provides a brief history of the provision of formal education for young children in Australia since colonisation, exploring its complexities in a way that we hope helps readers better understand why things are the way they are today.

First we describe the establishment of the earliest schools in colonial Australia and outline the origins of Australian public schooling systems. We then focus on the development of early childhood education as a specific field of professional endeavour. We explore the establishment of kindergartens and day nurseries/crèches at the turn of the nineteenth century, the establishment of the

Australian Association for Pre-School Child Development and the creation of Lady Gowrie Child Centres in the 1930s–40s and the expansion of preschools in the 1960s. We describe the rise of child care and the introduction of the *Child Care Act* in 1972. We finish by outlining the commercialisation of child care and the accompanying development of an accreditation system for ECEC in the 1980s. Our aim in this chapter is to demonstrate links between these past events and the current configuration of ECEC.

FORMAL SCHOOLING IN COLONIAL AUSTRALIA

Prior to the late nineteenth century most colonial children received informal education from their families, not from formal school institutions (Ward & Macnab, 1962). Children of the poor learnt the skills they needed to survive and, hopefully, thrive from working alongside their parents. Children of wealthy colonists, on the other hand, were mostly educated at home by governesses and then, when older, sent back to England for further education. Aboriginal and Torres Strait Islander children were taught culture and skills through participation in song, music and dance, as well as through direct observation and instruction.

The very earliest colonial schools were established by governments in the early nineteenth century, under the direction of governors of the colonies (Campbell & Proctor, 2014). At this time, schooling was viewed as an important instrument for shaping the moral development of the colony and maintaining social order. The convicts who populated Australia as a penal colony were considered morally and socially corrupt and it was feared that their children would grow up to be similarly dangerous and uncontrollable, thus endangering the stability of the fledgling society. There was, however, belief in the redemptive power of education. By intervening early in children's lives and providing them with a moral education, it was believed the children of convicts could be shaped into respectable and compliant citizens.

In these early colonial schools, both boys and girls were taught reading, writing and basic arithmetic (Barcan, 1965). The curriculum was closely tied to religious and moral instruction, often using religious texts. Instruction was largely through rote learning, memorisation and drill. Children were also taught gendered work skills considered important for preparing them for their 'place' in society. For instance, boys learned gardening and carpentry, and girls needlework. These schools were highly structured, children were tightly controlled,

The development of early childhood education and care in Australia

and discipline was often harsh and included corporal punishment. Interestingly, and somewhat ironically, because of a shortage of teachers in the colonies, the teachers in these schools were often convicts (Campbell & Proctor, 2014).

As the population expanded, the number and diversity of schools increased. From the early 1800s, schools were established by religions of various persuasions. There was also an increase in private schools. Some, such as Dame schools (usually run by widows or spinsters), charged small fees and catered for the children of poor families. Others, such as boarding schools and preparatory schools, catered for the emerging middle class, and were often run by families of teachers. Governments also established schools for particular groups of children, including 'Orphan' schools and 'Native' schools, where children—some of whom were orphans, but many of whom were coercively or forcefully removed from their families—lived out their childhood in highly regulated institutions (Barcan, 1965). The quality of schools varied considerably. As schooling expanded, there was limited supervision, and most schools were staffed by teachers who had little pedagogical training, were often poorly paid and had little access to support.

In these early days only a small percentage of children attended schools, and attendance was often sporadic (Weiss, 1993). School attendance was optional for all but orphans and other state wards. It was the children of the poor who were the least likely to attend as many poor parents relied on their children's work to support the family, either labouring or working in the home. Moreover, as the establishment of schools was haphazard, many children, especially those living in remote areas, were not within reach of a school. Formal schooling for Aboriginal children remained largely a role of the churches and missionary societies (Dickey, 1979). In a naïve and racist plan to assimilate Aboriginal children, they were often separated from their families and transported to schools where attempts would be made to convert them to Christianity and/or to teach them work skills that would make them 'useful' to white settlers. Often such schooling merely committed them to a life of servitude.

Until the mid to late 1800s, the provision of schools across the colonies was unsystematic. Different types of schools catered for different classes of people and upheld class and religious divides. Much of this situation changed in the late nineteenth century with the introduction of 'compulsory, free and secular' education in all colonies.

Compulsory secular education begins

By the late 1800s there was strong support for public education (Cook, Davey & Vick, 1979). Some argued that schooling was necessary to ensure an educated population to fulfil its (male) franchise responsibilities because 'An intelligent democracy must be founded on education' (Black, 1893, p. 6750). Others argued that education was necessary for developing a knowledgeable, skilled and capable workforce that would in turn lead to greater prosperity for the nation. Yet others envisaged public schooling as an equalising and socially just endeavour that would improve the prospects and potential of the poorest in society.

Nevertheless, the concept of universal education faced strong opposition. Churches vigorously resisted public schooling, fearing that secular education would result in a godless society. Others argued against education for the working class on the grounds that educating the 'under-class above their station' could lead to civil uprising. Despite such objections, the provision of state-funded public schools was broadly supported by the growing populace and by the end of the century each colony had introduced Education Acts (see Table 1.1).

Figure 1.1: Woolloomooloo Day Nursery, 1906
Source: Sydney Day Nursery Association, image courtesy of SDN Children's Services

Table 1.1: Passing of Education/Instruction Acts and establishment of early childhood organisations in Australia

State	Passing of Education Acts	Beginning of early childhood organisations	Establishment of first free kindergarten/ day nursery	Teachers' colleges established
Western Australia	*Education Act 1871*	1911: Kindergarten Union of Western Australia	1912:	1913: Western Australia Kindergarten Training College
Victoria	*Education Act 1872*	1908: Free Kindergarten Union of Victoria	1901: Carlton	1922: Kindergarten Training College (later Melbourne Kindergarten Teachers' College)
		1910: Victorian Association of Crèches		
South Australia	*Education Act 1875*	1905: Kindergarten Union of South Australia	1906:	1907: Adelaide
Queensland	*Education Act 1875*	1907: Crèche and Kindergarten Association		1907: Brisbane Kindergarten Training College 1907
New South Wales	*Public Instruction Act 1880*	1895: Kindergarten Union of New South Wales	1896: Woolloomooloo	1896: Sydney Kindergarten Teachers' College
		1905: Sydney Day Nursery Association	1905: Woolloomooloo	1932: Nursery School Training Centre (later Nursery School Teachers' College)
Tasmania	*Education Act 1885*	1910: Hobart Free Kindergarten Association (Kindergarten Union of Tasmania formed in 1938)	1910: Hobart 1910: Launceston	No training college was established in Tasmania. In 1967 a training course commenced at Hobart Teachers' College

Source: Adapted from Brennan, 1998, p. 18; Wong & Press, 2013, p. 100

Historical, theoretical and philosophical perspectives of ECEC

Figure 1.2: Children at Lady Gowrie Child Centre, South Australia, c. 1940–50
Source: Courtesy of Gowrie South Australia

It is often stated that the introduction of Education Acts made public provision of schooling 'free, secular and compulsory', but this is not strictly accurate. First, they were not 'free'; most public schools charged a small fee for attendance from all but the poorest families. Second, education in public schools was not completely secular; it was broadly based on Christian values, often with a considerable part of the day devoted to scripture. Third, compulsion was not really enforced by Education Departments as many poorer families were dependent on their children's labour, while many middle-class families objected to their children attending schools with children from lower-class, 'less desirable' families. Towards the end of the century, when the idea of public schooling became more entrenched, non-attendance began to be taken more seriously by School Inspectors, except with regard to Aboriginal children. Many Aboriginal parents sought school education for their children, but in practical terms Aboriginal children were often denied access. Although they were not officially excluded from public schools, in some cases non-Aboriginal parents would remove their children from schools that Aboriginal children attended, and, for want of sufficient pupils, the schools were forced to close. Moreover,

The development of early childhood education and care in Australia

many Aboriginal children lived in more remote areas where public schools were not established. For those who did attend school, the practices they experienced were often aimed at assimilation and preparation for low-paid manual and domestic work. Further, the language of instruction was English and traditional languages and cultural practices were prohibited. At the same time, some Aboriginal parents actively refused to send their children to public schools as a way of resisting schooling's colonising influence.

Each colony had its own curriculum, but they all included reading, writing and arithmetic. Gradually, curricula and curricula materials developed an Australian flavour, reflecting a growing national identity that culminated in Federation in 1901 (Clarke, 1981). Students began to learn about Australian as well as British history (albeit from an Anglo-European perspective) and school 'readers' began to depict Australian scenes, flora and fauna, replacing the previous ones from the United Kingdom and Ireland.

Supervision of schools increased. School inspectors would visit schools to assess their conditions and compliance with regulations. Teachers were assessed on the basis of their students' success. Inspectors would 'test' the children on arithmetic and reading and should children's knowledge be found wanting, the teacher's salary could be docked. There are anecdotes of teachers banning their less able students from school on the day the inspectors came to visit so that their pupils' test scores would remain high. We hear of similar stories in relation to today's high-stakes tests.

From the mid-1800s, new pedagogies had begun to emerge (Campbell & Proctor, 2014). Teachers newly arrived in Australia brought with them progressive educational ideas that had emerged in Europe (the New Education). Proponents argued for a movement away from the 'mass' production model of the monitorial system, largely based on rote learning, towards more individualised pedagogies that explained the underlying principles of 'facts' and which were geared to students' ages and stages of development. To support this style of learning, children were separated into 'infants' and 'primary' classrooms. These pedagogies required skilled teachers, and so began a more systematic approach to teacher education (Whitehead, 2003). Beginning in Sydney in 1896, teacher education colleges were established in many states to train teachers for the public schools and teachers' associations and unions were established to support the professionalisation of teaching.

19

Despite these positive developments in public education, school practices largely remained ill-suited to the needs of young children. Thus, at the end of the nineteenth century, advocates for progressive education established separate educational settings for children younger than six years of age.

BEGINNINGS OF EARLY CHILDHOOD EDUCATION AND CARE

A number of educational reformers made some progress in bringing about changes to pedagogy in the public school system in New South Wales based on Fröebelian kindergarten methods (Walker, 1964; Wong, 2013). Indeed, several parliamentarians commented on the value of the kindergarten in debates in the House. Sir George Houston Reid (MP), for instance, referred to kindergarten as having 'converted what used to be a barbarous system of learning into a system of education which makes education a positive delight and a source of strength to those children who are taught by it' (1893, p. 6740).

By and large, however, attempts to introduce kindergarten methods into schools were thwarted by complacency, and a lack of clear understanding of its pedagogical approach. Complicating the uptake of kindergarten methods in schools was the new practice of excluding very young children. Despite compulsory attendance at school beginning from six or seven years of age, there had been a tradition of younger children attending, often with their older siblings (Snow, 1989). In the late 1890s, however, when the colony was in the depths of an economic depression and there was a need to reduce public expenditure, funding for children younger than six, who were not required by law to attend school, was an easy target for cost cutting. It was asserted that their education posed a danger to their health and that they were too young to learn. Consequently, with fewer young children attending school, there was no longer an imperative to reform education to better meet their needs (Wong, 2007).

Frustrated with the speed and lack of fidelity of uptake of kindergarten methods in public schools, a group of educational reformers, led by Maybanke Anderson, established the Kindergarten Union of New South Wales in 1895. The main objectives of the Kindergarten Union were: 'To set forth Kindergarten Principles. To endeavour to get those principles introduced into every school in New South Wales. To open Free Kindergartens wherever possible in poor neighbourhoods' (Anderson, 1911, p. 19).

The Kindergarten Union of New South Wales established free kindergartens in poor areas of Sydney, the first being Woolloomooloo Free Kindergarten, established in 1896 in what was then one of Sydney's poorest suburbs.

In ways that would be familiar to today's early childhood educators, education in Free Kindergartens was described by Ridie Lee Buckey, a member and staunch supporter of the Kindergarten Union (Waters, 2002), as a means of channelling children's natural curiosity towards 'useful' activities, providing children with experiences that familiarised them with basic academic concepts, and fostering positive attitudes towards learning:

> We teach the children how to learn . . . We lay the foundation in geography by giving the children clay with which to model islands and other forms of the earth's surface: In mathematics by getting the children to use counters in their games . . . In science we give them the chance to watch germs growing, and so stimulate observation. (Kindergarten schools: A chat with Miss Buckey, 1897, p. 5)

Free Kindergartens were to also be 'establishment[s] for organising and propaganda' (*Sydney Morning Herald*, 1898, p. 3) of kindergarten methods. Advocates worked tirelessly giving public speeches and demonstrations, and Free Kindergarten doors were always open to visitors. Regardless, Fröebelian kindergarten methods were never fully taken up in public schools, although later in the new century Maria Montessori's educational methods were implemented much more broadly (Simpson, 1911). Fröebelian kindergarten ideas did, nonetheless, spread across the country, largely due to the work of Lillian De Lissa (Whitehead, 2009), so that by 1911 there were Kindergarten Unions in all Australian states (see Table 1.1).

The development of a separate system of education for children younger than six years reflects the desire of advocates for a progressive education for young children and their concerns for a socially just society (Mellor, 1990; Wong, 2013). At the end of the nineteenth century, many families lived in abject poverty. Infant mortality, morbidity and injury rates were high. Child care was virtually non-existent, and, without access to any form of financial support, many mothers were forced to leave their young children unattended while they went to work. Kindergarten Union members argued that Free Kindergartens would contribute to improvements in conditions of the poor by educating mothers and thus improving child welfare, and keeping children safe while their mothers worked. However, the child care function of kindergartens was only ever minimal, as they were open for just a few short hours each day. Further, many Kindergarten Union supporters were reluctant to extend their operations to child care, viewing this as outside their purview of education. Thus, in most states, separate organisations established day nurseries and crèches in order to provide child care (see Table 1.1). It was from this initial split that today's perceived dichotomy between early childhood 'education' and 'care' originates.

In addition to providing kindergartens, the state Kindergarten Unions established Kindergarten Teacher Colleges soon after forming (see Table 1.1). In addition, a Nursery School Teachers' College, which provided training for those working with very young children, was established by the Sydney Day Nursery Association in New South Wales in 1932.

The establishment of early childhood education and care (ECEC) was strongly connected to first wave feminism (Brennan, 1998). Advocates for kindergartens and day care were mostly women, many of whom were also involved in advancing women's rights. Further, all those working in the services were women. ECEC gave women a 'legitimate' and, largely, socially acceptable form of employment, although it was not without controversy; some people argued, for example, that female employment contributed to the decreasing national fertility rate. ECEC continues to be a female-dominated profession in Australia today.

The separation of education for children younger than six years from that of older children contributed to consolidating early childhood education as a specialisation. It also maintained ECEC as a charitable endeavour, rather than an educational entitlement as was the case with schools for older children. Consequently, state government financial support for ECEC varied. It was not until the late 1930s that the Commonwealth Government became involved in the provision of ECEC, when it funded the establishment of the Lady Gowrie Child Centres.

The Australian Association for Pre-School Child Development and Lady Gowrie Child Centres

In the late 1930s concerns about the poor health of the nation drew attention to the potential for early intervention in children's development to ensure children received adequate nutrition and education, and to detect and remedy 'problems'. In response, the Commonwealth Government committed funding to provide services that would both demonstrate 'best practice' in early years' education and provide opportunities for research into children's development (Press & Wong, 2013).

To take advantage of the opportunity to obtain such funding, the six state-based Kindergarten Unions recognised they needed to unite, thereby forming the Australian Association for Pre-School Child Development (AAPSCD). AAPSCD obtained Commonwealth funding to establish demonstration preschools in each state capital city, the Lady Gowrie Child Centres. Named after Lady Zara Gowrie, the wife of the then Governor–General and a strong advocate for preschool education, the 'Gowries' still provide early childhood education and care as well as training and resourcing to the early childhood field. The first of the centres opened in Carlton, Victoria, in December 1939. The remaining five centres—in Brisbane, Adelaide, Perth, Sydney and Hobart—opened in 1940.

Funded by the Commonwealth Department of Health, the Gowries were established to demonstrate best practice standards for preschools in relation to factors such as staff qualifications, ratios of teachers to children, buildings, equipment and hours of operation; and to study 'the problems of physical growth, nutrition and development' (Cumpston, np, cited in Clements & MacPherson, 1945). Partly driven by a desire to know whether 'a distinct racial type is evolving in this country' (Hill, 1949, p. 13), they were to only enrol healthy children, born in Australia of Australian-born parents. Ironically, Aboriginal children were excluded (Brennan, 1998).

Informed by an emerging emphasis upon scientific principles for child development, each centre employed a non-teaching director to demonstrate and interpret its work to the general public and those with a professional interest in children's development. Each centre also employed a kindergarten teacher, a social worker and a nurse (Spearritt, 1980). In recalling the early days of the Brisbane Lady Gowrie Centre, Jean Ferguson wrote:

> Child study both from a medical and educational perspective was a vital element in the Centre's programme. Each child had a medical check on arrival each morning ... pictures were taken of

Historical, theoretical and philosophical perspectives of ECEC

> the child's posture on a regular basis; the food he ate at the Centre was scientifically balanced; his home was visited twice yearly by the social worker . . . each week the whole staff [including] five fully-qualified kindergarten teachers sat down and considered a variety of reports on two or three specific children . . . After discussion, the reports would be summarised, the child's needs identified and recommendations made for parents. (1997, cited in Gahan, 2005, pp. 6–7)

As well as child study, parent education was a central remit of the Lady Gowrie Child Centres and the AAPSCD. The centres were sites for newsreel documentaries on topics such as children's nutrition and physical development. In Western Australia the Centre director wrote a series of articles for the local newspaper on parenting and child development. In the 1950s the Executive Officer of the AAPSCD, Gladys Pendred, delivered a series of radio broadcasts on parenting (Press & Wong, 2013). Upon enrolment, Gowrie parents were to sign an agreement that they would cooperate with staff in the 'proper guidance of the child' (cited in Brennan, 1998, p. 41). The AAPSCD, especially through the Gowries, was very successful in promoting the value of preschool education to the general public.

However, the years in which AAPSCD and the Gowries were established were tumultuous. War had been declared in 1938 and, as war raged in Europe and later the Pacific, considerable strain was placed on the resources available for the centres and their capacity to attract and retain qualified staff. As the war came closer to Australian shores, concerns for the safety of children resulted in kindergartens in Perth and Brisbane being closed. The closure of Perth kindergartens prompted the idea of kindergarten by radio. This idea was supported by the Kindergarten Union of Western Australia and the ABC agreed to trial a daily radio program called *Kindergarten of the Air* (Graham-Taylor, 1996). This soon became a very popular national program and was later recorded for broadcast to Britain, South Africa and the United States (Press & Wong, 2013).

The formation of the AAPSCD, the establishment of the Gowrie Centres, and the instigation and success of Kindergarten of the Air, pointed to a burgeoning popular interest in preschool education. This interest in initiatives to support children's development in the kindergarten and the home was also linked to broader ideals about the role of education in building a peaceful post-war world. The following quote from Helen Paul, Principal of the Melbourne Kindergarten Training College, in her 1941 address to the students, is somewhat typical of the sentiment of the time:

> if we can help to build up people through our understanding of them, we are doing something in some small way to help peace . . . next to the men, children in our communities must be supported. (cited in Jackson-Nakano, 1993, np)

The other significant, but short-lived, development in ECEC during these years was the establishment of wartime children's centres. The war made industries dependent upon women's labour, and child care was required so that mothers could enter paid work. A number of wartime centres were established, funded by the Department of Labour and National Service, and overseen by a coalition of interests, including representatives from trade unions, health and social work and, somewhat begrudgingly, the AAPSCD. Many members of the AAPSCD did not approve of mothers being in paid employment and thus regarded child care as something to be tolerated in only exceptional circumstances (Brennan, 1998; Davis, 1988). This was a continuation of the kindergarten and day nursery split earlier in the century and was to once again divide the ECEC sector with the rise of child care from the 1970s onwards.

The spread of preschool education

The Gowrie centres and the work of the AAPSCD more generally helped generate widespread interest in preschool education, especially among middle-class families. Even during the war a number of preschools were established, usually in 'better-off' neighbourhoods. After the war, demands for preschool education increased even further and, in response, some of the Gowries changed their attendance patterns so that more children could participate. In 1950, for example, the Lady Gowrie Child Centre in Perth began offering two preschool sessions a day, morning and afternoon, rather than a 9.00 a.m. to 3.00 p.m. daily program (Kerr, 1994).

From the 1950s onwards, preschool education expanded significantly. At first, growth occurred mainly in parent-run preschools in middle-class communities.

Reflecting this changed environment, the AAPSCD became the Australian Pre-School Association (APA) in 1954. The objectives of the new Association included the promotion of 'the optimum development of the preschool child', the provision of support to parents, and the formulation and promotion of standards for preschool services (Press & Wong, 2013).

In the 1960s a number of state governments began to take an interest in the provision of preschool education. Reports and initiatives from the United Kingdom (the Plowden Committee Report) and the United States (especially Project Headstart) piqued the interest of education departments in the role that preschool could play in improving students' outcomes at school. Tasmania and Western Australia began to manage and run preschools through their education departments (Brennan, 1998). In the Australian Capital Territory preschool provision expanded through 'a co-operative effort between the Department of Education and Science, the National Capital Development Commission and the community' (Martin, 1968, p. 21). In Victoria and New South Wales preschool largely remained the province of voluntary agencies. However, in Victoria preschool provision (kindergartens) had been strongly supported since the 1940s by its Department of Health, due to the efforts of Dr Vera Scantlebury Brown, Director of Maternal, Infant and Preschool Welfare and a champion of the kindergarten movement. Thus, in a survey of preschool attendance released in the early 1970s, 29 per cent of eligible children in Victoria attended preschool while in New South Wales the figure was a low 3 per cent (Brennan, 1998, p. 58).

As a result, preschool provision grew in distinct ways in each state and territory. In some jurisdictions the growth of preschools was closely aligned with schools, and many preschools were located on school grounds. Some preschools fell under the policy umbrella of departments of education, others under health or community services. Some were directly managed by education, others by parent committees or voluntary agencies (such as the Kindergarten Unions in New South Wales and Victoria or the Crèche and Kindergarten Association in Queensland). As a result, there was not universal access to preschool education for children on a national basis. The national commitment of universal access only emerged as part of the Early Childhood Reform Agenda introduced by the former Federal Labor Government (2007–13).

The rise and rise of child care

ECEC services are commonplace in contemporary Australian life, yet there was a time when formal child care services (rather than preschool) were rare and the desirability of government support for them hotly contested.

The need for child care, as well as preschools, became a prominent issue during the 1960s, a time of significant social upheaval. Throughout this decade the workforce participation of married women continued to rise and women themselves became increasingly vocal about their right to work, and the need for social attitudes to change. Take, for instance, this excerpt from *The Australian Women's Weekly* (Smith, 1966, p. 21):

> This article is addressed to all women on behalf of their daughters. It is addressed to the coming generation of men and women.
>
> The three main points:
> - Equal opportunity for education regardless of sex.
> - The recognition that the dignity of housework should be shared by working partners.
> - Official provision for the children of working mothers.
>
> These are all ingredients of a new attitude, essential if society is to come to terms with the married female working force. Not until society changes its attitudes will it be able to make the most of the potential lying largely dormant in half its population.

The Child Care Act 1972

Such views clashed with a prevailing belief that mothers of young children should not be in the workforce and, following the work of psychologist John Bowlby, that child care was harmful to children. Yet it was a conservative Liberal-Country Party Coalition federal government that introduced the *Child Care Act 1972* impelled by three trends: widespread concern for the welfare of young children who were left at home alone because their mothers needed to work (so-called 'latch-key' children); the need of the manufacturing industry for access to women's cheap labour; and the increasingly vocal demand of the women's liberation movement for child care so that mothers were supported to enter the paid workforce. The Act was introduced by the Minister for Labour and National Service, Phillip Lynch, who described it as 'a tangible expression of our real and proper concern for the welfare of children' (cited in Jackson-Nakano, 1993, np). It was a watershed moment in early childhood policy, triggering ongoing national government investment in ECEC.

In its initial phases, funding under the *Child Care Act* often was used to fund the expansion of preschool education, reflecting in part the influence of the Australian Pre-school Association. However, funding preschool rather than child care drew the ire of many feminist groups critical of the inability of preschools to address the needs of working women. Divisions between advocates for preschool and advocates for child care ran deep. Preschool advocates emphasised the need for professionally staffed high-quality services and were largely unsupportive of mothers entering the paid labour force, while child care advocates sought the rapid expansion of services to enable women to participate in the paid workforce and/or undertake higher education. In the face of such debates, Commonwealth funding moved predominantly to support child care services. In the 1980s such funding became entrenched in social policy through the Prices and Incomes Accord introduced by the Hawke Labor Government.

The Prices and Incomes Accord (the Accord)

From 1983 onwards, the planned and systematic expansion of community-based facilities occurred as part of the Accord—an agreement between the Australian Council of Trade Unions and the Australian Labor Party. Under the Accord, unions undertook to exercise wage restraint in return for government expenditure on the 'social wage'. The social wage, broadly defined, included expenditure on benefits and services with broad social impact. These included significant policy initiatives, such as Medicare, the extension of superannuation, and an increase in subsidies to support the increased availability of child care places. The Accord was renegotiated several times during this period of ALP Government and increases in child care provision were consistently and successfully put forward as part of social wage claims. As more child care services became funded, so did a number of culturally specific programs. From 1987, the federal government began funding Multifunctional Aboriginal Children's Services (MACS) to provide a mix of services, for example, child care, outside school hours care and preschool to Aboriginal and Torres Strait Islander communities. From 1989, the government also funded Aboriginal and Torres Strait Islander crèches. At the time of writing there are currently 33 MACs and 36 crèches throughout the country (Australian National Audit Office, 2010).

Privatisation and accreditation

Despite ever increasing federal government expenditure, demand for child care places always outstripped supply. In the early 1990s, in order to stimulate private sector investment in the market and thereby increase the availability of child care places, the then federal Labor government announced it would make fee subsidies available to parents using private (for-profit) child care facilities. This policy shift was in line with many other micro-economic reforms instigated during this period, whereby more and more public services were opened up to private investment. Nevertheless, the decision to support private child care was an extremely controversial policy decision. Early childhood advocates on both sides of politics had long opposed the profit motive for the provision of child care. To allay fears that private sector provision would have a detrimental impact upon the quality of care, the government promised a national system of child care accreditation to oversee the quality of all child care centres. In 1990, in announcing the introduction of accreditation, the then Prime Minister, Robert Hawke, stated:

> Parents are entitled to be confident they are getting quality attention for their kids whether they are using government funded or commercial centres. So we will work with all key interests in child care to develop a system of accreditation. (cited in Wangmann, 1992, p. 47)

This led to the development of the National Childcare Accreditation Council (NCAC) and quality improvement and accreditation systems for all early childhood programs supported by the federal government. Initially applicable only to long day care centres (LDCs), in subsequent years accreditation systems were also developed for family day care and outside school hours care. The NCAC was a precursor to today's Australian Children's Education and Care Quality Authority.

The extension of fee subsidies to parents using commercial LDCs was a very successful stimulant for market provision, with LDCs quickly becoming the

Historical, theoretical and philosophical perspectives of ECEC

fastest growing 'industry' in Australia. By 1996, 75 per cent of LDCs were run by for-profit providers (Loane, 1996) and the provision of child care in Australia was transformed.

CONCLUSION

Today's complex system of ECEC has a long, turbulent and controversial history. It has been marked by debates about the role of women, and the suitability of education and care environments for young children. Taken as a whole, systems for the education and care of young children have been much more fragmented than those of schools, encompassing a range of for-profit and non-profit providers, direct government provision and diverse service types. Yet it has also been a site for innovation and strong advocacy for the rights of young children. Early childhood educators and advocates have initiated many far-sighted educational reforms in the establishment of kindergartens, day nurseries and child care and continue to transform the way we think about young children's learning.

FURTHER THINKING

1. Experience of ECEC is socially and historically contingent. What type(s) of early years' settings did you attend? Ask an older person about their experience of ECEC. How do the two experiences compare? What's the same? What's different?

2. Different forms of ECEC have emerged to cater for a range of needs. What types of early years' settings are in your local government area? Who manages these settings? What services do they provide? Who do they serve?

3. Both state and federal governments are now heavily involved in ECEC. Who is your state/territory Minister for Education? What is his/her role? Who is/are the federal minister(s) responsible for education and early childhood services? How do these roles differ?

4. ECEC serves many social functions. What are some of the purposes of school and ECEC? How do these purposes affect different groups in society (for example, women, ethnic minorities, Aboriginal people and employers)?

30

The development of early childhood education and care in Australia

5. Education for children older than six years is free, whereas education for younger children comes at a substantial cost to families. What are some arguments for and against the provision of free education for all children?

REFERENCES

Anderson, M. (1911). The Story of the Kindergarten Union of NSW. In Sydney Teachers' College Kindergarten Society, *The Story of Kindergarten in New South Wales*. Sydney: Sydney Teachers' College Kindergarten Society.

Australian National Audit Office (ANAO) (2010). *ANAO Audit Report No. 8, 2010–11*: Multifunctional Aboriginal Children's Services (MACS) and Crèches. Retrieved 5 October 2014, <http://anao.gov.au/Publications/Audit-Reports/2010-2011/Multifunctional-Aboriginal-Childrens-Services-MACS-and-Creches>.

Barcan, A. (1965). *A Short History of Education in New South Wales*. Sydney: Martindale Press.

Black, R.J. (1893). *New South Wales Parliamentary Debates*, First Series, Fifteenth Parliament, Fourth Session, Volume LXV, 19 April to 17 May 1893, p. 6750.

Brennan, D. (1998). *The Politics of Australian Child Care: Philanthropy to feminism and beyond*, rev. edn. Cambridge: Cambridge University Press.

Campbell, C. & Proctor, H. (2014). *A History of Australian Schooling*. Sydney: Allen & Unwin.

Clarke, C.M.H. (1981). *A History of Australia, Volumes V and VI: From 1888 to 1935*. Melbourne: Melbourne University Press.

Clements, F.W. & Macpherson, M. (1945). *The Lady Gowrie Child Care Centre: The health record*. Canberra: Government Printer.

Cook, P., Davey, I. & Vick, M. (1979). Capitalism and working-class schooling in late nineteenth century South Australia, *Australian and New Zealand History of Education Society Journal*, 8(2), 36–48.

Davis, L. (1988). The Brunswick Children's Centre: A forgotten model children's service? *Early Child Development and Care*, 34(1), 151–64.

Dickey, B. (1979). The evolution of care for destitute children in New South Wales, 1875–1901, *Journal of Australian Studies*, 4, 38–57.

Gahan, D. (2005). In Search of a Childhood Landscape: Historical narratives from a Queensland Kindergarten, 1940–1965. Doctoral dissertation. Brisbane: Queensland University of Technology.

Graham-Taylor, S. (1996). Graham, Margaret (1889–1966). In *Australian Dictionary of Biography*. Retrieved 5 October 2014, <http://adb.anu.edu.au/biography/graham-margaret-10339>.

Hill, E. (1949). *A First Analysis of Case History Records of Children Attending the Lady Gowrie Child Centres, 1939–1946*. Canberra: Government Printer.

Jackson-Nakano, A. (1993). From the Cradle: A history from the records of the Australian Early Childhood Association. Unpublished draft. Canberra: Early Childhood Australia.

Kerr, R. (1994). *A History of the Kindergarten Union of Western Australia 1911–1973*. Perth: Meerilinga Young Children's Foundation.

Kindergarten Schools: A chat with Miss Buckey, *Sydney Morning Herald*, 17 August 1897, p. 5.

Loane, S. (1996). *Who Cares? Guilt, hope and the child care debate*. Kew, Vic.: Mandarin.

Martin, S. (21 September 1968). Aim to give children confidence, *Canberra Times*.

Mellor, E. (1990). *Stepping Stones: The development of early childhood services in Australia*. Sydney: Harcourt Brace Jovanovich.

Multifunctional Aboriginal Children's Services (MACS) and Crèches. (2010). Retrieved 5 October 2014, <www.anao.gov.au/uploads/documents/2010-11_Audit_Report_No_8.pdf>.

Press, F. & Wong, S. (2013). A 'humanitarian idea': Using an historical lens to reflect on social justice in early childhood and care, *Contemporary Issues in Early Childhood*, Social Justice: Special Edition, 14(4), 311–23.

Press, F. & Wong, S. (2013). *Early Childhood Australia: A voice for children for 75 years*. Canberra: Early Childhood Australia.

Reid, G.H. (1893). *New South Wales Parliamentary Debates*, First Series, Fifteenth Parliament, Fourth Session, Volume LXV, 19 April to 17 May, p. 6740.

Simpson, M.M. (1911). Recent development in kindergarten in the state schools of New South Wales. In Sydney Teachers' College Kindergarten Society, *The Story of Kindergarten in New South Wales*. Sydney: Sydney Teachers' College Kindergarten Society, pp. 12–17.

Smith, S. (September 1966). There's too much talent tied to the kitchen sink. *The Australian Women's Weekly*.

Snow, D. (1989). 'But they're only babies': Policies and practices marginalising the very young from NSW state schools, 1788–1920. In N.J. Kyle (ed.), *Women as Educators in 19th and 20th Century Australia. Occasional Papers No. 1.* Wollongong: School of Learning, University of Wollongong.

Spearritt, J. (1980). *Working for the Pre-school Cause: The role of the Australian Pre-School Association.* Sydney: Macquarie University.

Sydney Morning Herald (21 February 1898). A Free Kindergarten at Newtown: A successful inauguration, p. 3.

Walker, M.L. (1964). The development of kindergartens in Australia. MEd thesis. Sydney: University of Sydney.

Wangmann, J. (1992). Accreditation: A right for all Australia's young children or a waste of time and money. In B. Lambert (ed.) (1992), *Changing Faces: The early childhood profession in Australia.* Canberra: Australian Early Childhood Association (AECA), pp. 46–57.

Ward, R. & Macnab, K. (1962). The nature and nurture of the first generation of native-born Australians, *Historical Studies*, 10(39), 289–308.

Waters (2002). (ed.) With Passion, Perseverance and Practicality: 100 Women Who Influenced Australian Children's Services, 1841-2001. Melbourne: OMEP Australia.

Weiss, G. (1993). A very great nuisance: Young children and the construction of school entry in South Australia, 1851–1915, *History of Education Review*, 22(2), 1–17.

Whitehead, K. (2003). *The New Women Teachers Come Along: Transforming teaching in the nineteenth century*, Australian and New Zealand History of Education Society Monograph Series Number 2. Sydney.

—— (2009). Contextualizing and contesting national identities: Lillian de Lissa, 1885–1967, *Vitae Scholasticae*, 26(1), 41–60.

Wong, S. (2007). Looking back and moving forward: Historicising the social construction of early childhood education and care as national work, *Contemporary Issues in Early Childhood*, Special Edition, 8(2), 144–56.

Chapter 2

Historical perspectives on children and childhood

Joanne Ailwood

In this chapter you will find:
- an overview of western ideas about childhood
- an account of the 'Stolen' and 'Forgotten' children
- a guide to children's work and mass schooling in Australia
- social and historical studies of children and childhood.

Until the mid-twentieth century, historical work was largely silent about children. Like women, children's experiences were less widely recorded than those of men, and most children were unable to record their experiences for themselves. In terms of the historical record, our understanding of the various experiences of childhood is incomplete. As Kociumbas (1997) points out, any history of childhood is dependent on adult recollection and documentation, so we rarely have access to the direct experience of childhood. Taking children seriously as a historical subject of inquiry is also quite recent. In 1962, Philippe Ariès' book *Centuries of Childhood* was translated into English from the original French. This book is usually noted as the indicator of when histories of childhood began to be recognised as important in and of themselves. While Ariès' book has since been widely critiqued, it remains important for its major contribution to the early establishment of the history of childhood as a field of study.

This chapter is divided into several sections. First, I consider the important question of how we understand children and childhood. In this section I also put forward some definitions of children and childhood, considering some

34

of the significant historical themes and ideas about western childhood and children. This is followed by some specifics relating to Australian history and how these have impacted our understandings of children and childhood. I then move on to one of the most significant historical shifts for western children, that of compulsory schooling. Finally, I note some of the more recent (late twentieth century) changes with the introduction of the United Nations Convention on the Rights of the Child (UNCRC) in 1989 and the solidification of the idea that children are worthy of serious attention and understanding in and of themselves.

WHAT IS CHILDHOOD? SOME (WESTERN) HISTORICAL IDEAS

Childhood is a temporal phase of life all humans experience; it is commonly recognised as a period of dependence on others for basic needs, such as food, shelter and care. The ways in which these needs are met and how the lived experiences of childhood are understood varies across time and place. Ariès (1973) suggested that the idea of childhood could be considered an invention; or, as Hendrick (1997) puts it, the concept of childhood is historically variable. Childhood is clearly a biological phase of growth; but how we define that phase, how we understand it, and what we think is or is not right for that phase is historically, socially and culturally invented. This idea is often referred to as the social construction of childhood. The social construction of childhood should not be understood as meaning there is a single way of thinking about children and childhood. Instead, there are many conceptualisations of childhood, some of which are contradictory or conflict with each other. Some ideas about children and childhood come to be more dominant than others, to the point that they are so taken for granted that it might seem difficult to challenge them. For example, take the idea that not only should children be at school, but that school should be divided into year levels linked to children's age. We might consider this normal in Australia. It's the way things are. But this is not necessarily a natural, normal experience of childhood. It is one that we construct together, as a society, based on a number of dominant discourses or ideas that we hold about children and childhood. These discourses become so historically fixed and self-evident that it is easy to forget that mass schooling, as we know it in Australia today, is an idea that is not much more than 100 years old (see Chapter 1 for more on this). Before this, for centuries education was either provided privately through home-based

Historical, theoretical and philosophical perspectives of ECEC

tutors and governesses for wealthy families or, for the majority, located within communities as children lived and worked alongside adults. This section of the chapter provides an overview of some of the dominant understandings of childhood evident in western history.

To understand ideas of childhood it is useful to begin by noting some of the shifting definitions of childhood. Age is now 'such an important framework for assessing the capacities, rights, and obligations of children that it is difficult for contemporary societies to comprehend a time when this was not so' (Lassonde, 2013, p. 212). There have been times where childhood was simply the period of most dependence, from infancy until about five years, after which children contributed to the community, family and household through their labour. In the 1830s in Britain, for example, childhood was declared over at thirteen years old (Hendrick, 1997). Contemporary definitions of childhood are now linked to compulsory school age, as children have become more removed from everyday adult worlds and work and are relegated to home and school. Currently, in the UNCRC (UN, 1989), children are defined as persons aged up to eighteen years. Within this, the period of early childhood is widely recognised as birth to eight years. This definition means that early childhood extends across the period of time before schooling and into the first few years of compulsory primary schooling.

In the West, childhood has historically been valourised as a time of innocence and children are often viewed as incomplete, weak and needy (Hendrick, 1997; Moss & Petrie, 2002; Cunningham, 2005). Of course, to challenge this view of childhood is not to simplistically suggest that children are not vulnerable or in need of care and protection; rather it is to suggest that we need to recognise their strengths and personhood in the childhood moment. Children have likes, dislikes, opinions, strengths and weaknesses just as adults do. Rather than focusing on the negative and understanding children from a position of lack, it is important to overlay this with an understanding of what children are capable of and what they already have.

Sometimes the institutions we provide for children are historical accidents; school starting age is one example. In Australia, most children are required by law to be in school at the beginning of the year they turn six; that is, when they are five turning six. However, formal schooling begins the year before for many children; for example, in the preparatory year (prep) in Queensland. However, in Finland, one of the countries that currently outranks Australia in various

Historical perspectives on children and childhood

international testing results, formal schooling does not begin until seven years of age. Prior to this most children attend informal, play-based early childhood education settings. In other words, in Finland children attend early childhood education settings for up to six years, followed by twelve years of primary and secondary education as opposed to Australia, where children spend up to five years, and for most fewer, in early childhood education settings and then up to twelve years in primary and secondary settings. Furthermore, in Finland the most common teacher education degree is a master's degree rather than a bachelor's degree and teaching is a socially valued occupation (Finnish National Board of Education, 2014). These kinds of international comparisons can help us to understand the point about the construction of our social worlds.

This section of the chapter has highlighted two key points. First, definitions of children and childhood are not fixed and unalterable; rather they shift and are changeable across varying historical times and societies. Second, these definitions impact our treatment of children, including the kinds of opportunities and provisions societies create. How adults 'think' about children and childhood leads to the kinds of institutions, laws, policies and provisions we create for children (Moss & Petrie, 2002; Woodrow & Press, 2007). These ideas have been recognised for some time (for example, Cleverley and Phillips, 1988) and are often referred to within the umbrella concept of the social construction of childhood. As Hendrick (1997, p. 35) points out, 'there is always a relationship between conceptual thought, social action and the process of category construction and, therefore, definitions of childhood must to some extent be dependent upon the society from which they emerge'.

You'll notice that this question of definition, of 'who we think children are', sits beneath all the chapters in this book. It is a key point of reflection for any educator. One historical example of the two key points above is the forcible removal and/or emigration of children in Australia. How the Australian and British governments and societies have 'thought' about children, race and education enabled them to remove children from their families, relocating them with little or no recognition or care for their experiences and personhood as children. Institutions provided for these 'removed' children also reflected what kind of future the government predicted for the children, often as domestic workers and labourers.

CONFRONTING AUSTRALIA'S HISTORY: STOLEN AND FORGOTTEN CHILDREN

One of the many significant consequences of colonialism for the history of children and childhood in Australia is the removal of children from their families. The recent history of Australia has many stories of children being transported from Britain to Australia as convicts, workers, or as good 'British stock'. The removal of children from Aboriginal and Torres Strait Islander families remains a shameful reminder of the nation's treatment of the Indigenous Peoples of this country. Stolen children refer to the Aboriginal and Torres Strait Islander children taken from their families, while the Forgotten children refer to children sent unaccompanied to Australia from Britain. The stories we have of Stolen and Forgotten children are the recollections of adults. These stories could not be heard and understood until our social and historical understandings of children changed, and until the children who were removed from their homes and families became adults and were able to have their voices taken seriously. While children their experiences were invisible, silenced and marginalised. As a nation we are still learning about the experiences of those children who were taken and the long-term, intergenerational impact on their lives, families and communities.

Children were taken away from their families by the successive British and Australian governments for multiple reasons. British children were certainly among the convicts transported to Australia and were also included in the early voluntary migration of British families during the second half of the nineteenth century. Kociumbas (1997) suggests that about 15 per cent of the individuals transported from Britain to Australia between 1788 and 1868 were unaccompanied and below eighteen years of age. Coldrey (1999) puts the number of children involved in transportation at closer to 25 per cent. It is difficult to get precise figures as while children's ages were recorded in sailing logs, children often did not know their birth date or how old they actually were—what is recorded may have been a best guess. Regardless, it is clear that children were a significant component of the convict story.

The trauma of the Stolen Generations of Aboriginal and Torres Strait Islander children and their families is vividly recorded in the *Bringing Them Home* report (Human Rights and Equal Opportunities Commission [HREOC], 1997). This report investigated the Australian government's practice throughout most of the twentieth century, right up until the 1970s, of forcibly removing Aboriginal and Torres Strait Islander children from their families. The damage that policy such as this has caused to multiple generations of Indigenous families continues to be inherited in their communities and beyond. The *Bringing Them Home* report led, in part, to the former Rudd Federal Government apologising to the Stolen Generations for our governments' actions as the first act of the then incoming federal parliament in 2008.

Bringing Them Home documentation and evidence suggests that 'many Indigenous children were removed when they were less than 10 years old. Between one-half and two-thirds of those who were forcibly removed were taken in infancy (before the age of five years)' (Australian Human Rights Commission, 2010, np, p. x). We now know that separation from families and at a young age has long-term and intergenerational effects, including poor mental and physical health, behavioural problems and loss of cultural heritage. This last effect was one intention of the policies; Aboriginal children who were taken away to government institutions or white families were not allowed to speak their own language and were not able to learn their community's cultural knowledges, beliefs or practices.

BRINGING THEM HOME

Below are two of the many personal stories provided in testimony at the Stolen Generations inquiry from the *Bringing Them Home* report.

The policeman, who no doubt was doing his duty, patted his handcuffs, which were in a leather case on his belt, and which May [my sister] and I thought was a revolver ... 'I'll have to use this if you do not let us take these children now'. Thinking that the policeman would shoot Mother, because she was trying to stop him, we screamed, 'We'll go with him Mum, we'll go' ... Then the policeman sprang another shock. He said he had to go to the hospital to pick up Geraldine [my baby sister], who was to be taken as well. The horror on my mother's face and her heartbroken cry! (Tucker, 1984 in HREOC, 1997, p. 37).

Because [my mother] wasn't educated, the white people were allowed to come in and do whatever they wanted to do—all she

Historical, theoretical and philosophical perspectives of ECEC

> did was sign papers. Quite possibly, she didn't even know what she signed . . . The biggest hurt, I think, was having my mum chase the welfare car—I'll always remember it—we were looking out the window and mum was running behind us and singing out for us. They locked us in the police cell up here and mum was walking up and down outside the police station and crying and screaming out for us. There was 10 of us.
>
> (Confidential evidence 689, New South Wales: woman removed in the 1960s and placed in Parramatta Girls' Home in HREOC, 1997, p. 40)

The policy of removal was devastating. As Read points out:

> It used to be said that by the end of the first world war, there wasn't a single British family that had not been touched, by injury or death, by the fighting in Europe. It is probably fair to say that except for the remotest region of the nation, there was not a single Aboriginal family which had not been touched by the policy of removal. Everybody had lost someone. (1998, p. 9)

There are many prominent Aboriginal artists, activists and community elders who were stolen but have found a way to tell their stories through their art or activism; for example, Archie Roach, Ruby Hunter, Deborah Cheetham, Doris Pilkington Garimara and Charles Perkins. As Read (1998) and the National Sorry Day Committee (nd) suggest, the experience of removal cannot be universalised; there are stories of great strength and deep bonds of friendship formed between children, alongside genuine love and care provided by white foster or adoptive parents and staff in institutions. However, 'the end result is a deep sorrow in the psyche or spirit for many Aboriginal and Torres Strait Islander individuals, families and communities throughout Australia' (National Sorry Day Committee, nd).

Running parallel to the removal of Indigenous children, but on a smaller scale and in a different legislative environment, was the forced, and occasionally voluntary, migration of white British children. The Child Migrants Trust (National Archives of Australia, nd) suggests that 'It is estimated that child

Historical perspectives on children and childhood

migration programmes were responsible for the removal of over 130 000 children from the United Kingdom to Canada, New Zealand, Zimbabwe (formerly Rhodesia) and Australia' (www.childmigrantstrust.com/our-work/child-migration-history). This policy was explicitly designed to provide 'good British stock' in those countries (Coldrey, 1999). In Australia, the number of children forcibly emigrated was small compared to the thousands of children sent to Canada. These children have become known as the Forgotten children.

Children sent to Australia were usually suffering terrible poverty in Britain, sometimes as orphans. They were regularly placed in specially built institutions such as the Fairbridge Farm (www.migrationheritage.nsw.gov.au/exhibition/fairbridge-farm-school/child-migration-to-australia/). Here they laboured—girls in domestic work and boys in the outside farm work—to maintain themselves. They also attended school and church. As we know from current government inquiries, these unaccompanied children were vulnerable to multiple forms of exploitation and abuse. Again, our federal government has apologised for the nation's treatment of these children. The then Prime Minister, Kevin Rudd, delivered his apology to the Forgotten children in 2009.

This historical removal and movement of children, some only weeks old in the case of the Stolen Generations, is a significant part of Australia's colonial and postcolonial history. It has impacted generations of Australian families, both Aboriginal and non-Aboriginal, as multilayered and explicitly racist social policies were put into practice by successive British and Australian governments (Burns et al., 2013). Even after the Second World War, children were considered the best immigrant. They constituted a particularly attractive category of migrant because they were seen to assimilate more easily, were more adaptable, had a long working life ahead and could be cheaply housed in dormitory style accommodation' (National Archives of Australia, nd). While many governments at state, territory and federal level have apologised for this historical treatment of children, it should be noted that as I write this chapter, and in breach of their human rights, refugee children remain in detention; indeed, some are born there. Children, it seems, remain vulnerable to silencing and marginalisation, despite the historical examples available to adults.

Having an historical understanding of childhood and how children have been viewed helps us to understand children and childhood in our contemporary world. It enables us to see that the social institutions, educational practices and policies for and about children have a past—and, importantly, that they can be changed. How a society understands childhood—our 'image' of childhood—impacts how we engage with children, the kind of education we provide and the kinds of laws and policies that governments enact. As a nation we need to publicly debate how children are treated in this country, how we think about who they are and what kinds of provisions are available to children and their families.

CHILDREN'S WORK AND MASS SCHOOLING IN AUSTRALIA

As is evident in accounts of the lives of Stolen and Forgotten children and in various histories of children's lives, children have always worked, usually alongside their families and other adults. Work, whether paid or unpaid, is one part of contributing to and maintaining societies. Historically, children worked alongside adults in a range of roles as soon as they were physically capable (Heywood, 2013). There is an important distinction to make between rewarding, valued and appropriately renumerated work and exploitative, unvalued or undervalued and under or unpaid work. Many children were, and still are, proud to work. As Heywood (2013) suggests, it is important to remember in our historical accounts to not only focus on the overwhelming stories of abject poverty and abusive or degrading work conditions for children. Histories indicate that in Britain in the nineteenth century 'organised child labour, for the poor, became the pattern that was accepted' (Gorton & Ramsland, 2002, p. 52) and this organised labour was often for long hours and low wages; in this context children were clearly at risk of significant abuses and neglect. History is rarely simple or clear-cut so the picture is always more complex, and it is important to note that while there is no doubting this appalling history of children's work, some children enjoyed their work, were well treated and took pride in their accomplishments and contributions to the family.

Children sent to Australia as convict children worked, many as indentured labour or apprentices. Gorton and Ramsland (2002) suggest that in New South Wales children were preferred as workers by some big landowners, who actively sought out children from prisons and children's homes. Boys were often apprenticed for trades (for example, as tailors, carpenters, milliners or factory workers)

(Gorton & Ramsland, 2002), while girls were generally confined to domestic labour.

As noted in the previous chapter, until the late nineteenth century, schooling in Australia was piecemeal. The introduction of widespread mass schooling in Australia reflected the western trend across the United Kingdom, Europe and the United States of moving children out of full-time workplaces and into schooling (Heywood, 2013). In the closing decades of the nineteenth century, children in Australia were expected to attend school regularly, but many did not. For example, some were needed to continue working to contribute to family maintenance and some children were living too far from the closest schools.

At the turn of the twentieth century in Australia, the growth of schools, crèches and child care settings as new institutions where children spent long periods of time provided scientists with a laboratory through which to study children. The Child Study movement flourished during this period, as scientists sought to understand human development through the observation of children. Within the discourses of the early twentieth century, this research tended to focus on children's health and development with the aim of creating standards for normal development to encourage the creation of future citizens who fitted into the scientists' vision of normal. The surveillance and socialising of children underpinning early ideas about schooling has many modern remnants, from assemblies or parades to the content and routine of the school day. Schooling was, and is, a means of socialising children within a society's vision of normal. The invention of mass schooling enabled the filtering and sorting of children into future adult occupations and the production of citizens (Lassonde, 2013). The emphasis of mass schooling has long been on children as interesting only for the adults they will become, with a focus on how to grow good future adults, who are then good citizens and workers.

This emphasis gradually extended to children before school age, as crèches and various forms of child care became part of the education picture. For example, the Crèche and Kindergarten Association of Queensland (C & K), the Sydney Day Nursery (SDN) and other similar organisations in Australia have philanthropic roots. These organisations were created to provide care and early education for children who might otherwise be considered vaga-bonds or 'larrikins' (see also previous chapter). The C & K was established in 1907 'to specifically support underprivileged families in the Brisbane area'

(Fazldeen, 1997, p. 1). The formation of the C & K was initiated by the Reverend Loyal Lincoln Wirt who passed through the poor areas of Brisbane on his daily travels to and from his church. It was the visibility of poor children on the streets of poverty-stricken inner-city areas—and the attendant discourses that linked poverty with sickness, crime and immorality—that aroused his philanthropic action (Logan, 1990). The children who attended the C & K centres were mostly poor children and children whose mothers 'had' to work. At a C & K centre the children were fed, cared for or educated while mothers were instructed in how to properly care for their children (Logan, 1990). Initial support for the C & K was via wealthy upper-class and middle-class patronage; many were the wives of leaders in Brisbane society and government. As Logan (1990, p. i) states, 'the Association in its first decades can readily be seen as an instrument of the State and, more generally, as an instrument of society's governing elite.' In this sense it was very much a source of charitable work for the ruling classes and its services were reminiscent of the charity or ragged schools in the United Kingdom (Hilton & Hirsch, 2000).

Hendrick (1997) has suggested that the creation of separate child and adult worlds has not occurred quickly, and it has not occurred in isolation from broader social issues. Several important factors have contributed to the separation of childhood from adulthood and of play from work. Two suggested by Hendrick (1997, pp. 42–7) are ideas that first came to prominence during the late eighteenth century and into the nineteenth century of the 'delinquent child' and the 'schooled child'. Out of these ideas, particularly in Britain and other western nations, such as Australia, laws were developed defining and regulating childhood. For example, legislation in Britain early in the nineteenth century concerning child labour prohibited particular employment situations for children under nine and regulated the working hours of children aged between nine and thirteen. Towards the end of the nineteenth century the idea of the 'schooled child' became the more acceptable understanding of children. This is the period of time in which universal, compulsory schooling legislation was enacted in Australia; for example, in Queensland this was evidenced in the *Education Act 1875*. These shifting ideas about children and childhood meant that the 'proper' place for children changed from work to school.

Within the context of the Australian constitution, written in 1901, schooling is the residual constitutional responsibility of the states and territories. The newly formed Commonwealth Government of Australia was concerned at the time with issues that affected the whole country, such as immigration and defence. Schooling was considered local and therefore left to the state and territory governments. It is for this reason that schooling remains variable from state to state. It is why it has taken decades of debate and negotiation to agree upon the need for a national curriculum. This is a good example of the political nature of education and curriculum development. This is also evident in the current situation where, since there has been a change of federal government, the Australian Curriculum remains in development but also under review; even before the curriculum has been fully 'rolled out' into schools.

The social acceptance of compulsory schooling was linked with changing understandings of family life and of work. It was a time of intensification of the perceived need for children to be 'free' to 'have a childhood' while simultaneously creating a schooling system that required children's attendance. Social understandings of families shifted to emphasise a male in paid labour and a woman at home with children (Ailwood, 2008; van Krieken, 2010). Indeed many Australian governments legislated for this, as women working for governments were sacked upon marriage. Despite this family type being neither as dominant nor necessarily as desirable as thought, this ideal dominated after the Second World War and stayed in place until the late 1960s and varied from state to state and federal governments. In the second half of the twentieth century, views about families and women's work began changing and the provision of child care became more pressing. During this period childhood came to be viewed more and more as a time for education rather than work, and play came to be known as the work of children. In early childhood education and care more recent theorising about play and children recognises the significance of children's inventive, imaginative, creative, social and cultural competence.

STUDIES OF CHILDREN AND CHILDHOOD

Social and historical studies of childhood have provided educators with three new and interconnected approaches to reflecting upon our ideas about children and their childhoods. First, the overall invisibility of children and childhood, including the way in which they had been regularly subsumed within studies of family, has been addressed; instead children have been viewed as actively

Historical, theoretical and philosophical perspectives of ECEC

engaged in their current worlds. For example, as early sociology of childhood researchers Qvortrup et al. (1994, p. xi) have pointed out, historically:

> revolutionary events have ... both dramatically and tragically underlined and pinpointed one major tenet of our project: children are not only future members of society, but they are also indeed participating in it—for better or for worse.

Second, childhood is relational. We understand childhood through our adult perspectives and in relation to what it means to be an adult in our society. It is therefore important for us as adults to reflect on 'what it means to be a particular kind of child at a particular time and specific location' (Walkerdine, 1998, p. 231). Third, childhood is constructed and understood through social institutions and provisions. This is reflected in widespread and narrow debates about the need for child care so mothers can return to paid work; imagine how different this debate would sound if instead the focus was on children and childhood and the kinds of spaces and environments adults create for them (Moss & Petrie, 2002).

The ideas developed through historical, geographical and sociological studies of childhood have provided evidence of children's participation in society and the role of childhood within our social structures (Mayall, 2013). In Australia, historical and sociological studies of childhood have not moved far from the margins (van Krieken, 2010). We depend to a large extent on European developments of childhood studies.

Cregan and Cuthbert (2014, p. 4) suggest that the United Nations Convention on the Rights of the Child (UNCRC) 'is the keystone in contemporary constructions of childhood and the demarcation of the child as a specific form of human being on a global scale'. While the UNCRC has certainly provided a lever for children to be thought of as 'rights holders', we should also remain vigilant, for, as Cregan and Cuthbert (2014) go on to argue and Mindy Blaise also suggests in her chapter in this book, this is not an unproblematic position for children and the societies they live in. For example, there is a separate charter written for African children, the African Charter on the Rights and Welfare of the Child (African Committee of Experts on the Rights and Welfare of the Child, 1999). This charter was written as the UNCRC is based in developmentalism and understandings of children that are Euro- and US-centric;

these ideas do not take into account the specific situation of children across African nations.

CONCLUSION

Various discourses or understandings of children and childhood will circulate through society at any time. Right now there is an increasing awareness that children are more capable and competent than previously thought. This is not to suggest children are not also growing, developing and in need of adult guidance or support. Rather it is to suggest that children are not growing from a position of 'emptiness'. They are not empty vessels to be filled with knowledge or empty slates to be written upon. Instead they are actively and capably engaged in their worlds.

In this chapter I have given an introductory overview of some of these images of childhood and children, and of how those images have enabled particular government policies, practices and institutions to be created. Fass (2013, p. 2) notes that:

> childhood in the West is a privileged state, a status to which some children have historically had much more access than others. One of the clear conclusions that historians have come to is that modern childhoods and children's experiences are deeply affected by circumstances such as status, class, wealth, and poverty.

This variation in circumstances is reflected in our understanding of the range of Australian childhoods. As teachers, it is useful to reflect on how you understand children and childhood as this will impact how you think about your role as a teacher and what early childhood education is for, and what provision looks like.

FURTHER THINKING

1. What is your image of children and/or childhood? Where does your image of children and childhood come from? How does it shape the way you think about your role as an early childhood teacher?

2. Find out more about children who are born/held in immigration detention centres or jails. What are their rights? Are Australian governments attending

to the rights of these children and their families? What does that say about our nation and how we currently 'view' childhood and children?

3. Explore the National Sorry Day Committee's website. What was the image of children that the Australian government of the day had of Aboriginal and Torres Strait Islander children? How is this evident in the policies, practices and institutions the government provided for the children?

4. Watch the movies *Rabbit-Proof Fence* and *Oranges and Sunshine*. Discuss these stories of Stolen and Forgotten children.

5. Interview an older friend or relative about their childhood. What experiences are similar/different to your own memories of childhood?

REFERENCES

African Committee of Experts on the Rights and Welfare of the Child (1999). African Charter on the Rights and Welfare of the Child. Retrieved 20 August 2014, <http://acerwc.org/acrwc-full-text/>.

Ailwood, J. (2008). Mothers, teachers, maternalism and early childhood education and care: Some historical connections, *Contemporary Issues in Early Childhood*, 8(2), 157–65.

Ariès, P. (1973). *Centuries of Childhood: A social history of family life* (trans. R. Baldick). London: Jonathan Cape.

Australian Human Rights Commission (2010). *Bringing Them Home: Effects across generations*. Retrieved 20 August 2014, <www.humanrights.gov.au/publications/rightsed-bringing-them-home-4-effects-across-generations-resource-sheet>.

Burns, A., Burns, K., Menzies, K. & Grace, R. (2013). The Stolen Generations. In J. Bowes, R. Grace & K. Hodge (eds), *Children, Families and Communities: Contexts and consequences*. Melbourne: Oxford University Press, pp. 239–54.

Child Migrants Trust (nd). *Child Migration History*. Retrieved 21 November 2013, <www.childmigrantstrust.com/our-work/child-migration-history>.

Cleverley, J. & Phillips, D. (1988). *Visions of Childhood: Influential models from Locke to Spock*. Sydney: Allen & Unwin.

Coldrey, B. (1999). *Good British Stock: Child and youth migration to Australia*. Retrieved 15 September 2014, <http://guides.naa.gov.au/good-british-stock/>.

Cregan, K. & Cuthbert, D. (eds) (2014). Knowing children: Theory and method in the study of children. In *Global Childhoods: Issues and debates*. London: SAGE Publications, pp. 3–18.

Cunningham, H. (2005). *Children and Childhood in Western Society Since 1500*. 2nd edn. London: Pearson.

Fass, P.S. (ed.) (2013). *The Routledge History of Childhood in the Western World*. London: Routledge.

Fazldeen, A. (1997). *The Crèche and Kindergarten Association of Queensland: A brief history 1907–1997*. Brisbane: C & K.

Finnish National Board of Education (2014). *Finnish Education in a Nutshell*. Retrieved 15 September 2014, <www.oph.fi/english/education_system>.

Gorton, K. & Ramsland, J. (2002). Prison playground? Child convict labour and vocational training in New South Wales, 1788–1840, *Journal of Educational Administration and History*, 34(1), 51–62.

Hendrick, H. (1997). Constructions and reconstructions of British childhood: An interpretative survey, 1800 to the present. In A. James & A. Prout (eds), *Constructing and Reconstructing Childhood: Contemporary issues in the sociological study of childhood*. London: Falmer Press, pp. 34–62.

Heywood, C. (2013). Children's work in countryside and city. In P. Fass (ed.), *The Routledge History of Childhood in the Western World*. Abingdon: Routledge, pp. 125–41.

Hilton, M. & Hirsch, P. (eds) (2000). *Practical Visionaries: women, education and social progress 1790–1930*, London: Longmans.

Human Rights and Equal Opportunities Commission (HREOC) (1997). *Bringing Them Home: Report of the national inquiry into the separation of Aboriginal and Torres Strait Islander children from their families*. Retrieved 5 November 2013, <www.humanrights. gov.au/publications/bringing-them-home-stolen-children-report-1997>.

Kociumbas, J. (1997). *Australian Childhood: A history*. Sydney: Allen & Unwin.

Lassonde, S. (2013). Age, schooling, and development. In P. Fass (ed.), *The Routledge History of Childhood in the Western World*. London: Routledge, pp. 211–28.

Logan, G. (1990). 'Mother State' steps in: The origins of state preschool education in Queensland, 1907–1973, *The Educational Historian*, 3(3), i–iv.

Mayall, B. (2013). *A History of the Sociology of Childhood*. London: Institute of Education Press.

Moss, P. & Petrie, P. (2002). *From Children's Services to Children's Spaces: Public policy, children and childhood*. London: RoutledgeFalmer.

National Archives of Australia (nd). *Child Migration to Australia—Fact Sheet 124*. Retrieved 5 November 2013, <www.naa.gov.au/collection/fact-sheets/fs124.aspx>.

National Sorry Day Committee (nd). The History of the Stolen Generations. Retrieved 20 August 2014, <www.nsdc.org.au/stolen-generations/history-of-the-stolen-generations/the-history-of-the-stolen-generations>.

Qvortrup, J., Bardy, M., Sgritta, G. & Wintersbeger, H. (eds) (1994). *Childhood Matters: Social theory, practice and politics*. Aldershot: Avebury.

Read, P. (1998). The return of the Stolen Generation, *Journal of Australian Studies*, 59, 8–19.

United Nations (1989). *United Nations Convention on the Rights of the Child (UNCRC)*. Geneva: United Nations.

van Krieken, R. (2010). Childhood in Australian sociology and society, *Current Sociology*, 58(2), 232–49.

Walkerdine, V. (1998). Children in Cyberspace: A new frontier. In K. Lesnik-Oberstein (ed.), *Children in Culture: Approaches to childhood*. London: Macmillan Press Ltd, pp. 231–47.

Woodrow & Press (2007). (Re) Positioning the Child in the Policy/Politics of Early Childhood. *Educational Philosophy and Theory*, 39(3), 312-325.

Chapter 3

Theoretical perspectives on early childhood

Mindy Blaise

In this chapter you will find an overview of:
- developmental psychology
- sociology and the child
- feminist perspectives on early childhood education and care
- critical theory perspectives.

This chapter introduces four major theoretical perspectives about children's learning in early childhood education and care: developmental psychology, sociology, feminisms and critical theory. A theory is a system of ideas or concepts intended to help explain something. Theories can be thought of as 'top-down' or 'bottom-up', depending on where they come from and how they are produced. The theories discussed in this chapter are considered to be top-down because they have three elements in common: they are all formal in that they can be recognised as a consistent set of concepts; they are associated with theorists who have played a role in developing a particular line of thinking; and they have all been developed through research. Theories can influence what educators notice and do in their practice.

Theories are not static. As new knowledge is produced—whether these are ideas about infant brain development or issues raised by children and families seeking asylum in Australia—theories are modified. As all theories are broad-based attempts to make sense of the world, they will overlap to some extent. Within each theory there are various key thinkers and knowledge communities that struggle over key ideas and put them together in different ways that lead to new concepts. Sometimes these thinkers and knowledge communities question common ideas found within the theory and as a consequence new concepts emerge. This is how theories develop and change.

These four top-down theories are not the only ways that educators understand their work. All educators come to the classroom with their own theories, such as how children learn 'best' or what it means to be a 'good' early childhood educator. These are considered 'bottom-up' theories because they emerge from the field and are made up of an educator's values, beliefs and experiences.

Bottom-up theories are informal and have been developed through practitioner research. Because these theories have been generated by practitioners and are related to their local needs and interests, the findings are usually not published for others to read. Instead, they are used to improve practice. Bottom-up theories can also be thought of as 'situated knowledges'; because they have been produced out of a particular situation or site, they are local and specific (Haraway, 1988). This chapter concludes by pointing readers towards situated knowledges as they are generated by early childhood professionals. This shows how educators can potentially reconstruct top-down theories about early childhood education.

THEORETICAL PERSPECTIVE 1: DEVELOPMENTAL PSYCHOLOGY

Developmental psychology is interested in how children grow and learn. It understands children's thinking as developing over time and through a series of universal stages. This theoretical perspective shows how children develop across the lifespan.

Developmental psychology emerged at the end of the late nineteenth and early twentieth centuries during a time when positivism was growing strong in the sciences. Positivism is a philosophical position that values empirical data and scientific methods. It believes that you can know the 'real' world in different ways, placing a high value on observing. Researchers in developmental psychology worked hard for this field to be seen as the scientific study of children and wanted it to be associated with the sciences, like medicine. By aligning itself with the sciences and using scientific methods to observe children, developmental psychology produces research that is rarely questioned and functions as 'the truth'.

Key ideas: the individual child, ages and stages, and the power of science

Three interrelated key ideas that come from developmental psychology are a focus on the individual child; the use of ages and predetermined stages to understand the developing child; and the power of science. It is worth noting the significance that positivism has on developmental psychology in terms of the methods and practices used to understand how children develop and learn. Many of the methods used in developmental psychology to determine a child's stage of learning include classifying how the child learns, ordering a child's cognitive abilities from concrete to abstract, and predicting what a child can do (James & James, 2012). All of these methods contribute to building a common sense and taken-for-granted understanding of development, based on rational logic. By focusing on the individual child, developmental psychology generates knowledge that is considered universal, predictable and 'true' for all children. In recent years this has come under question as being the only way to view children's learning and we are now looking at the range of influences that impact a child's learning, including community and culture.

Key thinkers

Jean Piaget (1896–1980) has been regarded as the leading authority on the cognitive development of young children. His theories laid out children's cognitive and moral development in a series of discrete stages. In his research, Piaget described children as initially egocentric and over time developing their reasoning abilities so that they become rational adults.

Other key thinkers within developmental psychology include Arnold Gesell (1880–1961), Lev Vygotsky (1896–1934) and Lawrence Kohlberg (1927–87). Although their contributions to cognition, maturation, cultural mediation and moral development have been important, there are also several women who have been pioneers in this field, but are less well known. For example, Lois Barclay Murphy (1902–2003) and Florence L. Goodenough (1886–1959) offered perspectives on children's strengths, rather than their deficits, and created new methods of studying children (Pickren, Dewsbury & Wertheimer, 2012).

Research in practice: developmental psychology

Mamie Phipps Clark (1917-83) initiated a series of studies about racial identification and preference among African American children. She found that young black children preferred to play with white dolls over black ones and that the children ascribed negative attitudes towards the black dolls. This research helped end racial segregation in US public schools. Almost 50 years ago, Clark suggested a range of parenting strategies to promote racial understandings and oppose prejudice with young children (Rutherford, 2012). Many of these have now become common practices in Australian early childhood settings, such as reading books with characters with diverse backgrounds to children to help them learn about people from different cultures and religions to their own.

Questioning the assumptions of developmental knowledge

Erica Burman (1994) and Valerie Walkerdine (1990; 1993), two feminist and critical developmental psychologists, question the practices used in developmental psychology and how they produce dominant images of childhood. Their critique is important because developmental psychology has such a powerful impact on how educators think about children, learning and what is considered 'normal' development.

Some of the assumptions found within developmental psychology include:

1. Development is portrayed as 'natural' and inevitable.
2. Developmental tasks are presented in clear and discrete age categories.
3. Developmental descriptions are segmented into domains, such as physical, social, emotional and cognitive.
4. Measurement tools, such as checklists and rating scales, unproblematically classify and categorise children.
5. The child is presented as always growing, progressing, and moving from an irrational and incomplete individual towards *becoming* a rational, complete and civilised adult.
6. The child is presented as an abstract 'knower', who sits outside culture, gender, family or any social context.

Although developmental psychology continues to play an important role in early childhood education, other theoretical perspectives help educators gain a critical and complex understanding of children's learning.

THEORETICAL PERSPECTIVE 2: SOCIOLOGY

Sociology is interested in understanding society, and sees childhood as a significant part of society. Sociology seeks to understand education as a social system and a social experience. Different approaches to sociology (such as interaction, functional and conflict theories) help to answer the purposes of education, how education is organised and works, what the experiences of education are for different groups, and what children learn (Leighton, 2012).

Understanding society, social institutions and childhood

Cultural reproduction theories were developed in the second half of the twentieth century to better understand the role of social institutions. These theories suggest that those who dominate capitalist systems mould individuals to suit their own purposes. These sociological approaches consider how families and schools pass on forms of culture to shape individuals' views of their worlds (Bowles & Gintis, 1976).

In the 1970s Pierre Bourdieu (1931–2002) introduced the concept of cultural capital and habitus to explore education's influences on stratification and social class. He wanted to know more about how social structures influence individuals' experiences. Cultural capital refers to various cultural practices, including how a person dresses, what kind of food or movies they prefer, or what they do in their leisure time. Everyone has differing amounts and types of cultural capital and this is related to their social class background. Habitus is the accumulation of beliefs, practices and attitudes that create a set of dispositions towards life, including school, and this influences what people say and do. Habitus is the environment that people are a part of and it is shaped by a family's history, where they live, their experiences of education and work, and their social networks. All children have a home habitus and they bring this with them to school.

Research in practice: sociology

Liz Brooker's ethnographic study of an English reception (preschool) class shows how different kinds of social and cultural resources in families, communities and early childhood services affects social inclusion and exclusion for particular groups of children (Brooker, 2002). For example, Brooker (2008) shows how three- and four-year-old Saskia's and Sonia's different home cultures develop and what happens when these girls bring their home habitus to school. Saskia's parents were self-assured about their own lives and relaxed about their daughter's early experiences, prioritising fun and happiness. Sonia's family lacked confidence about their daughter's ability to succeed in school and did not feel capable of providing her with the knowledge she would need to thrive in school. Saskia and Sonia's home habitus influenced how the girls transitioned to school. Saskia's home habitus matched the expectations of the Reception classroom, and she easily settled in, whereas it took Sonia more time to trust her teachers, make friends and make sense of her teachers' expectations.

Key ideas: socialisation, society and childhood

Sociological approaches are concerned with issues of socialisation and how children learn to conform to social norms and become a part of society (Kehily, 2009). What makes a sociological approach unique is that it specifically addresses childhood as a phenomenon worthy of studying. It encourages educators to see childhood and its status as socially, culturally, politically and historically constructed. This is a move away from the emphasis that developmental psychology places on understanding the individual child, towards seeing the child in relation to others. Making this shift from focusing only on the individual child to also acknowledging the child as gendered, raced, classed, and part of a family and society requires educators to see the child as social, competent and capable.

Childhood studies

While Bourdieu's ideas were influencing how sociologists understood society, a new paradigm for studying children was emerging within the social sciences. This recognised that children were a part of, rather than separate from, society. This new thinking, often referred to as childhood studies, stated that if we are to understand how society works then children and their views must be included (Mayall, 2002). It called for children to be recognised as social actors and for their views and perspectives to be heard (James & Prout, 1990).

Although sociology sees the child and childhood within context, socialisation and developmental approaches both position the child as *becoming* a responsible member of a family, a child within an educational setting or a citizen of society (Kehily, 2009). Childhood studies takes an interdisciplinary approach to think differently about childhood. Two key features of childhood studies include understanding childhood as a social construction and seeing children as active social agents.

Understanding childhood as a social construction

Understanding the social construction of childhood highlights children as competent and capable. It also works against reducing childhood to a universal and static concept. This view recognises that:
- childhood is a social phenomenon
- there are multiple childhoods
- children's development is considered a social and cultural process
- childhood is political.

Children constructing their own lives

Children's active participation in their environments and the part they play in constructing their own lives is important. As a result, childhood studies argues for studying children in their own right, which is a move from researching *on* or *about* children towards researching *with* them. Inspired by these changing perspectives in regards to adult-child researcher relationships, early childhood educators are seeking ways to transform their relationships with young children. This change in the status of children has been seen as important and has been taken up by those who believe in children's rights.

Children's rights

The concept of children's rights has been developed as part of childhood studies because the child is seen as a social actor capable of creating and communicating views about the social world and has a right to participate in it. From this perspective, young children have a right to participate in matters that affect them. The principles of children's rights are outlined in the United Nations Convention on the Rights of the Child (the Convention) (United Nations, 1989). This Convention supports the argument that children have a set of rights that are legally binding. Across the world, 191 countries, including Australia, have ratified the Convention.

The Convention has influenced a 'children's rights movement' across the world. Researchers have outlined conventions and policies pertaining to the status of children's language use in education (Phatudi & Moletsane, 2013), and new ethical research procedures with children (Smith, A.B, 2011) and have demonstrated how to use rights-based approaches to observe and assess young children (Smith, K., 2013).

In Australia, there is a national children's commissioner, who plays an important role in promoting and protecting the rights of all children. According to the Australian Human Rights Commission (2010), the issues facing Australian children include homelessness, bullying and harassment.

In addition, children's rights has encouraged interest in and research about all kinds of issues, such as the status of asylum-seeking and refugee children, child poverty, children and the law, and the international migration of children. These areas of interest bring a global perspective to the field. They encourage educators to think outside their limited preschool, kindergarten and long day care contexts, and consider how they may be connected to these diverse childhoods. Making connections between wider issues and local early childhood contexts requires the field to rethink the role of an early childhood professional.

Questioning children's rights

Children's rights produces an image of the child as a social actor with rights and has been helpful in spurring advocacy for children across the globe. Nonetheless, it has also challenged the field to ask some hard questions about childhood. For example, the Convention clearly spells out that these rights are related to the special needs related to childhood, which assumes all children have such needs. This is considered problematic because a universal framework takes for granted that childhoods are similar across the world. This assumption works against much of the progress made by childhood studies in advocating for the recognition of local and diverse childhoods (James & James, 2012).

Reflections

1. How do we balance rights that are in conflict? For example, when children's rights clash with parents' or other adults' rights, what should be done?
2. Whose concerns about these rights are prioritised?
3. How is it problematic that these ideas are constructed by the West and then imposed on children in other-than-western contexts?
4. If children cannot enforce their rights, then what use are they?

Considering these questions allows advocates for children to ask hard questions about the continuing power that adults have over children.

The rights of Aboriginal children and their families and communities

As traditional owners of the land, Aboriginal Australians hold a distinct place in Australian society along with distinctive rights. According to the Australian Human Rights Commission (2010) these include:

- **The right to a distinct status and culture**, which helps maintain and strengthen the identity and spiritual and cultural practices of Aboriginal communities.

Historical, theoretical and philosophical perspectives of ECEC

- **The right to self-determination**, which is a process where Aboriginal communities take control of their future and decide how they will address the issues facing them.
- **The right to land**, which provides the spiritual and cultural basis of Aboriginal communities.

These are important rights and should be acknowledged within early childhood services. In 2013, a dedicated Commissioner for Aboriginal Children and Young People was appointed in Victoria to ensure these rights. Arguably Aboriginal children's rights should be addressed in early childhood because early childhood services has been identified by Aboriginal communities as a site to address the disadvantages experienced by Aboriginal people due to colonisation. This will require educators to figure out how to honour Aboriginal rights, even (or especially) when Aboriginal Australian families or educators are not currently part of their services. One way that educators can support Aboriginal Australians' rights to a distinct culture is to acknowledge the traditional owners of the land the centre is built on. Another strategy is to find out, in partnership with the local Aboriginal community, about their histories and stories, and bring this knowledge into the curriculum. Focusing on the local Aboriginal community in particular interrupts the idea of a homogenous Aboriginal Australia. In a similar way to questions raised in regard to enforcing children's rights, it is critical to ask how we support Aboriginal children to exercise these rights. These are hard questions about children's rights in general and Aboriginal children and families in particular. They are useful, however, for helping educators clarify their own values and beliefs in regards to all children's rights.

THEORETICAL PERSPECTIVE 3: FEMINISMS

Four feminist knowledge communities that influence early childhood education include liberal, essentialist, poststructuralist and 'new' materialist. Although these feminisms might understand knowledge differently, they are united in their common interest in how gender mediates, shapes and constitutes our lived experiences (Measor & Sikes, 1992). The following section explains the different ways they aim to reach this common goal.

Theoretical perspectives on early childhood

Key ideas: gender equality and gender equity

Feminist theories have made important contributions to how educators approach gender equity and include the concepts of equality and equity (Carelli, 1988). The concept of equality falls within an equal opportunities paradigm, arguing that children should have an equal chance to achieve in schools regardless of their backgrounds.

Gender equality in practice

- Promoting equal access to play experiences and materials for girls and boys.
- Guaranteeing that boys and girls have the same opportunities in the curriculum.
- Ensuring that same-sex families are treated with the same respect as heterosexual families.

An equity pedagogy exists when educators adapt their pedagogies to the unique talents, needs and differences of a diverse population. An equity pedagogy recognises the historical inequities of children and families from different social groupings, such as gender and sexuality, and that children and families do not all start from a level playing field. It believes in redistributing resources more fairly to those who need them. Gender equity also recognises that different gender relationships of power and privilege exist within educational settings and society.

Gender equity in practice

- Rewriting registration forms to include terms such as 'primary caregiver' and 'caregiver' instead of Parent/Mother/Father.
- Having a 'special person in my life' celebration, rather than 'father's day' or 'mother's day' celebrations.
- Addressing newsletters with 'Dear Families' rather than 'Dear Mums and Dads'.

Historical, theoretical and philosophical perspectives of ECEC

Feminist knowledge communities and key thinkers

Liberal feminism
Liberal feminism is associated with the Enlightenment, as both theories draw upon ideas about natural rights, justice and democracy. Liberal feminism sees females as equal citizens, entitled to the same rights and opportunities as males. Education is seen as a social institution that can facilitate progress and social reform. Access to education is important because it is claimed that by providing equal education to girls and boys an environment is created in which everyone's individual potential can be developed.

> ### Liberal feminism in practice
> The block area is often associated with boys, whereas writing is usually seen as an activity that girls prefer or enjoy. To ensure that the girls have opportunities to build with blocks, a teacher working from a liberal feminist perspective might have a 'girls only' block-playing day, where only girls are allowed to go to the block area.

Essentialist feminism
Instead of concentrating on the similarities between women and men, essentialist feminism focuses on the differences in an effort to draw attention to the inequalities between the genders, especially within patriarchal social structures. Some essentialist feminists affirm that women and girls are born with 'natural' feminine qualities (such as caring, nurturing and interdependence) and these are sources of both pride and strength (Martin, 1984; Noddings, 1984). This idea about gender differences has also been used to explore and critque the feminisation of the early childhood profession and why girls and boys are perceived to construct knowledge and solve problems differently.

Like the liberal perspective, essentialist feminism promotes equality in the classroom. However, essentialist feminism views girls as different, therefore requiring curriculum and teaching strategies that support their alleged learning differences.

Similar thinking about gender differences has been mobilised within the policy arena and public debates to continuously frame girls' success in relation to the failure of boys (Ringrose & Epstein, 2008). Feminist scholars show how these debates fail to highlight the continuing problems experienced by girls in terms of performance and classroom interactions (Francis & Skelton, 2005).

Essentialist feminism in practice

To encourage more girls to build with blocks, a teacher working from a radical feminist perspective might include 'feminine' materials (pink blocks, dolls, cooking utensils, etc.) in the block area. An essentialist feminist practice would not encourage a 'boys only' time in the dramatic play area because it only reinforces the patriarchal relationships that males already possess.

Poststructural feminism

In the late 1980s poststructural feminism emerged to challenge liberal over-reliance on Enlightenment and rationalism. It rejects the logic of gender differences, binary oppositions and the unified subject. It is considered anti-structural and sets out to create new ways of understanding gender, while seeking to analyse the workings of inequity in all of its distinct and obscure forms.

Michel Foucault's (1926–84) theories of power and knowledge have been used with poststructural feminism and offer a conceptual framework for producing knowledge about gender. Foucault (1980) argued that power is a process operating in our social world that functions within all relationships and is expressed through discourse. From this perspective power is understood as something that circulates and produces particular kinds of gendered subjects. Knowledge and power are tied together and expressed through language. Since power exists within fields of knowledge, it produces and exercises particular forms of gender power relations.

Poststructural feminism is interested in how gender is constructed through power relations. It is concerned with how discourses operate as normalising and naturalising processes, and this is considered a source of gender inequity. This theory allows educators to recognise how children (and families) are constituted, positioned and sometimes marginalised through gender discourses. This perspective illuminates the necessity for early childhood educators to understand the parts that children, knowledge and power play in the construction of gender.

Poststructural feminism in practice

A teacher working from the poststructural feminist perspective sets out to rethink many of the current gender equity strategies she is employing. Instead of trying to make these strategies 'work', she uses new concepts such as language, discourse and power to understand and trouble children's play. By recognising how children play a part constructing what it means to be a 'girl' and boy', this teacher might intervene in children's play in order to question who benefits from the play taking place.

'New' material feminisms

Extending on poststructural feminist questioning of Enlightenment thinking, 'new' material feminism further challenges what counts as knowledge. This feminist perspective can be thought of as a practice, conceptual frame and political stance that refuses to focus exclusively on language and discourse to understand the world (Dolphijn & van der Tuin, 2012). As a practice it turns to studying the material world, stressing the complex materiality of bodies (child, teacher, animals, nature, objects, etc.) immersed in social relations of power. This provokes new thinking around meaning as emerging within dynamic entanglements of all sorts of matter. To do this kind of conceptual work requires reconsidering certain binaries (nature and culture; mind and body; boy and girl; material and discursive) and focusing instead on the intra-actions and entanglements of these elements. Material feminisms offer a radically different way of looking at reality and how educational institutions reproduce, sustain and shift gender inequalities (Taylor & Ivinson, 2013).

In early childhood, there is an emerging field of scholarship that draws inspiration from French philosophers Gilles Deleuze (1925–95) and Félix Guattari (1930–92) and feminist thinkers, such as Karen Barad, Rosi Braidotti and Donna Haraway. Feminist early childhood researchers foreground how materiality and relationality are significant in relation to gender and difference.

Theoretical perspectives on early childhood

'New' material feminism in practice

'New' material feminism encourages the educator to recognise the materiality of the blocks that the children are playing with and the relationality between blocks and children. It is a strategy that decentres the human child and makes room for the more-than-human, such as the blocks. Attention is paid to how the child and blocks are co-shaping each other. As a new methodology, it encourages an educator to trace the history of the blocks, finding out what materials they are made of, where they came from, how they were made and who made them. The educator might also consider their own memories of block play and how this influences what they notice or dismiss when considering gendered block play. This methodology does not position the educator as separate from the block play; they too are entangled in the female educator–girl child body-block-play.

THEORETICAL PERSPECTIVE 4: CRITICAL THEORY

Critical theory developed from various ideas emerging from the Frankfurt School in the twentieth century. It is grounded in a vision of a democratic society in which people live together in ways that are generous, compassionate and socially just. It is considered a socio-political theory because it is concerned with issues of power and oppression. In particular, critical theory is interested in how economies, race, social class, sexuality and gender, abilities, age, etc. interact to construct a social system. Critical theory is relevant to the field of early childhood because it assumes that education is a social and political activity that affects the life chances (both positively and negatively) of children involved in it.

Key ideas: questioning and transforming

Critical theory offers educators a range of conceptual tools to consider how power operates in education in relation to knowledge and authority. Most importantly, educators use these tools to question taken-for-granted assumptions (ideologies) about teaching, learning and childhood.

By asking politically fraught questions, such as, 'Who gains and who loses in this preschool from seeing things in particular ways?' or 'Who would gain and who would lose if an alternative view were accepted?', critical theory sets out to locate and understand inequalities and oppressions. By uncovering *whose* values and knowledge perpetuate particular truths about early childhood education, a critical perspective makes possible the creation of more inclusive and socially just forms of curriculum.

The main aim of critical theory is to critique *and* change society. This is different from other social theories, which usually intend to understand and explain society, not transform it. In this sense critical theory is considered radical, emancipatory and a theory for change.

Transformational teaching

In the field of education, Paulo Freire (1921–97) is most closely identified with critical theory. He was a Brazilian educator who taught peasant farmers to read and to understand how the power structures of the dominant society worked to oppress them. He was devoted to work that would transform the lives of marginalised groups of people.

In order to do transformational work, critical early childhood educators, like the farmers that Freire worked with, must first become conscious about the ways that their own thinking, and the traditional early childhood curriculum that they have enacted, can be limiting and oppressive. Early childhood educators have become critically aware of these limitations by drawing from a range of theories that take a critical stance on particular forms of oppression. For example, building on the important gender research that poststructural feminism provided, scholars have used insights from queer theory to critique heteronormativity, which is the expectation that everyone in society should be, or at least act, heterosexual. Mindy Blaise and Affrica Taylor (2012) show how early childhood educators can develop a 'queer eye' (p. 91) to analyse how children negotiate their gender identities and the gender/sexuality power relations associated with them. This enables educators to understand how heteronormativity plays out in the curriculum and develop ways to disrupt this knowledge.

Educators can also use critical theory more generally to raise questions about oppression by placing themselves and their values and beliefs within social, cultural, historical and philosophical frameworks. This allows them to gain a sense of how different groups of people (girls, single mothers, Indigenous children and their families, second-language learners, etc.) are situated within the wider world and early childhood. Critical educators do not stop at becoming aware of these issues. Instead, they name these inequities, critically reflect on them, and then act.

Critical theory teaches us that education is always political and that educators are part of this process. Education can be transformational, but it can never be an individual process. Therefore, critical educators must build alliances with others (colleagues, families, students) to reconstruct new knowledge together.

Critical theory in practice: the Revolutionary Planning Group

In Victoria, a small group of critical early childhood professionals, who call themselves the Revolutionary Planning Group (RPG), work together to question and reconceptualise some of their own taken-for-granted early childhood practices. For instance, they became frustrated with the traditional practices of program planning and felt that these ways of documenting children's learning valued only one kind of knowledge. They were concerned that the ways in which they were encouraged to document children's learning tended to focus on what children could not do, rather than what they were doing. They wondered if the observations that they were expected 'to do on children' even focused on children's learning at all. Because of their dissatisfaction and critique, they started to experiment with other ways of 'knowing' children. One of the RPG members decided to see what would happen if she did not do program planning for a week. Instead, she spent the week 'being with' children. Another member reconsidered the checklists that she used to determine children's readiness skills. Both of these educators were finding new approaches that focused on what children were like and who they were as people. It soon became apparent how limiting the current program planning model and assessment tools were because they got in the way of developing relationships with children. As a result, these educators began experimenting with 'learning stories', creating and inventing new pedagogies that helped build relationships with children and families, and support their learning.

Historical, theoretical and philosophical perspectives of ECEC

As a group, the RPG created a manifesto that represents how they were envisioning critical and transformational education for young children. *The Manifesto of the Revolutionary Planning Group* includes the following points:

1. Indigenous culture should be central to all early childhood services.
2. Learning should focus on children's strengths rather than weaknesses.
3. Early childhood should embrace complexity.
4. Learning is only meaningful when it engages with real life.
5. We want transformation, not acceptance of the status quo.
6. Advocacy for children and their rights is central to our teaching.
7. Early childhood is fundamentally about relationships.
8. Children's identities are fundamental to their lives and learning.
9. Children's voices should dominate the curriculum.
10. Early childhood services must be owned by their community.
    (Blaise, 2007; pp. 46-7)

These ten principles all address, as a political issue, some aspect of early childhood practice that these educators believe is damaging to less-privileged groups of children.

CONCLUSION

This chapter has introduced four theoretical perspectives (developmental psychology, sociology, feminisms and critical theory) that are part of early childhood education. Although these are considered to be 'top-down' theories, many educators generate their own 'bottom-up' theories. Sometimes this is done by applying theories into their practice and modifying them in ways that work best within their local context. Other times they build knowledge from the bottom-up through experimentation. In doing so, they are producing new knowledge that will eventually contribute to building contemporary theories about childhoods, teaching and learning. Early childhood educators, rather than theorists (who often do not work with young children on a daily basis in educational settings), can take the lead in transforming and advancing the field.

This chapter concludes with an example of early childhood professionals who are producing new, specific and situated knowledge in their communities.

Working together, Kerry Mundine, a Wiradjiri Bunjalung woman and early childhood educator, and Miriam Giugni, a white educator, show how three- to five-year-old children in a long day care centre use a range of strategies to include and exclude others in their play (Mundine & Giugni, 2006). In order to find out more about children's understandings of beauty, Aunty Kerry, Miriam and other educators had discussions with children about whiteness. Although such discussions can be challenging for those with existing race privilege, they show how young children understand the workings of power and knowledge in relation to skin colour and culture.

FURTHER THINKING

1. Locate more examples of situated knowledges in early childhood education and read how early childhood professionals are producing new knowledge. Identify the ways in which the four theories influence their projects.

2. Write down three reasons why you want to work with young children. Consider how the four theories will help you achieve this goal.

3. Look through Belonging, Being and Becoming: The early years learning framework for Australia and identify how the four theories are present in this document. Do you think the Framework uses one perspective more than the other? If so, which one? What leads you to think this?

ACKNOWLEDGEMENT

Mindy would like to acknowledge the generosity of Dr Sue Lopez Atkinson, a Yorta Yorta woman who gave important advice regarding the rights of Aboriginal children, their families and communities.

REFERENCES

Australian Human Rights Commission (2010). *An Australian Children's Commissioner: Discussion paper*. Retrieved 9 June 2014, <www.humanrights.gov.au/sites/default/files/document/publication/2010_commissioner_children.pdf>.

Blaise, M. (2007). Revolutionising practice by doing early childhood politically: The Revolutionary Planning Group. In S. Edwards & J. Nuttall (eds), *Professional learning in early childhood settings*. Rotterdam/Taipei: Sense Publishers, pp. 27–47.

Blaise, M. & Taylor, A. (2012). Research in review: Using queer theory to rethink gender equity in early childhood education, *Young Children*, pp. 88–98.

Bowles S. & Gintis H. (1976). *Schooling in Capitalist America: Educational reform and the contradictions of economic life*. New York: Routledge.

Brooker, L. (2002). *Starting School: Young children learning cultures*. Buckingham: Open University Press.

—— (2008). *Supporting Transitions in the Early Years*. Berkshire: Open University Press.

Burman, E. (1994). *Deconstructing Developmental Psychology*. New York: Routledge.

Carelli, A. (1988). *Sex Equity in Education: Readings and strategies*. Springfield, IL: Charles C. Thomas Publisher.

Dolphijn, R. & van der Tuin, I. (2012). *New Materialism: Interviews and cartographies*. London: Open Humanities Press.

Foucault, M. (1980). *Power/Knowledge: Selected interviews and other writings 1972–1977*. New York: Pantheon Books.

Francis, B. & Skelton, C. (2005). *Reassessing Gender and Achievement: Questioning contemporary key debates*. London: Routledge.

Haraway, D. (1988). Situated Knowledges: The science question in feminism and the privilege of partial perspectives, *Feminist Studies*, 14(3), 575–99.

James, A. & James, A. (2012). *Key Concepts in Childhood Studies*, 2nd edn. London: SAGE Publications.

James, A. & Prout, A. (eds) (1990). *Constructing and Reconstructing Childhood*. London: Falmer Press.

Kehily, M.J. (2009). *An Introduction to Childhood Studies*, 2nd edn. Berkshire: Open University Press.

Leighton, R. (2012). Sociology of education. In J. Arthur & A. Peterson (eds), *The Routledge Companion to Education*. New York/London: Routledge, pp. 58–65.

Martin, J.R. (1984). Bringing women into educational thought, *Educational Theory*, 34(4), 341–54.

Mayall, B. (2002). *Towards a Sociology for Childhood: Thinking from children's lives*. Buckingham: Open University Press.

Measor, L. & Sikes, P.J. (1992). *Gender and Schools*. New York: Cassell.

Mundine, A.K. & Giugni, M. (2006). *Diversity and Difference: Lighting the spirit of identity*. Canberra: Early Childhood Australia.

Noddings, N. (1984). *Caring: A feminine approach to ethics and moral education*. Los Angeles: University of California Press.

Phatudi, N. & Moletsane, M. (2013). Restoring indigenous languages and the right to learn in a familiar language: A case of black South African children. In B.B. Swadener, L. Lundy, J. Habashi & N. Blanchet-Cohen (eds), *Children's Rights and Education: International perspectives*. New York: Peter Lang Publishing, pp. 150–68.

Pickren, W.E., Dewsbury, D.A. & Wertheimer, M. (eds) (2012). *Portraits of Pioneers in Developmental Psychology*. New York: Psychology Press, Taylor & Francis Group.

Ringrose, J. & Epstein, D. (2008). Gender and schooling: Contemporary issues in gender equality and educational achievement. In D. Richardson and V. Robertson (eds), *Introducing Gender and Women's Studies*, 3rd edn. Hampshire & New York: Palgrave Macmillan, pp. 144–59.

Rutherford, A. (2012). Mamie Phipps Clark: Developmental psychologist, starting from strengths. In W.E. Pickren, D.A. Dewsbury & M. Wertheimer (eds), *Portraits of Pioneers in Developmental Psychology*. New York: Psychology Press, Taylor & Francis Group, pp. 261–76.

Smith, A.B. (2011). Respecting children's rights and agency: Theoretical insights into ethical research procedures. In B. Perry, D. Harcourt, & T. Waller (eds), *Young Children's Perspectives: Ethics, theory, and research*. London: Routledge, pp. 11–26.

Smith, K. (2013). A rights-based approach to observing and assessing children in the early childhood classroom. In B.B. Swadener, L. Lundy, J. Habashi, & N. Blanchet-Cohen (eds), *Children's Rights and Education: International perspectives*. New York: Peter Lang Publishing, pp. 99–114.

Taylor, C.A. and Ivinson, G. (2013). 'Material feminisms: New directions for education', *Gender and Education*, 25(6), pp. 665–70.

United Nations (1989). *United Nations Convention on the Rights of the Child (UNCRC)*. Geneva: United Nations.

Walkerdine, V. (1990). *Schoolgirl Fictions*. London: Virago.

—— (1993). Beyond developmentalism? *Theory and Psychology*, 3, 451–70.

Chapter 4

Practical approaches and philosophies in early childhood education and care

Linda Henderson and Susan Edwards

In this chapter you will find an overview of the:
- Highscope approach
- Cultural historical approach
- Reggio Emilia educational project approach
- Forest Schools approach
- Montessori approach
- Multiple Intelligence Theory and Practice.

Western-European approaches to early childhood education are informed by various beliefs about young children and their learning. These beliefs are reflected in philosophical positions about the purpose of learning and, therefore, how educators should teach. They are also evident in theoretical ideas that have been created to explain children's development and learning. Early childhood education is an interesting field because it has drawn on a mixture of such philosophies and theories to create different 'approaches' to learning and teaching with very young children (Arthur et al., 2015). This is one of the reasons why Belonging, Being and Becoming: The early years learning framework (EYLF) for Australia (Department of Education, Employment and Workplace Relations [DEEWR], 2009) recognises that there are a range of theories and philosophies that early childhood educators draw upon in their work (p. 11).

In this chapter we outline some practical approaches to early childhood education. These approaches apply theoretical concepts about young children's learning and development. Some of these practical approaches draw on the theories discussed in the previous chapter. Some, such as the cultural historical approach, draw on other theories influencing early childhood education and care (ECEC). Each approach is introduced with a reflection from an educator on how and why they use those ideas and philosophies in their own work with young children. The approaches considered in this chapter include the HighScope approach, cultural historical approach, Reggio Emilia educational project approach, Forest Schools approach, Montessori approach and the Multiple Intelligences approach.

HIGHSCOPE APPROACH

Children need to have direct hands-on experiences with their world if they are to learn. When I set up my room I look at children's interests and divide the room into interest areas. In each area there are baskets and labels. The baskets are filled with different materials and labelled with words and pictures describing their contents. This allows children to purposefully choose an area and engage in meaningful learning experiences. On the mat area I have a message board. Central to my teaching approach is predictable and well-structured routines for the children. Every morning the children and I gather on the mat for 'greeting time'. I also read the message board explaining the day's routines. Then the children move into small group time, inside and outside time, as well as whole group time. I embed into each of these routines deliberate learning intentions. When the children come together for whole group time I might read a story about the different seasons. I ask specific questions that will help children make connections between the story and real life. During 'greeting time' I will deliberately ask questions of children about their previous learning to encourage them to review their learning. So I believe learning is "active participation" (Epstein, 2007) where children must be involved in planning, carrying out and reflecting on their intentional activities and my role is to support and extend their learning.

> **—Mary reflecting on her practices as a HighScope educator**

Historical, theoretical and philosophical perspectives of ECEC

HighScope is a curriculum approach developed in the United States by the HighScope Education Research Foundation, an independent non-profit organisation. HighScope is based on the idea that combining teaching practices with curriculum provides the most effective means of supporting young children's learning (Conner, 2008). We can see this in Mary's reflection on HighScope when she talks about embedding deliberate learning intentions for the children into their planned group time experiences. According to the HighScope approach, teaching practices are about *how teachers work with children* and curriculum is *what children learn*. Teaching practices are characterised by:

- shared control during discussions between teachers and children
- active participatory learning relationships with children, and
- provision of materials for children's direct exploration. (HighScope, 2011)

HighScope teaching practices are influenced by concepts from constructivist learning theory. This includes ideas developed by Piaget and Dewey regarding the need for children to explore objects when learning about the properties of materials, and the role of children's active problem solving and thinking in constructing knowledge (Hohmann & Weikart, 1995). These ideas are evident in Mary's work when she talks about placing objects and materials in baskets located in different areas of the classroom. Children are invited to select from these materials and to use them to support their own learning interests.

In the HighScope approach, the curriculum focuses on defined content areas so that what children learn during their periods of exploration can be readily identified. The main content areas are:

- language, literacy and communication
- social and emotional development
- physical development, health and wellbeing
- arts and science (including mathematics), and
- approaches to learning. (HighScope, 2011)

An important aspect of HighScope is that the teaching practices and curriculum are aligned so children learn content knowledge via intentional teaching. This does not mean that educators 'tell' children what to do. Instead, educators use daily routines that help them participate in the 'Plan/Do/Review' process with children. The 'Plan/Do/Review' process is a central aspect of the

HighScope approach, where children make choices about what they will do during a session. They then carry out their planned ideas, and finally reflect on what happened during the implementation of their ideas. The 'planning' phase occurs early in the session, the 'doing' phase during the middle part of the session and the 'reviewing' phase towards the end of the session. Children appreciate that their learning will be deliberate in terms of planning, and discovery-oriented in terms of what they will experience during their 'doing' phase. They also learn that reflection helps them to make connections between their ideas and experiences. Mary indicates that this type of routine is important for supporting children's learning. She values the 'greeting time' and helps children to understand the range of experiences that will occur during the day. Intentional teaching is embedded in each experience to ensure children access content knowledge, as well as actively engage with objects and materials.

HighScope is considered to promote children's curiosity, decision-making, cooperation, persistence, creativity and problem solving (Hohmann & Weikart, 1995). HighScope is acknowledged as a significant international approach to early childhood education. This is because the effectiveness of the approach was researched by randomly assigning groups of children to a 'no program' and a 'HighScope program' approach. Initially conducted over 30 years ago, the research followed children assigned to the 'no program' and the 'HighScope program' into adulthood. Now aged in their forties, the findings show that the original child attendees of the 'HighScope program' were more likely to complete high school and be in sustained employment during adulthood than their 'no program' peers. HighScope participants were also less likely to have been in trouble with the law, to have used drugs of dependence and to be reliant on social security (Schweinhart et al., 2005). The HighScope approach is a research-informed approach to early childhood education that makes strong connections between how teachers teach and what children learn.

CULTURAL HISTORICAL APPROACH

> I believe that the child comes into the kindergarten with a range of experiences. Each child may have learned differing concepts from similar experiences. It is my task as the teacher to support the children in extending that knowledge and skills base. I believe

Historical, theoretical and philosophical perspectives of ECEC

in supporting children to have experiences that will enable them to function successfully as a social person within our community and culture. I acknowledge the child's individual background when designing learning experiences. I have a child, Finley, at the moment and he is very quiet and often stands watching what is happening around him. I noticed that Finley loved watching the other boys build with the large indoor blocks but he would not participate even when asked by the children or staff. One day Finley mentioned that he had been to the zoo on the weekend. He was very excited about this. I suggested we go and build a zoo with blocks. To my delight he agreed. I was able to actively work with Finley, talking about what we might build, how we might use small blocks for the animals and where we might place the animals. We spent about half an hour working on the zoo. The next day Finley returned to this zoo play and over the next couple of weeks he would work with me. But he was also happy to have a peer join in. Slowly over a period of many weeks Finley began to take on more initiative in this play to the point where he was able to initiate this play independently. This shows how I set up a social situation from an experience and interest of the child. I was also able to work on an experience that I felt was going to provide Finley with new learning skills, especially in developing social skills with peers. I could also provide opportunities for learning mathematical concepts with input from me as the teacher. Learning using the child's interests is critical because it acknowledges what the child already knows, what experiences he may have already had with his family or community, and the importance of working within a child's zone of proximal development to enhance learning.

—**Elizabeth reflecting on her practices as an educator using cultural historical ideas**

A cultural historical approach to early childhood education draws on ideas about children's learning and development that were first proposed by Lev Vygotsky. Vygotsky was a Russian theorist who was interested in how children learn and develop within a cultural context. We can see this in Elizabeth's reflection on her practice when she talks about connecting Finley's experience of having been to the zoo to provide him with a play-based activity. Elizabeth deliberately draws on Finley's contextual experiences as a basis for his play. An important idea in cultural historical theory is that people learn to use the tools associated with their community (Vygotsky, 1997). Learning to use tools is important because it helps people to achieve particular 'objects' or things they would like to do. Children learn to use cultural tools by interacting with other people. Elizabeth shows this idea when she reflects on using the blocks with Finley to achieve the object of 'playing zoos'. She shows him how to use the blocks as 'tools' for building enclosures and then how the enclosures can be used to 'categorise' the different animals. By using the blocks as tools in this way Elizabeth exposes Finley to mathematical concepts, such as length and categorisation. Vygotsky believed that tools could be both physical (such as the blocks) and conceptual (such as measuring). Conceptual tools include language and symbolic means of communicating ideas, including musical notation or mathematical symbols. Cultural tools change over time because they are adapted by people as they use them to achieve their objects of activity (Wertsch, 2007).

Language shows how cultural tools change over time. Early language was predominantly spoken. The invention of the printing press meant more people had access to written language. This meant that reading as well as speaking became important. In recent years, the widespread use of technologies in post-industrial societies means that language is increasingly understood as 'multimodal', meaning that it now includes visual images and audio in addition to written text (Kalantzis & Cope, 2012). Text messaging has also changed the form of language and resulted in 'new' ways of communicating. As a cultural tool, language has a history of development over time. This is why Vygotsky's work is understood by some scholars to be 'cultural historical'—tools have a historical pattern of development within the culture from which they are derived (Daniels, 2008). People use and adapt cultural tools to suit their purposes and needs.

Vygotsky's work suggests that adults are important for young children's acquisition of cultural tools (Hedegaard & Fleer, 2008). This is because adults have learned how to use cultural tools and have acquired cultural knowledge over time. Adults share cultural knowledge and the use of cultural tools with children through social interactions. Elizabeth is very clear that she has an intentional role in supporting Finley's play using physical and conceptual tools—she

Historical, theoretical and philosophical perspectives of ECEC

provides materials, identifies and builds on his interests, connects him with his peers, promotes access to mathematical concepts and knowledge about zoo animals, and engages him in discussion about his activity. Elizabeth's practices and decisions are grounded in her understanding of how children's experiences and interactions with others inform their acquisition of cultural tools as a basis for learning. This is a core idea in cultural historical theory that is useful for thinking about how the concept of 'intentional teaching' (DEEWR, 2009, p. 15) can be used in practice.

REGGIO EMILIA EDUCATIONAL PROJECT APPROACH

Our kindergarten is inspired and provoked by the Reggio Emilia Educational Research Project. We are constantly involved in a process of interpreting what this inspiration means for our context so we can create unique, authentic and meaningful spaces for learning. This means the kindergarten is not a separated space from the community but rather an open space embedded within the community. By embracing this philosophy in all our engagements with children and families we strive to respectfully foster experiences and interests that reflect the children, their families and the community in which they live and learn. Our provocations and possibilities for play and learning are offered and shared by the educators, as well as the educators responding to the provocations and ideas of the children. To do this we value the many 'languages' children possess to express their inquiries, curiosities, competencies, wonder and learning. We also respect children as individuals and share individual relationships with each child. However, we are also mindful of the social context within which we play and learn. The group is of equal importance as are the individuals that make up the group. No one comes to kindergarten in social isolation and so of central importance is the process of learning about the sense of belonging to a group, including what each individual can bring to the group and our responsibilities to the group. We believe that it is only through such encounters children learn trust, respect, reciprocation of relationships, listening for meaning, participation and more. Intricately entwined within these understandings is the use of documentation, which is considered a research tool for educators in their role as observers and listeners of children's learning. Documentation gives us a window into children's thinking and learning and provides us with a tool to engage in rich pedagogical dialogue with each other. When we undertake documentation we first ask the children if we can share their time at a particular learning experience. When invited we record some of the children's conversations and photograph some of the processes they are engaged in. During this time we listen with our eyes, our ears and our heart. We note the children's exchange of rich language, of ideas and views, the formation, expression and debate of differing theories and each child's ability to use all manner of materials as a medium of expressing their 101 languages.

—Leanne reflecting on her practice using principles derived from the Reggio Emilia project

The Reggio Emilia Educational Project originated in the Italian town Reggio Emilia over 40 years ago and can best be described as a community coming together to engage in a pedagogical experiment (Dahlberg & Moss, 2006). Following the Second World War an increasing awareness of the importance of early childhood education was combined with the belief that schools should be open democratic spaces in dialogue with the local community. According to Loris Malaguzzi, the founding theorist and leader of the Reggio Emilia Education Project, the purpose of education was to provide people with a dignified and civil meaning to their existence within community. This existence would develop clarity of mind and purpose along with a yearning for the future of humankind (Millikan, 2003). We can see this in Leanne's reflection when she talks about the kindergarten being an open space embedded within the local community and the group being a place of encountering others as they learn about trust, respect, reciprocation of relationships, listening for meaning and participation. Central is an understanding that education should be a shared experience rather than an individual commodity (Edwards, Gandini & Forman, 2012).

Historical, theoretical and philosophical perspectives of ECEC

Reggio Emilia educators believe that children are guardians of democracy (Lepicnik, 2012). Both children and teachers are co-founders of knowledge, and, together, they play a role in creating a democratic society (Moss & Dahlberg, 2005). This means the role of early childhood education is to draw the community's attention to the rich culture of childhood (Rinaldi, 2006). Teaching becomes a form of dialogue that aims to unsettle prior understandings to bring about transformation within the individual and at the community level (Rinaldi, 2006). For the Australian context, this means that it is difficult to label a preschool or kindergarten as 'Reggio'. The translation of specific cultural understandings around notions of 'community' and 'dialogue' is never straightforward. For Leanne community and dialogue means listening with her 'eyes, ears and heart'. Malaguzzi (1993) has likened this process to teachers knowing about Piagetian ideas of development and learning, and then placing these ideas aside so as to deeply listen to children.

It is not possible to exactly replicate Reggio Emilia as it is practised in the region from which it came. Instead, the principles that inform the practice of Reggio Emilia can be used in different cultural contexts (Millikan, 2003). For example, the role of the kindergarten in relation to the community is a central principle. Leanne indicates her relationship with the community as one of respecting the community's interests and values and fostering these within the kindergarten. Leanne is also careful to promote another important principle for Reggio Emilia. This is one that holds an image of childhood that recognises children as:

- competent
- intelligent
- co-constructors of knowledge, and
- active participants in democratic societies.

Foregrounded in these principles are practices such as listening, learning from and with peers and adults, and provoking and evoking thinking (Chaille, 2002). Leanne works with these principles when she talks about asking children for their permission to enter their learning space to document their ideas. She acknowledges that her role is to listen to children's exchange of ideas. She is interested in how children form, express and debate different explanations for what they see and experience. Leanne believes that children are theory makers who co-construct knowledge with peers and adults.

Documentation is a tool that helps educators and children co-construct knowledge (Schroeder-Yu, 2008). Documentation illustrates the different stages associated with children's thinking and problem solving. It uses photographs, transcripts of children's dialogue and examples of children's use of materials to create these illustrations. The environment is important because the aesthetic display of documentation reveals how children plan, carry out and complete projects. Documentation invites educators, families and children to engage in dialogue about children's ideas, theories and experiences. Documentation is core to a Reggio Emilia approach because it takes the community on a journey that refuses to follow a straight pathway (Giamminuti, 2009), reflecting an understanding of children's learning as complex. Using a Reggio Emilia approach is a political and an ethical choice made by a community because the principles mean that together educators, families and children will actively engage in pedagogical practices aimed at transforming knowledge and society (Olsson, 2009).

FOREST SCHOOLS APPROACH

In our preschool community we have developed a philosophy around connecting children with nature. By embracing the concept of 'Being and Belonging' from the EYLF (DEEWR, 2009, p. 7) we bring together these concepts with the practice of connecting children with nature. We consciously pay attention to the importance of embedding Indigenous perspectives into our everyday practice because we understand that Indigenous children learned on Country everyday. For this to happen we have developed strong partnerships with an Indigenous woman. Through such partnerships we have become conscious that society today is always looking to the future instead of the now. Educating with nature provides opportunities for children, families and educators to appreciate the now and be in the moment. In practice this is a program that reaches beyond the gate where children are able to explore wild spaces: wetland, forest area, national park and the beach. Each week, no matter what the weather, the kindergarten children head down to the beach to engage in exploration. We do this because we believe that children

Historical, theoretical and philosophical perspectives of ECEC

grow and learn when they are able to make choices, take risks and are trusted by the educators. Outdoor learning provides many opportunities and possibilities to provide these conditions. There are also rich opportunities for extending children's skills as they explore changing environments: climbing trees, scrambling across large boulders, walking on unsteady rocks at the rock platforms, and lighting fires with flints. Integral here is the development of: resilience, observations skills, awareness of the environment and how to care for it and create a strong sense of place and belonging. What this means is that children are able to be successful and participate at a level that works for them.

—Karen reflecting on her Beach Kinder program based on ideas derived from Forest Schools

Forest Schools originated in Scandinavia and are particularly associated with Denmark, where young children learning in the outdoors is highly valued (Maynard, 2007). There is no one definition or explanation for what a Forest School is or how to develop and implement a Forest School. However, a core idea is that the children experience their learning outdoors. Karen reflects this idea when she says her use of Forest School means reaching 'beyond the gate where children are able to explore wild spaces: wetland, forest area, national park and the beach'. Central principles for using a Forest School approach include:

- viewing children as active learners
- providing children with opportunities for social interaction
- privileging access to first-hand experiences, and
- promoting problem solving and experimentation. (Williams-Siegfredsen, 2012)

Natural settings, such as woodlands or meadows (in the United Kingdom or Scandinavia) or the bush and beach (in Australia), are considered strongly aligned with these principles. This is because natural settings offer children opportunities for unstructured outdoor play. Unstructured outdoor play is believed to provide opportunities for children to create their own play situations. In these situations children need to draw on what is offered by the environment to meet their play needs and so need to experiment with different materials, such as sticks, leaves, logs and stones. They may need to solve problems about how to access different materials and work out which materials are most suitable for their needs. Karen identifies these possibilities when she says that using a Forest School approach means that the children can extend their skills by participating in challenging activities, such as climbing and balancing on natural structures and/or lighting fires with flints. Social interactions between peers and adults are also supported in Forest Schools as groups of children focus on meeting their play goals through first-hand experience of the natural environment.

Some settings run Forest Schools as part of a traditional program and visit an outdoor location once a week for several hours. Others run primarily from an outdoor site. Children attend Forest Schools in all types of weather with a focus on wearing clothing appropriate to the climate. The main idea is that children spend time in the outdoor setting in a relatively unstructured way (Ridgers, Knowles & Sayers, 2012). The learning and development associated with the outdoor experience emerges from the children's activities and is supported by adult guidance. In Australia, Forest Schools are described as 'Bush Kindergartens'. There are also some 'Beach Kindergartens'. These kindergartens draw on the principles of Forest Schools, but also focus on fostering children's ecoliteracy (Reidy, 2012). Ecoliteracy refers to children learning more about their local context. Local context involves understanding the biodiversity of plants and animals living in the area. It includes a focus on understanding the local cultural and Indigenous history (Elliot, 2013). Karen talks of working closely with an Indigenous woman so that the children learn the cultural knowledge associated with their experiences at the beach. This means the children are learning to understand the cultural meanings associated with the space they visit, and so develop the capacity to see how people engage with their environments. This is important because understanding the relationships between people, environments and cultural meaning helps children develop respectful relationships with living and non-living things.

Other benefits associated with children's participation in Bush Kindergartens include building children's resilience, increasing motivation and concentration, and improving physical stamina and gross and fine motor skills. Karen believes that this occurs in her Beach Kindergarten because 'children grow and learn when they are able to make choices [and] take risks'. Being outdoors at the beach provides a range of opportunities for these choices and

Historical, theoretical and philosophical perspectives of ECEC

risks that might not occur in a traditional kindergarten setting. Forest Schools are committed to the belief that the natural environment creates learning and play experiences for young children that foster relationships, build respect for the environment, and challenge young children's learning and skills development in authentic ways.

MONTESSORI APPROACH

As a Montessori teacher I regard myself as an observer of children's activity. Observations inform my pedagogy. This is important because an essential element to my pedagogy is a firm belief that my role is to prepare the classroom so children can determine their own engagement in learning. My classroom is equipped with Montessori materials designed with the specific purpose of allowing children to direct their own learning. The materials are tools that take on the role of 'teacher' by directing children's attention to the work task and preventing the child from becoming distracted. In the morning I come early to set up the classroom. I check the materials to ensure they are in order and in the right location. When the children arrive I wait by the front door and greet each child. When greeting the children we shake hands and exchange personal greetings. The children have learned this through our lessons in grace and courtesy, which are a part of their practical life lessons. The children enter the classroom and know what to do. They will put their bags in the appropriate place and select a tray with a collection of materials. For example, a child may select the tray with the bells designed for sensory exploration. The learning will be both direct and indirect. As the child orders the bells according to pitch they are directly learning the principles of ordering according to pitch. Indirectly they are also developing auditory discrimination. I don't need to tell the child how to order the bells by pitch as previously I presented the bells using exaggerated movement and language that the children can imitate and develop through repetition. Stepping in to help them as they engage in this repetition would only be putting up an obstacle to their development. I believe children learn through

84

movement directed by the mind. My task is to help children build their desire to engage in this movement as learners so they build their own intelligence.

—**Barbara reflecting on her practice as a Montessori educator**

Dr Maria Montessori was the founder of the Montessori Method of Education. She was an Italian physician, anthropologist and pedagogue who studied children from different cultures and socio-economic backgrounds (Montessori Australia, nd). Her studies informed her belief that children have an inner drive to learn that pushes them towards independence and powers development. There is no 'real' or 'authentic' Montessori approach, but rather quality Montessori approaches (Ungerer, 2014). Quality approaches are committed to Maria Montessori's beliefs about children's abilities to reason, develop habits of concentration and be driven by a deep internal desire to learn (Grebennikov, 2005).

Montessori believed that educators should enter the classroom with a mind free of assumptions about children's learning (Isaacs, 2010, 2012). When educators are free of assumptions about children's learning they are capable of seeing childhood for its inner developmental drive, nature and learning potential (Weinberg, 2009). This is evident in Barbara's reflection when she says that her role is to help children tap into their natural desire to learn and build their own intelligence. Barbara sees her role as preparing the classroom so that children can determine their own engagement in learning. The educator's preparation of the classroom using Montessori materials is central to the approach (Lillard, 2005). The materials are designed to capture children's interest and attention while encouraging independence in learning. They foster the development of perception and dexterity as well as promoting independence in learning. Barbara describes these materials as tools that take on a teaching role as they direct children's attention to the task and help prevent distraction. Time is also important so that children are involved in extended periods of uninterrupted work (Larson, 2010). During these periods children select materials from one of the four learning areas: practical life exercises; sensorial exercises; language exercises; and mathematical exercises. Practical life exercises allow children to learn self-control and to build willpower (Feez, 2010). They involve culturally sensitive exercises using functional objects, such as child-sized jugs to learn pouring, and shoes for lacing and polishing. Through these exercises children learn how to regulate movement and attention. Sensory exercises allow children to isolate percepts and construct sensory impressions, which lay the foundation for creativity and imagination. Materials also include rods of differing lengths to sort according to size and glass jars to order according to pitch. Mathematics and language materials involve using materials such as chains of beads for skip counting or sandpaper letters to trace with a finger (Weinberg, 2009).

A Montessori approach recognises early childhood as a time when cognitive capacities are laid and developed. It argues that children need to engage in work that allows them to form and act on their own judgements (Tregenza, 2009). The teacher's role is to 'guide' and 'direct' children's learning. This helps children to enter extended periods of work and to reach their full potential (Bragdon, 2014). Imitation and repetition is a principle used by Montessori teachers, and is applied to guide learning. Using precise and purposeful gestures and language, educators show children what is needed to participate in each exercise. For example, Barbara greets the children as they enter her classroom. She shakes their hand and exchanges personal greetings. She says this teaches the children grace and courtesy as part of their practical life exercises. Once children have been provided with guidance they are free to engage with these exercises on their own, correcting themselves as necessary. The central aim of imitation and repetition is to allow the child to train themself to become an observer of life, making comparisons and forming judgements (Larson, 2010).

MULTIPLE INTELLIGENCE THEORY AND PRACTICE

I believe all children are intelligent and capable. A traditional 'educational' understanding of intelligence sees it as something determined at birth. Drawing on Multiple Intelligences I have come to understand that every child has a unique intellectual profile, which can be developed and improved in the right learning environment. As a teacher, my role is to develop approaches that allow children to engage in set tasks or problem-solving situations in various ways. For example, if we were investigating the lifecycle of a butterfly, previously I would have just read a story about it to all the children during circle time and had them all draw the lifecycle.

> Now what I do is I set up learning centres where the children engage in a range of tasks specifically designed to allow them to investigate the lifecycle so as to arrive at their own understandings. One centre might be designed for children with strong linguistic or verbal skills. In that centre I might have books about butterflies and writing materials. In another centre I might have a CD player and CDs with songs along with large pieces of material where the children could create a dance to act out the lifecycle. There might also be a centre with a board and material for the children to design a play about the lifecycle they could later perform for the class. A mathematical centre might have counters and cut out pictures of caterpillars, eggs, cocoons and butterflies for children to map out the lifecycle according to time. My role is to identify a child's strengths and then I notice patterns and relationships between their strengths. This way I build and stretch a child's intellectual abilities and meet their unique intellectual needs.
>
> **—Gabby reflecting on her use of Multiple Intelligences**

The concept of intelligence is complex. Traditional theories of intelligence focused on genetic determination. These perspectives believed that intelligence was determined by children's genetic history and could be measured using psychometric tests to identify their intellectual levels (Tannenbaum, 2000). Gardner (1983) challenged these ideas when he studied a number of well-known people identified for their 'intelligence'. He argued that intelligence is about being able to solve problems, or create products that are valued by one or more cultures. This was an important shift in thinking about intelligence because it focused on what people do in social and cultural contexts, instead of seeing intelligence as relatively fixed. Gardner argued that because intelligence is related to problem solving and creation, humans possess a blend of intelligences (Gardner, 1999). Currently he names the intelligences as musical intelligence, visual intelligence, verbal intelligence, logical-mathematical intelligence, bodily-kinesthetic intelligence, interpersonal intelligence, intrapersonal intelligence, naturalistic intelligence and existential intelligence (Gardner, 2006).

Some scholars in the field of psychology question Gardner's ideas because his description of intelligence does not use traditional approaches (Waterhouse,

2006). However, in the field of education, Multiple Intelligences has been well received (Gardner & Hatch, 1989). This is evident in Gabby's reflection when she talks of her shift in thinking about 'intelligence' and how this has impacted on her curriculum planning according to the different intelligences. She creates 'centres' that focus on different aspects of intelligence and help children focus on their intellectual strengths (see, for example, Arnold, 2007; Schiller & Phipps, 2011). Using the example of the lifecycle of a butterfly Gabby explains how using Multiple Intelligences helps children to arrive at their own understandings about the lifecycle, instead of her just telling them the information. Gabby's use of learning centres is one of the unique features of applying Multiple Intelligences in educational settings (Bernard, 2014a). Therefore, she acknowledges that every child has their own set of intelligences and the teacher's role is to foster these intelligences through individualised learning activities (Bernard, 2014b).

Gardner's theory of Multiple Intelligences has transformed teaching across early childhood and school settings (Vialle & Perry, 1995). But lessons have been learned since it was first introduced to education. Multiple Intelligences is a complex theory that can too easily be reduced to simply providing children with a range of learning activities. To be effective the approach must be underpinned by a pedagogical framework where 'putting understanding up front' is foremost (Perkins & Blythe, 1994). This means the focus is on creating pedagogical conditions that advance the development of children's 'intellectual character', which emphasises depth over breadth and concepts over facts, and is grounded in real-world issues that children care about or need to know (Ritchhart, 2002).

CONCLUSION

Philosophies and theoretical perspectives about children's learning and development are evident in different approaches to ECEC. Approaches to ECEC describe how they view and understand children and children's learning. Approaches to ECEC articulate teaching and curriculum practices based on these views and understandings. Multiple approaches to ECEC are available for educators to consider as a basis for their own practice. This is an important aspect of working in Australian ECEC settings because the EYLF does not prescribe a particular approach. Instead, educators are invited to reflect on different approaches and how these connect with their own beliefs and values according to contexts in which they work.

FURTHER THINKING

1. Think back to your own experiences in early childhood. What do you remember about your learning? What do you value for young children's learning today?

2. Consider the approaches to ECEC presented in this chapter. What similarities and differences in their perspective about children's learning and development do you notice? How do these perspectives seem to be represented in teaching and curriculum practices?

3. Consider the approaches to ECEC presented in this chapter and the links each approach makes with the key principles, practices and learning outcomes presented in Belonging, Being and Becoming: The early years learning framework for Australia. (DEEWAR, 2009)

ACKNOWLEDGEMENTS

Linda and Susan would like to thank the early childhood educators who generously gave of their time to contribute to this chapter in the form of vignettes.

REFERENCES

Arnold, E. (2007). *The MI Strategy Bank: 800+ Multiple Intelligence ideas for the elementary classroom*. Chicago: Zephyr Press.

Arthur, L., Beecher, B., Death, E., Dockett, S. & Farmer, S. (2015). *Programming and Planning in Early Childhood Settings*, 6th edn. South Melbourne: Cengage Learning.

Bernard, S. (2014a). How to address Multiple Intelligences in the classroom, *Edutopia*. Retrieved 4 March 2014, <www.edutopia.org/multiple-intelligences-immersion-enota-how-to>.

—— (2014b). Elementary school kids show their Multiple Intelligences, *Edutopia*. Retrieved 4 March 2014, <www.edutopia.org/multiple-intelligences-immersion-enota>.

Bragdon, J. (2014). What every family should know about Montessori, *Montessori Life*, 26(1), 7.

Chaille, C. (2002). Reflections on the notion of investing in children, *Childhood Education*, 78(4), 234–5.

Conner, J. (2008). *Learnings from HighScope: Enriching everyday practice.* Canberra: Early Childhood Australia.

Dahlberg. G. & Moss, P. (2006). Introduction. In C. Rinaldi (ed.), *In Dialogue with Reggio Emilia: Listening, researching and learning.* Abingdon: Routledge, pp. 1–22.

Daniels, H. (2008). *Vygotsky and Research.* London: Routledge.

Department of Education, Employment and Workplace Relations (DEEWR) (2009). Belonging, Being and Becoming: The early years learning framework for Australia. Retrieved 4 March 2014, <http://docs.education.gov.au/system/files/doc/other/belonging_being_and_becoming_the_early_years_learning_framework_for_australia.pdf>.

Edwards, C., Gandini, L. & Forman, G. (2012). *The Hundred Languages of Children: The Reggio Emilia approach—Advanced reflections*, 3rd edn. Santa Barbara, CA: Praeger.

Elliott, S. (2013). Play in nature: Bush kinder in Australia. In S. Knight (ed.), *International Perspectives on Forest School: Natural spaces to play and learn.* London: SAGE Publications, pp. 113–30.

Epstein, A.S. (2007). *The Intentional Teacher: Choosing the best strategies for young children's learning.* Washington, DC: National Association for the Education of Young Children.

Feez, S. (2010). *Montessori and Early Childhood: A guide for students.* London: SAGE Publications.

Gardner, H. (1983). *Frames of Mind: The theory of Multiple Intelligences.* London: Fontana.

—— (1999). *Intelligence Reframed: Multiple Intelligences for the 21st century.* New York: Basic Books.

—— (2006). *Changing Minds: The art and science of changing our own and other people's minds.* Boston: Harvard Business School Press.

Gardner, H. & Hatch, T. (1989). Multiple Intelligences go to school: Educational implications of the theory of Multiple Intelligences. *Educational Researcher*, 18(8), 4–9.

Giamminuti, S. (2009). Pedagogical Documentation in the Reggio Emilia Educational Project: Values, quality and community in early childhood settings. Unpublished PhD thesis, Crawley, Western Australia: University of Western Australia.

Grebennikov, L. (2005). The normalised child: A non-traditional psychological framework, *Australian Journal of Early Childhood*, 30(2), 8–18.

Hedegaard, M. & Fleer, M. (2008). *Studying Children: A cultural–historical approach.* Maidenhead, UK: McGraw-Hill.

HighScope (2011). *Getting to know HighScope's preschool curriculum*. Retrieved 4 March 2014, <www.highscope.org/Content.asp?ContentId=584>.

Hohmann, M. & Weikart, D. (1995). *Educating Young Children: Active learning practices for preschool and child care programs*. Ypsilanti, USA: HighScope Press.

Isaacs, B. (2010). *Bringing the Montessori Approach to Your Early Years Practice*. New York: Routledge.

—— (2012). *Understanding the Montessori Approach: Early years education in practice*. New York: Routledge.

Kalantzis, M. & Cope, B. (2012). *New Learning: Elements of a science of education*. New York: Cambridge University Press.

Larson, H. (2010). The Montessori method: Educating children for a lifetime of learning and happiness, *The Objective Standard*, 5(2), 41–59.

Lepicnik, V. (2012). The Reggio Emilia Concept or different perspectives on preschool education in kindergartens, *Euromentor Journal*, 2, 13–26.

Lillard, A.S. (2005). *Montessori: The science behind the genius*. New York: Oxford University Press.

Malaguzzi, L. (1993). For an education based on relationships, *Young Children*, 49(1), 9–12.

Maynard, T. (2007). Forest schools in Great Britain: An initial exploration, *Contemporary Issues in Early Childhood*, 8(4), 320–31.

Millikan, J. (2003). *Reflections: Reggio Emilia principles within Australian contexts*. Castle Hill, NSW: Pademelon Press.

Montessori Australia (nd). *Montessori Approach*. Retrieved 4 March 2014, <http://montessori.org.au/montessori/approach.htm>.

Moss, P. & Dahlberg, G. (2005). *Ethics and Politics in Early Childhood Education*. Abingdon: RoutledgeFalmer.

Olsson, L. (2009). *Movement and Experimentation in Young Children's Learning: Deleuze and Guattari in early childhood education*. Abingdon: Routledge.

Perkins, D. & Blythe, T. (1994). Putting understanding up front, *Educational Leadership*, 51(5), 4–7.

Reidy, C. (2012). Back to nature, *Inspire*, 6, 23–5.

Ridgers, N., Knowles, Z. & Sayers, J. (2012). Encouraging play in a natural environment: A child focussed case study of Forest School, *Childhood Geographies*, 10(1), 49–65.

Rinaldi, C. (2006). *In Dialogue with Reggio Emilia: Listening, researching and learning*. Abingdon: Routledge.

Historical, theoretical and philosophical perspectives of ECEC

Ritchhart, R. (2002). *Intellectual Character: What it is, why it matters, and how to get it*. San Francisco: Jossey-Bass.

Schiller, P. & Phipps, P. (2011). *The Daily Curriculum for Early Childhood: Over 1200 easy activities to support Multiple Intelligences and learning styles*. Silver Spring, MD: Gryphon House.

Schroeder-Yu, G. (2008). Documentation: Ideas and applications from the Reggio Emilia Approach, *Teaching Artist Journal*, 6(2), 126–34.

Schweinhart, L.J., Montie, J., Xiang, Z., Barnett, W.S., Belfield, C.R. & Nores, M. (2005). *Lifetime Effects: The HighScope Perry preschool study through age 40*. Monographs of the HighScope Educational Research Foundation. Retrieved 4 March 2014, <www.highscope.org/content.asp?contentid=219>.

Tannenbaum, A. (2000). A history of giftedness in school and society. In K. Heller, F. Monks, R. Sternberg & R. Subotnik (eds), *International Handbook of Giftedness and Talent*, 2nd edn. Oxford: Elsevier Science Ltd, pp. 23–54.

Tregenza, V. (2009). Developing judgement in young children: Ideas from a Montessori perspective, *Critical and Creative Thinking*, 17(2), 153–64.

Ungerer, R. (2014). What is Montessori education, and who defines it? *Montessori Life*, 26(1), 3.

Vialle, W. & Perry, J. (1995). *Nurturing Multiple Intelligences in the Australian Classroom*. Melbourne: Hawker Brownlow Education.

Vygotsky, L.S. (1997). Research Method. In R.W. Rieber (ed.), *The Collected Works of L.S. Vygotsky*, vol. 4. New York: Plenum Press, pp. 27–65.

Waterhouse, L. (2006). Multiple Intelligences, the Mozart effect, and emotional intelligence: A critical review, *Educational Psychologist*, 41(4), 207–25.

Weinberg, D. (2009). Maria Montessori and the secret of tabula rasa, *Montessori Life*, 21(2), 30–5.

Wertsch, J. (2007). Mediation. In H. Daniels, M. Cole & J. Wertsch (eds), *The Cambridge Companion to Vygotsky*. Cambridge: Cambridge University Press, pp. 178–92.

Williams-Siegfredsen, J. (2012). *Understanding the Danish Forest School Approach: Early years education in practice*. Abingdon: Routledge.

Perspectives and practices in ECEC policy and provision

Chapter 5

Key ideas, research and challenges in early childhood education and care

Maryanne Theobald and Gillian Busch

In this chapter you will find:
- An overview of the ways young children learn, especially play-based learning
- International models of early childhood education and care (ECEC)
- What neuroscience tells us about early childhood
- Studies of young children
- Economic research and social justice principles
- Challenges and ways forward—the educational program for the early years, relationships with diverse families, professional accountabilities and changing constructions of childhood.

The Australian government has recognised the importance of ECEC in recent years. With over one million Australian children accessing ECEC provision every day (Productivity Commission, 2014), today's children are a generation who spend a large part of their early years in some form of out-of-home child care. Early chapters in this text have discussed a range of people, theories and approaches that inform the development of ECEC. Early childhood pedagogical practice is an eclectic mix of these ideas.

This chapter begins with an overview of the ways young children learn in ECEC highlighting play-based learning as a pedagogical response to our understandings about children. Next the chapter outlines areas that have more recently influenced ECEC, including international models of ECEC, neuroscience,

95

national studies of young children and their families, economic research and social justice principles. Drawing on the reflections of educators working in various ECEC contexts, the chapter then presents four topics encountered by educators as part of their everyday work with diverse communities. These topics include:

- the educational program for children in the early years
- relationships and partnerships with diverse families
- professional accountabilities and expectations
- changing constructions of childhood.

THE WAYS YOUNG CHILDREN LEARN

Early childhood is a time of immense growth and development. Growing interest in ECEC from government is driven by research that shows the early years are critical for positive trajectories in life, including being able to be an 'active and informed citizen' who contributes to and within their community (Ministerial Council on Education, Employment, Training and Youth Affairs [MCEETYA], 2008, p. 9). From theories and research with children, we understand children as inquisitive, active and competent learners.

Play-based learning is a key idea for ECEC and one of eight pedagogical practices that are endorsed in Belonging, Being and Becoming: The early years learning framework (EYLF) for Australia (Department of Education, Employment and Workplace Relations [DEEWR], 2009), Australia's first national framework for children birth to five years. Play is defined as a 'context for learning through which children organize and make sense of their social worlds, as they engage actively with people, objects and representations' (DEEWR, 2009, p. 6). ECEC is internationally recognised as serving the ages from birth to eight years of age; it extends therefore from birth through to the years of compulsory schooling. For educators working in the compulsory years, the Australian Curriculum (Australian Curriculum Assessment and Reporting Authority [ACARA], 2013) focuses on content that children will have the opportunity to learn in a range of areas, with educators drawing on their training and knowledge of how children best learn to implement the curriculum.

As one of the key pedagogical approaches for ECEC, play-based learning is designed to be meaningful and purposeful. Play-based learning is most effective when it is closely associated with children's lives and the contexts in which they

Key ideas, research and challenges in early childhood education and care

live (DEEWR, 2009). Children's active engagement and active thinking and a focus on a holistic approach to learning are central to play-based learning (DEEWR, 2009). Play-based learning is *learner* focused rather than subject focused, with learning controlled largely by the learner under the careful guidance of early childhood educators.

Educators have an active role as facilitators of children's learning. They work with children to design the learning environment, including the temporal environment; encourage children's active participation and ownership of their learning and extend children's higher-order thinking and learning through effective questioning, focused or intentional teaching. Educators may join also as co-players in the play.

Play is recognised as a fundamental right of all children (United Nations, 1989). Defining play is difficult, however. Some attribute particular characteristics to play, including that it is pleasurable, voluntary, self-motivated; others describe the social stages of play (Parten, 1932); while others note the cognitive stages of play (Smilansky, 1968). Overall, it is acknowledged that play incorporates a range of creative activities (Ebbeck, Yim & Lee, 2013).

To summarise , play-based learning involves:

- active engagement
- a learner focus
- purposeful but open-ended activities
- an inquiry approach
- child participation and ownership
- holistic approaches to development
- meaningful experiences, and
- symbolic and higher-order thinking.

Ailwood (2003) has suggested that we reconsider the ways that play is referred to and has identified the following play discourses: 'romantic/nostalgic discourse' of play and play as 'characteristics discourse and a developmental discourse' (p. 288). Such discourses create taken-for-granted assumptions that play is fun and innocent, and reduces the opportunity to address unequal power relations that might occur in play (Grieshaber & McArdle, 2010). Interrogating simplistic understandings of play enables educators to respond to and challenge matters of equity and social justice (Grieshaber & McArdle, 2010).

MORE RECENT INFLUENCES ON ECEC

Early theorists and researchers have influenced understandings about the ways children learn and the development and implementation of play-based learning in the early years (see Chapter 4 in this text). Many of these views are still influential today. More recently, however, international and national research in and out of the fields of education has influenced early childhood policy and practice in shaping how we think about and interact with children today. Areas of influence include international models of ECEC, evidence from neuroscience, studies of young children, economic research and social justice principles. Each of these areas will now be explained.

International models of early childhood education and care

International ECEC models that promote participation and democratic principles are considered exemplary ECEC models that continue to influence policy and practice in the Australian context (Theobald, Danby & Ailwood, 2011). The growing recognition of the Nordic countries (including Sweden, Norway, Switzerland, Denmark, Finland and Iceland) as leaders in ECEC is attributed to three areas: economic investment in the early years, societal values and pedagogical practices.

First, the economic contributions made by the governments in the Nordic early childhood systems are significant. Public investment in early childhood provision means that parents are guaranteed access to a preschool position, the costs associated with going to preschool are heavily subsidised and there is a focus on quality. The quality of early years provision is represented by high staff ratios, highly qualified educators with doctoral degrees and pedagogical design (Pramling & Samuelsson, 2011).

Second, success of ECEC programs in Nordic countries is closely associated with strong societal values of the importance of childhood. It is understood that government alongside the parents have responsibility to children and that preschools can positivity improve social outcomes (Bennett, 2010). Recognition and implementation of the United Nations Convention on the Rights of the Child (United Nations, 1989) and of a societal understanding that children are competent members of society, underpin early childhood provision and practice.

The third area of influence lies in the exemplary pedagogy used in the Nordic preschools. A historical-cultural perspective, influenced by Vygotsky, is dominant throughout the Nordic countries, along with understandings from the sociologies of childhood perspectives (see chapter 4). Educators practise participatory learning in which children are active in making decisions about what they study, with democratic principles underpinning practice. There is joint attention on the interaction and communication required in achieving intersubjectivity (Pramling & Samuelsson, 2011).

The Reggio Emilia educational approach (see chapter 4) has also been taken up in some Australian ECEC programs. Carlina Rinaldi, who worked closely with the founder, Loris Malaguzzi, challenges those interested in providing the best outcomes for young children to consider how 'what we believe about children . . . is a determining factor in defining their social and ethical identity, their rights and the education and life context offered to them' (Rinaldi, 2013, p. 15). In other words, pedagogical approaches that value children's participation and contributions can positively influence children's own sense of self.

Understandings from neuroscience research

Neuroscience research has had significant influence on the provision of ECEC within Australia. The importance of a loving, stable, secure and stimulating environment for the healthy development of children is recognised. Findings from neuroscience research provide evidence that the development of the brain in the early years, including in utero, has a significant influence on the child's trajectory, including physical and mental health, learning and behaviour. These findings outline that early experiences have a pivotal role in the 'architecture and function of the brain' (Mustard, 2007, p. 12). For example, touch is an important sensory experience for developing our thinking, feeling and social skills, thus encouraging educators to 'take the opportunity for caring touch during our time with children' (Linke, 2014, p. 14).

Mustard (2007, p. 14) notes that early experience shapes:

- the development of neural pathways
- emotion and regulates temperament and social development
- language and literacy capability
- perceptual and cognitive ability
- how we cope with our daily experiences
- physical and mental health in adult life, and
- physical activity and performance.

Neuroscience has recognised that nurturing and responsive relationships are significant in building brain architecture in young children, and supports their future health and wellbeing. Such research has alerted the Australian government to the importance of children's access to quality early childhood programs. High-quality programs are characterised by having responsive adults and secure attachments between children and their caregivers and these understandings underpin the principles for practice in the EYLF (DEEWR, 2009).

National studies of young children and their families

Key studies by a range of organisations (including the Australian Research Alliance for Children and Youth (ARACY), Murdoch Children's Research Institute and Telethon Kids Institute) support the government's investment in the early years. Data derived from the Australian Early Development Census (AEDC); the Longitudinal Study of Australian Children (LSAC), which began in 2004; and Footprints in Time, the Longitudinal Study of Indigenous Children (LSIC), commencing in 2008, have also given the field important understandings about the development of health and wellbeing in the daily lives of young Australian children and their families.

Utilising a framework that measures wellbeing among children and youth, the ARACY Report Card alerts all Australians to the challenges facing children, including the incidence of diabetes and asthma, and disparity between Indigenous and non-Indigenous children (ARACY, 2013). Educators collect AEDC data in children's first year of formal full-time schooling. Data from five developmental domains (physical, social, emotional, cognitive and language) informs both policy and service delivery to improve the wellbeing and trajectory of Australian children. Additionally, data can be used at an educational site level to identify strengths and vulnerabilities of the particular community in which the site is located. According to the 2012 data, while the majority of children are doing well, '22.0 per cent of Australian children were developmentally vulnerable on one or more domain/s and 10.8 per cent of Australian children were developmentally vulnerable on two or more domains'. Also explicated from the data are the disparity between Indigenous and non-Indigenous children and the relationship between socio-economic disadvantage and vulnerability in two or more domains. Such data suggests that supporting children's learning and wellbeing requires a collaborative approach that involves partnerships with families, other service providers, and local, state and federal governments, working together for the best outcomes for children.

Understandings from economic research

There are cost benefits for investment in ECEC. Having access to a quality early years program means children have a better chance at health, learning and wellbeing. In return there are significant returns to the broader community. These understandings are based upon research that shows that education is fundamental to improving individual life chances (Heckman, 2011).

Economic research has shown that investment reduces crimes, grade repetition and costs associated with intervention (Heckman & Masterov, 2004). If children have a successful transition to school and are encouraged to be confident learners they are more likely to do well in school and continue schooling to higher education and training. Continuing to higher education provides more opportunity to gain a job and make a contribution to the nation's economy.

Investment in education is a core economic strategy of the Australian government. The Melbourne Declaration on Educational Goals for Young Australians (MCEETYA, 2008, p. 4), a guiding document for education, outlined that improving educational outcomes is essential for children to be 'successful learners' and 'active and informed citizens' (p. 7). The goal of strengthening ECEC is noted as 'central to the nation's social and economic prosperity' (MCEETYA, 2008, p. 7).

Understandings from principles of social justice

Social justice principles challenge stereotypes of power, gender, culture, class and disability and promote the rights of all children regardless of socio-economic status, language, religion, culture, ability or class. Such principles have arisen from theoretical perspectives of feminism, children's rights and sociology that consider children as active and competent and have led to a review of children's social status. Curricular documents respect that children have varying capacities and rich cultural and linguistic heritages (DEEWR, 2009). Children are to 'respond to diversity with respect' and communicate effectively with others (DEEWR, 2009, p. 27). When children are connected to and contribute to their social environments they build 'rights and responsibilities necessary for active community participation' (DEEWR, 2009, p. 26). Valuing diversity and equity is also a key goal of the Melbourne Declaration (MCEETYA, 2008).

One example of a social justice policy is the Australian government's investment in the early years to ensure universal access for vulnerable groups of children. The term 'universal' means that everyone has an opportunity to attend a high-quality early years program regardless of ability, location or socio-economic status (ARACY, 2013). This includes children in need of additional support, Indigenous children, children with languages other than English and children from economically disadvantaged backgrounds.

Using social justice principles, children are encouraged to consider their participation and learning in the classroom as part of a collective 'community' rather than themself as an individual. Such a view entails learning values about participating as a moral citizen for the good of the community (Rinaldi, 2013). When the classroom is thought of as a reproduction of society, it is important for educators to continually reflect upon classroom practices to identify unjust practices that might be occurring (Grieshaber & McArdle, 2010). In response, educators might make adjustments to processes that may unintentionally reinforce unfair play and practice.

Drawing on the principles of social justice, an educator might provide opportunities for children to listen to each other in pairs, group meetings and in reflection. During these times, children are encouraged to discuss their learning or issues that might have arisen and how such problems might be solved. In this way, children are part of a learning community. For children to know that as members of a community they help each other, an educator may need to restrict their immediate involvement. For example, if a child bumped their knee, an educator might support children to take on duties of 'care' by offering aid to their classmate (Figure 5.1). In this example, children learn that the educator is not the only member of the class who can solve a problem.

So far, this chapter has outlined key ideas and international research that have influenced the provision of ECEC in Australia. It is well established that ECEC is important for children, families and the broader community. This under-standing has been strengthened with evidence from fields outside education, including neuroscience and economics. The next section presents educators' views about their work in ECEC and highlights key considerations, challenges and ways forward for educators working with children and families.

Figure 5.1: Acting as members of a community: boys comfort a peer
Source: Theobald, Maryanne Agnes (2009). Participation and social order in the playground. PhD thesis, Queensland University of Technology.

CONSIDERATIONS, CHALLENGES AND WAYS FORWARD IN EARLY CHILDHOOD EDUCATION AND CARE

We asked five educators, working in various contexts of ECEC, to share their stories and consider their everyday practice. Analyses of their stories highlight the complex work of educators and their commitment to children's learning and their work with families. Four topics emerged as the key considerations and ones that provide challenges for educators:

- an educational program for children in the early years
- relationships and partnerships with diverse families
- professional accountabilities
- changing constructions of childhood.

Topic 1: Educational program for children in the early years

Reflecting international research, key elements for high-quality educational programs include play-based learning where children actively interact with concrete materials and have multiple ways to approach problems and opportunities to explore their environment as part of their learning experiences. Visual representations, access to materials that support thinking, and opportunities

Perspectives and practices in ECEC policy and provision

to express ideas are effective ways to support children's auditory and written learning (DEEWR, 2009). Responsive adults who engage in respectful relationships with young children also characterise a high-quality educational program.

Continued inclusion of a play-based curriculum in the years prior to school and the early years of formal schooling is a challenge. More and more educators are faced with a 'push down phenomenon' (Hard & O'Gorman, 2007) of an academic curriculum. In other words, expectations about academic content are greatly influencing the pedagogical style and threatening play-based inquiry approaches in the years prior to school. An educational program with an academic focus is often focused on outcomes, particularly in the areas of literacy and numeracy. David Whitebread, a researcher of the 'Too Much Too Soon' campaign (2014), has called for early childhood educators to reconsider the 'earlier is better' approach and to examine more closely the value of play for children's learning (Save Childhood Movement, 2014).

Educators identified a push down of an academic curriculum in the years before compulsory schooling as a concern for pedagogy and practice. In their reflections Rachel*, Helen* and Anne* articulate challenges and proffer ways of countering such encounters. (*Pseudonyms have been used for the educators in this chapter.*)

The educational program: Rachel's story

Rachel discusses the pressure of parent expectations regarding the purpose of ECEC and academic performance:

> Many families arrive to my class after experiencing a program that values rote learning more than play. What I have noticed is that for some children this means that the development of their social skills and ability to articulate their emotions is less developed.

While the EYLF affirms the value of play within the non-compulsory years, within the contemporary context, some educators, particularly those in the first year of formal school, may implement programs that are more structured and teacher directed. In this way there is a clash of beliefs within the early childhood profession itself about the best way that children learn. Thus, Rachel identifies that, for educators who embrace play as pedagogy, it is critical to inform parents and other stakeholders of its value. Such a perspective places educators in the

Key ideas, research and challenges in early childhood education and care

position of educating parents of the benefits of play, particularly the higher order thinking involved within investigations through play-based learning.

The educational program: Helen's story

Helen outlines the learning that is afforded through children's investigations in a play-based program:

> Parents think they are doing the best for their children by pushing 'learning' and taking away play and time for exploration. The push down of curriculum also hinders the exploration and inquiry of children's interests and the time to just be.

Helen emphasises the need for time for learning so that children have time to explore, develop and act on their ideas. She recalls a project where, over the course of four months, the children explored pushing and rolling. This occurred through play spaces that were set up for and with the children, and involved in-depth interactions between the children and between the children and the adults, and multiple opportunities to explore pushing and rolling.

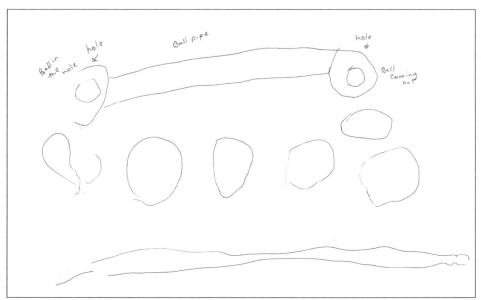

Figure 5.2: A child's representation of the balls moving
Source: Rainbow Valley Early Learning Centre

105

Figure 5.3: A child's representation of the ball run
Source: Rainbow Valley Early Learning Centre

The depth of understanding that the children developed about pushing and pulling was observable in their drawings and through the documentation of children's interactions collated by the educator.

As Helen explains, it takes confidence to slow down and to trust children and make time for investigations:

> By slowing down the curriculum and holding firm to the belief that both 'childhood and learning are not a race' we really see the child. We see when and where they are at each point in time. In this way, we take children on amazing learning journeys that afford deep understandings of concepts.

The educational program: Anne's story

Parental expectations that non-compulsory education settings should provide children with knowledge of how to read and write in preparation for formal schooling are considered a challenge. Anne shares strategies that they use to respond when faced with this situation.

> Information sessions are ongoing where as a teacher you share your goals for the year, demonstrate how you work, how you engage children's thinking and learning through their interests while covering the curriculum. It is also important for you as the teacher to know what goals parents have for their children so that later in the year you can reflect together on the accomplishment of the goals. We take every opportunity to speak to parents about how and why we have a play-based curriculum—parent interviews, roster days, committee meetings, newsletters, documentation and planning books which explain clearly what we do and why. Through making the children's thinking and learning visible, parents and children are more engaged and become active participants in the journey.

Anne's strategies outlined here are based upon building a partnership with parents throughout the year. Meeting regularly with parents and developing shared goals for the child help parents to understand the complexity of learning in ECEC settings. Documentation helps to show the thinking and learning accomplished by children, so that parents and the children are aware of their development and achievements.

> We meet with the teachers at school to find out their expectations of children entering the school system, and make adjustments to the last term of the year to help children to mentally and physically prepare for the transition. For example, we discuss how routines and facilities are accessed or may be different. For the children, this translates to how do we have our lunch, when will I play with my friend, how do I go to the toilet and how do I know what the bell means.

Anne reflects on the importance of smooth transitions for children. Transitions from one setting to another can be a significant challenge for young children and their families. Researchers report that successful transitions require the establishment of positive collaborative relationships between all stakeholders; underpinned by 'trust and respect' and a willingness to be responsive and adaptable to the emerging needs of all stakeholders (Dockett & Perry, 2001,

p. 13). By talking with school educators about what is expected of children when entering compulsory school, Anne forms a strategy to help stakeholders in this transition. Keeping open lines of communication with the local school, Anne is able to inform the school about each child's strengths and advocate for the play-based approach within a formal school setting. Anne's advocacy for a play-based approach contributes to building pedagogical continuity between prior-to-school settings and early years classrooms in the compulsory years. Smoother transitions for children are possible when educators from prior-to-school contexts and school settings develop deeper professional relationships (Boyle & Petriwskyj, 2014). It is critical that children are provided with information about the school context and it is vital that schools prepare for young children.

Reflection

1. As educator, how can you respond to a push down of an academic curriculum in the years prior to school?
2. How can you promote and support children's meaningful participation in their own learning in the early years of formal schooling?
3. As an educator in the first year of formal schooling, how can you create smooth transitions to school for young children?

Topic 2: Relationships and partnerships with diverse families

Working in partnership with families to build secure, respectful and reciprocal relationships with their children at home can support families to give children the best start in life. Parent involvement in children's learning, the supportiveness of the home learning environment, and quality educational programs in early education are important factors for children's optimal learning and success at school (Berthlesen & Walker, 2008).

Principles of partnerships include providing welcoming and inclusive environments, having effective communication and shared decision-making. Chapter 11 details the practice of forming relationships between staff, children and families in ECEC. The next two stories from the field highlight factors about the diversity of families that educators might consider in their daily interactions with families.

Working with families: Marie's story*

> Many families we encounter are usually blended in some way. This sometimes means that a variety of people will drop off or pick up. Parents or step-parents may be working; sometimes one parent may be away for extended periods of time. Grandparents may also drop off and pick up children and in some instances, they may be the primary caregivers. The implications of these situations are the difficulties that arise with having a consistent conversation regarding the children's development. To summarise—it's complicated!! The result is that I have to always be aware of the family situation of children in my care.

Marie's story highlights the many social and family arrangements in which children live. Families today are diverse in terms of structure and who is part of the family, living arrangements and relationships (Poole, 2005). Families can be constructed in many ways: couple families with children, sole-parent families, step-families, blended families, foster families, adoptive families, extended families and same-sex families. Contemporary family structures are the result of changing patterns over recent decades in marriage, divorce and cohabitation, a decrease in the significance of religion, and changing social attitudes (Poole, 2005). Increased migration means there is more cultural diversity of families.

As Marie notes, traditional ways of connecting with families may not be effective and Marie has embraced technology to communicate with families. Her communication methods include:

> Using group emails to send home stories/documentation of the day and other items each day; which helps to include those parents or caregivers that do not regularly come into the setting and also provides parents with a way of contacting us if they need to.

Perspectives and practices in ECEC policy and provision

In the next story, Rachel notes the changing lives of contemporary families.

Working with families: Rachel's story

> Parents have many external pressures placed upon their time. Taking the time to get to know and build positive relationships with families is crucial to foster children's learning and growth. This benefits their child and all children in the class.

Rachel, an educator in a school setting, considers time as one of the pressures for families today. Families face a range of social and economic pressures that may pose challenges for children's long-term outcomes. These might result from parents' employment patterns or working conditions, geographical isolation or social isolation due to linguistic differences or disability. Unemployment may mean financial hardship, less access to social support mechanisms and increased health problems (Baxter et al., 2012). Educators have a role to play in helping families gain support from social settings and services within a community (Bowes, Grace & Hodge, 2012).

In response to this consideration, Rachel emphasises the need to understand each family's unique situation, without casting judgement. She explains:

> We are proactive in becoming familiar with families at the beginning of the year, then build on this relationship throughout the year. During stories or general conversations with children we must be mindful of different family situations and demonstrate an understanding of these diversities. We must also help the children to develop their understanding of diversity.

Early childhood educators are well placed to provide stable and supportive environments for young children during their day at preschool. Educators can work with families to help them overcome challenges (Productivity Commission, 2012). Such work starts from a strengths-based approach; that is, determining what is working well for each family.

Reflection

A caring, supportive environment is one that fosters and nurtures relationships.

1. For children in the year prior to school, birth to five years, what might a caring, supportive environment look like, feel like and sound like?
2. For children in the early years of formal schooling, five to eight years, what might a caring, supportive environment look like, feel like and sound like?

Topic 3: *Professional accountabilities and expectations*

Educators' professional accountabilities and expectations are articulated in a number of policy texts. This includes the Australian Professional Standards for Teachers, which has identified seven 'interconnected, interdependent and overlapping' benchmarks that articulate what teachers should know and be able to do (Australian Institute for Teaching and School Leadership [AITSL], 2014). Also informing educators' professional accountabilities is curriculum texts developed by ACARA (2013) and the implementation and publication of school performance data. In the non-compulsory years of education, the EYLF (DEEWR, 2009) articulates educator accountabilities pertaining to the principles and practices that support the implementation of the framework and contribute to learning outcomes for young children. Also contributing to educator accountabilities in the non-compulsory years is the National Quality Standard (NQS) that articulates our responsibilities in seven quality areas, including programming, health and safety, and relationships with children (ACECQA, 2011).

Professional accountabilities and expectations: Olivia's story*

Olivia considers how system accountabilities have shaped the work of educators. Additionally, she wonders how some stakeholders may interpret the silencing of pedagogical advice in the Australian Curriculum (ACARA, 2013). While Olivia recognises that it is not the remit of the Australian Curriculum, as a syllabus document, to provide pedagogical advice regarding the implementation of the curriculum, she believes the silencing of pedagogy may influence classroom practices.

Olivia argues that when educators work from a perspective where curriculum outcomes drive classroom practice, ideological tensions are created that impact on everyday practices. The imperative to meet curriculum outcomes that are framed by weeks, terms and semesters conflicts with her beliefs about supporting children's positive dispositions to learning through play-based educational experiences. Olivia is concerned that such an emphasis shifts our focus from individual children and our responsiveness to their learning needs and interests. In their study of children's participation in preschool, Theobald and Kultti (2012) found that educators face tensions when implementing pedagogical beliefs about play-based learning while adhering to curriculum outcomes and the temporal constraints of a school system.

> Maintaining pedagogical approaches that focus on children's interests and curiosities is a significant challenge within the current educational landscape. The capacity to retain the integrity of pedagogical practice depends on several factors. Early childhood educators must first be able to articulate the benefits of play-based learning to all stakeholders in order to maintain support for this practice. At the same time they must also be able to demonstrate that learning outcomes are achieved successfully through play-based learning. To build a relationship that facilitates productive dialogue about play-based practice to accomplish the valuing of play-based practice takes time and trust and a knowledgeable team.

In response to this consideration, Olivia highlights the importance of pedagogical leadership to support the continuation of play-based practice, particularly in the preparatory year. The importance of pedagogical leadership is reflected also in the National Quality Framework (NQF) requirement for an educational leader in ECEC centres (Cheeseman, 2012) and is supported by research highlighting that pedagogical leadership contributes to outcomes for children (Sylva et al., 2004). A pedagogical leader is someone who has specialist knowledge about young children and how they learn, is actively engaging in learning, engages in reflective practice and mentors colleagues to build their knowledge and practice (Cheeseman, 2012).

Key ideas, research and challenges in early childhood education and care

Professional accountabilities and expectations: Helen's story

> We have been inspired by the work of the Reggio educators and have embraced the documentation of our projects. These projects unfold over time and are underpinned by our commitment to really see the child, to see their strengths and potentials and to engage with their perspectives and to really listen to children and to wonder about the questions they are pondering. Through documentation we advocate for the way children learn and the approach we have taken here. We display documentation in the centre and provide copies to families. My challenge as a pedagogical leader is to work with staff to support their documentation.

Drawing on the practices of the educators in Reggio Emilia, documentation of children's learning documents visible traces of children's learning. Thus, documentation is 'not considered . . . as the collecting of data in a detached, objective, distant way' (Gandini & Goldhaber, 2001, p. 125); rather educators offer their perspectives on what they observe. Artefacts that make learning visible might include images, drawings, constructions, videos and so on with these artefacts annotated by the teacher. Documentation requires a commitment to reflect critically on the 'experiences we are living and the projects we are exploring' (Vecchi, 1998, p. 142).

> My starting point is always working with staff to interrogate their existing image of the child. We engage in weekly conversations where participants proffer their perspectives about what they observed and how they see the project proceeding, while it is always tentative and up for re-negotiation with the children. Additionally, we talk about articles that appear in journals and about the books we are reading. I know that I need to read with my educators and to proffer challenges to share what they are reading. As a service, we engage in learning outside the centre, attending conferences and presentations.

Helen's story shows how engaging in documentation supports educators to learn about children's learning, and it contributes also to transforming our thinking and practice. Also linked to the process of documentation is the manner in which it has the potential to contribute to educational sites for the creation of culture by 'means of a democratic process' (Rinaldi, 2013, p. 33).

> ### Reflection
> 1. Identify and compare examples of documentation of children's learning.
> 2. How might you use documentation to support your professional role?

Topic 4: *Changing constructions of childhood*

Children today are spending more and more time in preschool, child care and community activities. This may be due to the increased participation of both parents in the workforce or employment in positions that require a parent to be away from the family for an extended period of time: a Fly In, Fly Out (FIFO) job in the mining industry, for example. These situations influence the ways families go about their everyday lives and the ways that childhood is experienced.

Another change is the increasing use of technology in children's everyday lives. For example, younger children have increasing access to and use of devices such as tablets and smart phones with touch screens (Danby et al., 2013). The pervasiveness of technology in children's lives has been described as the 'technologisation of childhood' (Plowman, McPake & Stephen, 2010, p. 63). Debates continue about the benefits of and challenges that arise with the proliferation of technology in the lives of children. Findings from an English study highlight the ways in which digital technologies can extend children's learning and communication skills (Plowman & McPake, 2013). Emerging findings from a large Australian study show that rich interactions that contribute to building literacy understandings can occur as children engage with technology in the home (Danby et al., 2013).

This next story from the field highlights the changing interests and pastimes for children in society today and the implications of these for educators.

Key ideas, research and challenges in early childhood education and care

Changing constructions of childhood: Rachel's story

> With the introduction of more screen time, play appears to happen less often outside as parents are time poor and living arrangements no longer always provide a back yard as a play space.

Rachel reflects on the changes that have occurred in children's everyday lives and the implications of these changes for children's development. Rachel's concern about some children's limited engagement with outdoor environments because of changes in the communities where children live has implications for educational settings and for advocacy around the benefits of outdoor play.

Typically, outdoor activity provides opportunities for children to engage with activities requiring exploration, discovery and connection with nature and risk taking (DEEWR, 2009). Children are also able to learn about caring for the environment and the importance of sustainability (Davis, 2010). Interactions in the playground provide rich experiences for children's language and cognitive development (DEEWR, 2009). The playground offers children social and relational development for learning and high-level thinking skills (DEEWR, 2009).

Given the importance of outdoor play, educational sites must continue to offer rich outdoor environments where there is 'space' and 'time' to engage with natural materials, trees, grass, dirt, animals and insects and 'space' and 'time' to run, to climb and to just be. Forest Schools, which originated in Scandinavia (Maynard, 2007), enable children to experience a natural outdoor environment (see Chapter 4 for more detail). Affording children opportunities to engage with the environment and to see things grow is at the core of projects such as Bush Kinder, Stephanie Alexander Gardens (Kitchen Garden Foundation, 2014), community gardens and the development of local vegetable gardens. The importance of such projects is heightened in locations where children may not have back yards to play and observe plants grow.

Reflection

1. What changes have you observed in the way in which children experience childhood?

Perspectives and practices in ECEC policy and provision

2. How might you promote the importance of outdoor play for young children?

CONCLUSION

This chapter has introduced key ideas, international educational models and research that have more recently informed early childhood practice in Australia. A wide range of research informs approaches to early childhood pedagogy and Australia's commitment to the education and care of young children, which is articulated in policy texts. Educators working within the field have shared stories about contemporary challenges for everyday practices. Observable within each of the educators' stories is their strong commitment to the principles of early childhood, to their role as advocates for children and for quality early childhood practice, and to thinking and reflecting deeply about their work with children and families as they navigate the terrains in which they work.

FURTHER THINKING

1. What strategies might you use to gain the views of families with whom you work, and include these in the educational program or decision-making processes?

2. Identify key understandings from neuroscience for ECEC.

3. Think of possible scenarios when processes or interactions perpetuate socially unjust practices. What strategies might you put in place to overcome these?

4. Investigate these websites:
   Longitudinal Study of Australian Children (LSAC) <www.growingup inaustralia.gov.au/>
   Footprints in Time, the Longitudinal Study of Indigenous Children (LSIC) <www.dss.gov.au/about-the-department/publications-articles/research-publications/longitudinal-data-initiatives/footprints-in-time-the-longitudinal-study-of-indigenous-children-lsic#2>.

ACKNOWLEDGEMENTS

We thank Carolyn Atkinson, Sandra Grant, Marion Hayes, Karen Renz and Diane Daley.

REFERENCES

Ailwood, J. (2003). Governing early childhood education through play, *Contemporary Issues in Early Childhood*, 4(3), pp. 286–99.

Australian Children's Education and Care Quality Authority (ACECQA) (2011). *The National Quality Standard*. Retrieved 15 September 2014, <www.acecqa.gov.au/national-quality-framework/the-national-quality-standard>.

Australian Curriculum, Assessment and Reporting Authority (ACARA) (2013). *The Australian Curriculum*. Retrieved 15 September 2014, <www.australiancurriculum.edu.au>.

Australian Government Department of Education (2012). *Australian Early Development Census*. Retrieved 25 September 2014, <www.education.gov.au/australian-early-development-census>.

Australian Institute for Teaching and School Leadership (AITSL) (2014). *Professional teacher standards*. Retrieved 15 September 2014, <www.aitsl.edu.au/australian-professional-standards-for-teachers/standards/list>.

Australian Research Alliance for Children and Youth (ARACY) (2013). *Report Card: The wellbeing of young Australians*. Retrieved 3 August 2015, <www.aracy.org.au/documents/item/104>.

Baxter, J., Gray, M., Hand, K. & Hayes, A. (2012). Parental joblessness, financial disadvantage and the wellbeing of parents and children. Australian Department of Families, Housing, Community Services and Indigenous Affairs (DFaHCSIA), Occasional Paper (48).

Bennett, J. (2010). Pedagogy in Early Childhood Services with Special reference to Nordic Approaches. *Psychological Science and Education*, 2010(3), 16–21.

Berthelsen, D. & Walker, S. (2008). Parents' involvement in their children's education. *Family Matters*, 79, 34–42.

Bowes, J., Grace, R. & Hodge, K. (2012). *Children, Families and Communities: Contexts and consequences*, 4th edn. Melbourne: Oxford University Press.

Boyle, T. & Petriwskyj, A. (2014). Transitions to school: Reframing professional relationships, *Early Years*, 34(4), 392–404.

Cheeseman, S. (2012). The educational leader, *E-Newsletter 33*. Melbourne, Vic: Early Childhood Australia.

Perspectives and practices in ECEC policy and provision

Danby, S., Davidson, C., Theobald, M., Scriven, B., Cobb-Moore, C., Houen, S., Grant, S., Given, L. & Thorpe, K. (2013). Talk in activity during young children's use of digital technologies at home, *Australian Journal of Communication*, 40(2), 83–100.

Davis, J. (2010). What is early childhood education for sustainability? In J. Davis (ed.), *Young Children and the Environment: Early education for sustainability*. Melbourne: Cambridge University Press, pp. 21–42.

Department of Education, Employment and Workplace Relations (DEEWR) (2009). Belonging, Being and Becoming: The early years learning framework for Australia. Canberra: Australian Government.

Dockett, S. & Perry, B. (2001). Starting school: Effective transitions, *Early Childhood Research and Practice*, 3(2), pp. 1–20.

Ebbeck, M., Yim, H.Y.B. & Lee, L.W.M. (2013). Play-based learning in D. Pendergast & S. Garvis (eds), *Teaching Early Years: Curriculum, pedagogy and assessment*. Sydney: Allen & Unwin, pp. 185–200.

Gandini, L. & Goldhaber, J. (2001). Two reflections about documentation. In L. Gandini & C. Pope Edwards, *Bambini: The Italian approach to infant/toddler care*. New York: Teachers College Press, p. 125.

Grieshaber, S. & McArdle, F. (2010). *The Trouble with Play*. Maidenhead, UK: Open University Press.

Hard, L. & O'Gorman, L. (2007). 'Push-me or pull-you'? An opportunity for early childhood leadership in the implementation of Queensland's early years curriculum, *Contemporary Issues in Early Childhood*, 8(1), pp. 50–60.

Heckman, J. (2011). The economics of inequality: The value of early childhood education, *American Educator*, Spring, 31–47.

Heckman, J. & Masterov, D.V. (2004). *The Productivity Argument for Investing in Young Children*. University of Chicago. Retrieved 3 August 2015, <http://jenni.uchicago.edu/human-inequality/papers/Heckman_final_all_wp_2007-03-22c_jsb.pdf>.

Kitchen Garden Foundation (2014). Retrieved 15 September 2014, <www.kitchengardenfoundation.org.au/>.

Linke, P. (2014). The importance of touch, *Every Child*, 20(1), 14–15.

Maynard, T. (2007). Forest schools in Great Britain: An initial exploration, *Contemporary Issues in Early Childhood*, 8(4), 320–31.

Ministerial Council on Education, Employment, Training and Youth Affairs (MCEETYA) (2008). Melbourne Declaration on Educational Goals for Young Australians. Canberra: Commonwealth of Australia.

Mustard, F. (2007). *Investing in the Early Years: Closing the gap between what we know and what we do*. Adelaide: Government of South Australia.

Parten, M. (1932). Social participation among preschool children, *Journal of Abnormal and Social Psychology*, 28(3), 243.

Plowman, L. & McPake, J. (2013) Seven myths about young children and technology. *Childhood Education*, 89(1), pp. 27–33.

Plowman, L., McPake, J. & Stephen, C. (2010).The technologisation of childhood? Young children and technologies at home, *Children and Society*, 24(1), 63–74.

Poole, M. (2005). *Family: Changing families, changing times*. Sydney: Allen & Unwin.

Pramling, N., & Samuelsson, I.P. (eds). (2011). *Educational encounters: Nordic studies in early childhood didactics* (Vol. 4). Springer Science & Business Media.

Productivity Commission (2012). *Schools Workforce: The Productivity Commission Research Report*. Canberra: Commonwealth of Australia.

——(2014). *Childcare and Early Childhood Learning: Overview*, Inquiry Report No. 73. Canberra: Commonwealth of Australia.

Rinaldi, C. (2013). Re-imagining childhood. Adelaide: Government of South Australia. Retrieved 20 September 2014, <www.thinkers.sa.gov.au/rinaldiflipbook/files/inc/d99b4762d1.pdf>.

Save Childhood Movement (2014). *Manifesto for the Early Years: Putting children first*. Retrieved 16 September 2014, <www.savechildhood.net/uploads/1/8/4/9/1849450/putting_children_first.pdf>.

Smilansky, S. (1968). *The Effects of Sociodramatic Play on Disadvantaged Pre-school Children*. New York: Wiley.

Sylva, K., Melhuish, E., Sammons, P., Siraj-Blatchford, I. & Taggart, B. (2004). *Technical paper 12. The final report: Effective pre-school education*. London: Institute of Education, University of London.

Theobald, M. & Kultti, A. (2012). Investigating child participation in the everyday talk of teacher and children in a preparatory year, *Contemporary Issues in Early Childhood*, 13(3), 210–25.

Theobald, M., Danby, S., & Ailwood, J. (2011). Child participation in the early years: Challenges for education. *Australasian Journal of Early Childhood*. 36(3), 19-26.

United Nations (1989). *United Nations Convention on the Rights of the Child (UNCRC)*. Retrieved 14 August 2006, <www.ohchr.org/english/law/crc.htm>.

Vecchi, V. (1998). The role of the Atelierista: An interview with Lella Gandini. In C. Edwards, L. Gandini & G. Forman (eds), *The Hundred Languages of Children*, 2nd edn. Greenwich, CT: Ablex Publishing Corporation, pp. 139–57.

Whitebread, D. (2014). *Too Much Too Soon: Reflections upon the school starting age*. Retrieved 15 September 2014, <www.toomuchtoosoon.org/>.

Chapter 6

Contexts, policy and frameworks of early childhood education and care

Megan Gibson

In this chapter you will find an outline of:
- contexts—centre-based child care/long day care, kindergarten/preschool, family day care, Multifunctional Aboriginal Children's Services (MACS), integrated child and family centres, outside school hours care (OSHC) and schools
- integrated early childhood education and care
- early childhood education and care policy in Australia
- the reform agenda.

Early childhood education and care (ECEC) is a dynamic field that includes a number of contexts. Understandings of ECEC contexts—how they operate and the programs that they provide—gives important insights into the field. These contexts are shaped, at least partially, through policies that are developed and implemented by governments, organisations and the ECEC centres or services. Alongside policy documents, curriculum frameworks and regulatory frameworks govern and shape the ways in which ECEC contexts operate. This chapter provides insights into ECEC provision in Australia through examination of different early childhood contexts, policy and regulatory frameworks for children from birth to eight years. Consideration of the diverse range of contexts will shape understandings into the different ways in which ECEC programs are provided. Attention is given to the contemporary policy context, both in Australia and internationally, and how this shapes the field. This chapter also addresses the

Perspectives and practices in ECEC policy and provision

development and provision of regulatory frameworks, with particular attention to recent changes concerning quality.

EARLY CHILDHOOD EDUCATION AND CARE CONTEXTS

The early childhood years, spanning birth to eight years, encompass both prior-to-school contexts and the early years of primary school. Within this age range children and families access a number of different formal and informal education and care arrangements. Formal education and care includes ECEC contexts that provide programs and services for children and families that are regulated and subsidised by governments. Informal care includes private arrangements where family or friends provide care for children, where there may or may not be a fee paid. Increasingly, grandparents are drawn on to provide care for children, particularly to support parents to re-enter or remain in paid work after the birth of a baby (Goodfellow & Laverty, 2003). For many families, care arrangements are made up of a combination of formal and informal care where, for example, a child may attend child care for some days and be cared for by a grandparent other days.

Terminology for formal ECEC contexts varies, but there are some common shared understandings, both within Australia and internationally. In this section of the chapter some of the different contexts that operate within ECEC will be outlined. An initial overview of these contexts is included, where key operational and programmatic elements of each are presented in a table. Next, we look at kindergarten/preschool and child care/long day care, given that these contexts provide the largest number of ECEC programs in Australia. Models of ECEC provision, including community-based/not-for-profit and for-profit are also considered.

Some of the formal early childhood contexts in Australia include family day care, centre-based child care, kindergarten/preschool and the lower years of primary school. Terms for early childhood are not consistent across states and territories in Australia. For example, an ECEC program for children in the year prior to the first year of schooling is referred to as preschool in New South Wales and kindergarten in Victoria and Queensland. Table 6.1 provides insights into the operation of these and other ECEC contexts. While not claiming to cover all formal contexts, this table provides an overview of key ECEC programs and services across Australia, in prior-to-school contexts (up to approximately five years of age) and school contexts (lower years of primary school, for children up to eight years of age or Year 3).

There is a wide range of ECEC programs available for children and their families, in response to the diverse requirements of society. Programs may meet particular cultural, linguistic or geographic needs, and even within one context-type there will be variation within the operation.

Attention is now turned to a more detailed description of a select number of the ECEC contexts from Table 6.1: centre-based child care/long day care, kindergarten/preschool, family day care, Multifunctional Aboriginal Children's Services (MACS), integrated child and family centres, outside school hours care (OSHC) and schools. A fuller description of these contexts is included for their unique operational features, relevance for the early childhood field and/ or the frequency of their usage (Australian Bureau of Statistics [ABS], 2011). This usage is drawn from the *Australian Bureau of Statistics Childhood Education and Child Care Survey*, a census carried out in Australia triennially. The data captures usage of ECEC contexts by type and provides insights into child care contexts, with emerging patterns of usage (ABS, 2011).

Centre-based child care/Long day care

Centre-based child care or long day care centres (terms used interchangeably, hereafter referred to as child care centres) provide education and care for children birth to school age. Child care centres typically operate a minimum of 48 weeks a year and up to 52 weeks of the year, and are open a minimum of eight hours per day. Child care centres in Australia are currently regulated through the National Quality Framework (NQF) and the National Quality Standard (NQS) (Australian Children's Education and Care Quality Authority [ACECQA], 2014a, 2014b). Additionally, child care centres use an accepted national curriculum document for children birth to school age, the Early Years Learning Framework (EYLF) (Department of Education, Employment and Workplace Relations [DEEWR], 2009a) being the most common.

Participation in child care in Australia has increased significantly over the past two decades (ABS, 2011). One reason for this increase has been attributed to changing patterns of women's engagement in paid work after motherhood. The increase in workforce participation, resulting in an increased demand for child care, has seen the number of child care centres grow considerably. The expansion

Table 6.1: Australian ECEC contexts at a glance

Prior-to-school-contexts	Operation
Centre-based child care/Long day care	Education and care program for children from birth to five years (or school age) Provided for up to 52 weeks of the year, and open for a minimum of eight hours per day
Kindergarten/ Preschool	Education and care program for children aged three to five years during school hours and during school terms
Family day care	Home based care for children birth to twelve years Provided by an educator who is registered with a family day care coordination scheme
Home-based care	Care offered in an educator's home, operating independently of family day care schemes and qualifying for subsidy from the government
Mobile children's services	Services that operate across rural and remote parts of Australia travelling by bus, equipped with resources
Multifunctional Aboriginal Children's Services (MACS)	Flexible services for Aboriginal and Torres Strait Islander children and their families Includes long day care, playgroups, before and after school care and school holiday care, and cultural programs
Integrated child and family centres	Education and care, through kindergarten/preschool and long day care May include a focus on health, child protection and early intervention
Occasional care	Short-term centre-based programs for children from birth to school age
Playgroups	Coordinated activities and experiences for birth to school-aged children accompanied by an adult
Outside school hours care (OSHC)	Programs that operate outside school hours: before school; after school care and vacation care during the school holidays Most often operated in school grounds
School contexts	**Operation**
Non-compulsory schooling	Full-time preparatory school year for children approximately five years of age/prior to Year 1 in Queensland only
Compulsory schooling	School-based programs that offer education that draws on national and state/territory curriculum documents
Home schooling	Education of children at home, usually by a parent or guardian

Source: Gibson, 2015

in the number of child care centres, alongside the changes to government policy in early childhood, has seen issues regarding workforce and quality as central to reform in ECEC (Council of Australian Governments [COAG], 2008; DEEWR, 2009b). ABS data shows patterns in child care usage increasing, especially for children aged birth to four years from 1996, when 13 per cent of children aged from birth to four accessed child care in any one week, to 2011, when 31 per cent of children in this same age group were in child care (ABS, 2011).

Alongside workforce participation, other reasons have been promoted in the expansion of child care, including the benefits for children, society and government (Organisation for Economic Co-operation and Development [OECD], 2006). In addition to the focus on addressing poverty and disadvantage (Tayler, 2011), the benefits for children's wellbeing (Moore & Oberklaid, 2010) and social development have been particularly highlighted, especially for children aged over three years (Berk, 2013).

Child care centres have historically provided education and care for young children birth to school age, so that parents (usually mothers) are able to participate in paid employment. With their roots in the provision of care, moves in recent years to shift some of the main focus of child care as 'care' have seen the renaming of centres as 'Early Learning Centres' or 'Early Years Centres'. While child care has operated quite distinctly from kindergarten/preschool this delineation is not neat, and increasingly arguments are made that child care does indeed include education (and conversely that kindergarten/preschool includes care). Child care centres are required to meet educational quality standards, as well as quality care requirements regarding health and safety (ACECQA, 2014a, 2014b).

Kindergarten/Preschool

Kindergarten/preschool provides an ECEC program for children aged three to five years prior to the commencement of formal schooling. As mentioned earlier in the chapter, the name given to an early childhood program may vary across states and territories (for example, in Queensland, kindergarten; New South Wales, preschool; and South Australia, reception). Historically, these programs included sessional kindergarten for shorter days (for example, 9.00 a.m. to 12.00 p.m. or 9.00 a.m. to 2.30 p.m.) where children attended for two to three days per week. Increasingly, kindergartens operate for a full-day session of six hours and are often open 'after' or 'before' school to meet the needs of working parents.

There have been changes in ECEC in Australia, partly through the Early Years Reform Agenda (EYRA) discussed later in this chapter. Significantly, since 2009 ECEC programs in Australia have been required to follow a curriculum framework—the EYLF (DEEWR, 2009a). In addition, kindergartens/preschools are now required to work through quality improvement and rating systems—the National Quality Standard (NQS) (ACECQA, 2014a), administered through state/territory-based government departments. Another key change within the EYRA has seen kindergarten/preschool programs increasingly offered within child care centre programs, advertised as an additional feature of the program. Additionally, more kindergartens/preschools are now co-located on school grounds, reflecting key policy initiatives. These centres may be either co-located with state/government schools or with independent/private schools.

Family day care

In the last wave of data from the child care census in Australia only 4 per cent of children from birth to four years and 1 per cent of children from birth to eleven years used family day care (ABS, 2011). This small though significant percentage of children represents for many families a philosophical choice for care in a home-based setting. Family day care takes place in a private home, with a small number (approximately four) of children. The focus is on home-based learning experiences, and may include regular outings to parks, the local library and shops. This type of ECEC differs to other in-home care as it is provided through a registered family day care coordination scheme. Unlike other informal home-based care arrangements, in a registered family day care program parents are able to access government subsidies and rebates, thus reducing the fees. Like child care and kindergarten/preschool, family day care programs are required to work with the EYLF curriculum document and the NQS.

Multifunctional Aboriginal Children's Services (MACS)

MACS are government-funded, not-for-profit, community-based early childhood programs that provide for the educational, social and developmental needs of Aboriginal and Torres Strait Islander children (Australian National Audit Office [ANAO], 2010). MACS may include long day care, alongside another form of care or program, such as OSHC, playgroup, nutrition programs or parenting programs. Though there are few MACS in operation, with just 33 government-funded services in 2009–10 (ANAO, 2010), funding is continually under the microscope. These ECEC services provide important supports for children and their families, with a focus on responsiveness to local needs. This operational model makes each MAC program unique.

Integrated child and family centres

There is wide recognition that the integration of education and care programs with multiple functions forging work across professional disciplines has immense benefits for young children and their families (Tayler et al., 2008). Increasingly in Australia these benefits have not gone unnoticed and there are small, though significant moves to bring education/care/cross-disciplines together through integrating services that may offer child care, kindergarten and other programs, such as health, child protection and/or early intervention.

Outside school hours care (OSHC)

Alongside increased patterns of child care use in Australia are growing numbers of children accessing OSHC programs. In 2011, 13 per cent of children accessed before/after school care (ABS, 2011), compared with 6 per cent of children in 2006. These programs are usually offered on school grounds and are often affiliated with the school or a peak community organisation (for example, the YMCA) or are privately operated. Programs are offered before school, often from 6.00 a.m., and after school, until 6.00 p.m. or later. Some programs provide meals for children; for example, breakfast and afternoon tea. OSHC have also come under key policy reforms and are required to work with the curriculum document My Time, Our Place (DEEWR, 2011). Programs are also required to comply with NQS and undergo a quality rating and assessment process.

School contexts: lower years of primary school

Every state or territory in Australia has a full-time school year prior to Year 1, although this first year of school is referred to by different names (for example, Queensland, preparatory; New South Wales, kindergarten; and South Australia, reception). In the new Australian Curriculum this first year of school is referred to as the foundation year (www.australiancurriculum.edu.au/). Some of these programs are not compulsory (for example, preparatory in Queensland); however, most children do access this year, with almost 100 per cent attendance.

The age for compulsory school attendance varies between states/territories, though in most cases children commence school the year they turn five. The school week is Monday to Friday for approximately six hours per day.

Home schooling

It should be noted that while school attendance is compulsory in Australia, each state or territory has regulation requirements to monitor home schooling, or home education, as an alternative approach to mainstream school. Although the number of children in registered home school arrangements is small, there have been marked increases across Australia (English, 2014). Each state and territory has home schooling associations that provide support for families who choose this option of education for their children.

EDUCATION AND CARE: INTEGRATED EARLY CHILDHOOD EDUCATION AND CARE

The discussion of education and care and moves towards the integration of these two interconnected aspects of early childhood programs is not new, and for some time those in the early childhood field have grappled with the competing discourses of care and/or education. More recently, a case has been made for the integration of education and care (OECD, 2006), and the phrase 'early childhood education and care' has emerged. Apart from the different contexts that have been outlined so far in this chapter, there are a number of terms drawn on to describe the field. 'Early years', 'early childhood', 'early childhood education', and 'early childhood education and care' are among the terms that appear in policy, curriculum, texts or position titles. In the United States, the phrase early childhood education (ECE) is frequently used, partly as an attempt to capture the idea that education and learning take place across all contexts (White, 2002), and are not isolated to preschool. The OECD's *Starting Strong* publications use the phrase early childhood education and care. *Starting Strong II* makes the point that 'services for young children should combine care, developmental and learning opportunities, and that education and care should not exist apart in approaches to young children' (OECD, 2006, p. 229). The addition of care to create the term 'early childhood education and care' signalled bringing together preschool education and child care. However, the split between care and education seems ongoing as 'longstanding division between child care and early education still operates in most of the English-speaking world' (OECD, 2006, p. 230). In Australia there have been a number of initiatives to develop integrated ECEC centres. For example, 38 Aboriginal and Torres Strait Islander Children and Family Centres were established in 2009 to provide integrated ECEC programs, along with professional services, for families (COAG, 2009).

The delineations between education and care can be attributed, in part, to the complexity in the purposes of early childhood. According to the OECD, it is:

> concerned with providing education and care to young children but it is also linked—with women's employment and equality of opportunity; child development and child poverty issues; labour market supply; children's health, social welfare and early education. (OECD, 2006, p. 47)

MODELS OF EARLY CHILDHOOD EDUCATION AND CARE PROVISION

The number of child care centres in Australia has grown, commensurate with levels of parental workforce participation (ABS, 2011). Included in this growth has been the emergence of different models of child care operation. Different business models of child care provision have seen three distinct types: not-for-profit/community-based; for-profit/private; and corporate child care (Press, 2014). A model of not-for-profit/community-based child care has been prominent in early childhood programs not only in Australia, but also internationally (OECD, 2006; Penn, 2011). Not-for-profit/community-based centres are driven by principles of working with families and are committed to the highest quality. The link between quality and not-for-profit principles has seen the not-for-profit/community-based business model touted as the most appropriate for children and for families (Penn, 2011). For-profit/private child care centres operate under two related business models: privately owned and operated child care, and corporate child care. Private/for-profit centres are owned by individuals or small businesses and operate independently. The corporate child care model includes a larger operation in which a number of centres are centrally managed by a company. In Australia, the provision of for-profit and not-for-profit ECEC care is the result, to an extent, of child care policy—who can provide it, how it is funded, and how it should operate

Perspectives and practices in ECEC policy and provision

(Penn, 2011). The next section of this chapter turns to an examination of the ECEC policy in Australia, with attention to some of the key international policy reforms that have shaped this landscape.

EARLY CHILDHOOD EDUCATION AND CARE POLICY IN AUSTRALIA

ECEC policy is shaped by social, political and economic imperatives. In order to understand the ECEC policy landscape it is important to know about how policies are developed and what these policies mean for early childhood contexts. With the ECEC policy landscape shifting significantly in the past decade, it is useful to look back and to capture some of the historical and political events that have shaped contemporary policy contexts in Australia.

In recent years there has been increasing government interest in ECEC, particularly in prior-to-school contexts, resulting in significant changes in the policy agenda, both internationally and within Australia. This attention has moved from programs providing primarily care for children so that workforce participation increases to a focus on education and quality (COAG, 2008). Compelling arguments have been made for investing in the early years, with positive outcomes for children's life trajectories and the associated monetary savings for government; for example, higher employability, lower crime rates, positive impact on social services and higher rates of education (Heckman, 2006). The broader benefits of investing in early childhood, beyond labour force participation, are mapped out in *Starting Strong II*, drawing on an argument that ECEC is for the public good:

> Early education and care contributes to the public good, e.g. to the general health of a nation's children, to future educational achievement, to labour market volume and flexibility, and to social cohesion. (OECD, 2006, p. 37)

Additionally, neuroscience/brain research has made a convincing case for the importance of the early years, with high-quality ECEC programs supporting children to reach their potentials. The growing body of neuroscience/brain research has become one of the most effective and powerful arguments for an increased focus on the early years (Shonkoff & Phillips, 2000). The science of brain research presents evidence as to the importance of the early childhood

Contexts, policy and frameworks of early childhood education and care

years through clearly defined critical periods in which the brain develops. These are put forward as windows of opportunity for the neurons in the brain to connect and develop.

Alongside investment and neuroscience/brain research is growing interest in international comparisons, with the *Starting Strong II* report positioning Australia last out of the twenty countries in expenditure on pre-primary education (three-to-six year olds) (OECD, 2006). Together these factors made a strong case for the government to scrutinise ECEC provision, and develop policies that respond to reports and research.

The relevance of policy

Policy and regulatory frameworks require early childhood educators to work within a complex legislative and regulatory environment (Fenech, Sumsion, & Goodfellow, 2006). The relevance of policy is important to consider. By knowing about how policies are developed, and the different levels of policy, early childhood educators are able to work in ways that acknowledge and implement policies. A skilful educator is able to work in ways where policies, curriculum documents and regulatory support procedures guide practice and shape pedagogy, without smothering these, or indeed the educator. Understanding the purpose of relevant policies enables educators to make informed decisions and promote 'wise practice' (Goodfellow, 2001).

Policy is a key part of ECEC, with different levels of policy providing governance and frameworks. On one level policy emerges from political contexts, as explored in the previous section. An example of a current government policy is the National Quality Standard (NQS). This framework requires centres to develop and document their own policies. This is clearly stated through Element 7.3.5, 'Service practices are based on effectively documented policies and procedures that are available at the service and reviewed regularly' (Australian Children's Education and Care Quality Authority [ACECQA], 2014b). Therefore, government policies provide foundations for organisation and, in turn, centre policies. Yet, there are different levels or layers of policy development and implementation that require careful consideration. Table 6.2 represents three layers of policy developments, with examples provided.

The complexity in early childhood policy is partially attributed to the points that have already been outlined in this chapter, the origins of child care and

Perspectives and practices in ECEC policy and provision

Table 6.2: Layers of policy

Government policy	Organisation policy	Context-specific policy

For example:
    Commonwealth or
    State
Policy example:
    National Quality
    Standard
	For example: C & K,
	    SDN, Goodstart
	Policy example:
	    Child Protection,
	    Health, Safety and
	    Environment
		For example: individual
		    centre
		Policy example: Food
		    and Nutrition Policy

kindergarten/preschool, the range of purposes for early childhood, and different government policy arrangements for the field. The various levels of government have different responsibilities for funding, curriculum and regulatory frameworks (Tayler, 2011). Additionally, and as previously outlined in this chapter, early childhood programs are auspiced differently depending on whether they are in prior-to-school contexts or in schools (lower years of primary school).

Table 6.3 revisits the key ECEC contexts that were outlined earlier in the chapter. Alongside these, divided into prior-to-school and school contexts, are the relevant curriculum, regulatory authority and policies that provide governance and support frameworks for practice.

EARLY YEARS REFORM AGENDA

In Australia, key shifts in ECEC policy occurred in 2007 when the then Rudd Federal Government announced a raft of reforms that were part of an 'education revolution'. These reforms included policy changes in both prior-to-school and school contexts, and focused particularly on responsibility shifting from states/ territories to the national level. The argument was made that by streamlining systems, structures and curriculum there would be greater consistency, parity and equity across education and care programs throughout the country.

The Early Years Reform Agenda (EYRA) for prior-to-school contexts was conceived in 2007. Many policy changes contributed to this agenda. One was to provide universal access to a preschool program for all children in the year before school, delivered by a university-qualified teacher (COAG, 2009; DEEWR, 2009b), which aimed to 'improve the quality of early childhood services' (Press, 2014, p. 15). Prior to these key policy shifts a number of events occurred, including a change of federal government and the aforementioned attention to key research on investment in early childhood and neuroscience/brain research.

Contexts, policy and frameworks of early childhood education and care

Table 6.3: ECEC contexts and associated curricula, regulatory authorities and policies

Prior-to-school-contexts	Curriculum and regulatory authorities
Child care/Long day care Kindergarten/Preschool Family day care Home-based care Mobile children's services Multifunctional Aboriginal Children's Services (MACS) Integrated child and family centres Occasional care Playgroups Outside school hours care (OSHC)	**Curriculum:** Belonging, Being and Becoming: The early years learning framework for Australia *(DEEWR, 2009a)* **Regulatory authority:** National Quality Framework (NQF) (Australian Children's Education and Care Quality Authority [ACECQA], 2014b); National Quality Standard (NQS) (Australian Children's Education and Care Quality Authority [ACECQA], 2014a). The NQF and NQS are enacted through the state/territory-based legislation (for example, Education and Care Services National Law [Queensland Government, 2011]. **Policies:** Developed through the regulatory authority documents outlined above, though also shaped by organisation (for example, SDN in NSW; C & K in Qld) and individual centre/service.
School contexts	**Operation**
Schooling, including both non-compulsory (foundation year) and compulsory years	**Curriculum:** *National Curriculum* (Australian Curriculum and Assessment Reporting Authority [ACARA], 2014) <www.australiancurriculum.edu.au/>. **Regulatory authority:** Both Commonwealth and state/territory-based government department. **Policies:** state and territory-based government department; organisation (Education Department; Catholic Education; Independent school); individual school.

Understandings of these events provide insights into decisions that were made and how they shaped the ECEC policy terrain in Australia.

The reform initiatives are a blueprint for early childhood policy and include 'all four year olds entitled to receive fifteen hours of learning per week' (p. 16) with delivery by a 'four year qualified teacher' (p. 16). Also proposed was a national early childhood curriculum to replace the previous curricula developed by each state and territory, resulting in Belonging, Being and Becoming: The early years learning framework (EYLF) for Australia (DEEWR, 2009a). In addition, these proposed reforms necessitated transference of responsibility for ECEC policy and infrastructure to the Commonwealth level (p. 1).

Key to early childhood policy reform in prior-to-school contexts has been attention to Indigenous children and families. Initiatives have been developed that provide support to promote children from Aboriginal and Torres Strait Islander backgrounds to have access to high-quality early childhood programs. Examples of initiatives include the National Partnership Agreement on Indigenous Early Childhood Development, developed to focus on outcomes for Indigenous children. The agreement has seen Aboriginal and Torres Strait Islander Children and Family Centres developed across Australia in urban, regional and remote areas where there are high Indigenous populations (COAG, 2009).

As part of the education revolution, school settings have also seen substantial policy reform, notably through the introduction of the Australian Curriculum, the first national curriculum in the country, auspiced through the Australian Curriculum Assessment and Reporting Authority [ACARA] (www.acara.edu.au). The Australian Curriculum (www.australiancurriculum.edu.au) is now compulsory for all schools in Australia to implement, although at the time of writing not all subject areas were available for delivery. ACARA oversees assessment through the National Assessment Program (NAP) (www.nap.edu.au), which administers the standardised test instrument National Assessment Program— Literacy and Numeracy (NAPLAN). Reporting is captured under the My Schools website, where a profile for each school in Australia (based on the NAPLAN test score results) is accessible (www.myschool.edu.au).

While there has been substantial reform to bring greater consistency across early childhood policy in Australia, this policy is, at least partially, auspiced by both federal and state education departments (kindergarten/preschool) and departments concerned with community, family and human services (child care) (Brennan, 2007). As mentioned earlier in this chapter, in recent years, there have been policy changes to bring together education and care (Press, 2014). Prior to the reform agenda, ECEC policy in Australia included different levels of legislation, policy and funding across Commonwealth, state/territory and, in some cases, local government. Adding to this policy landscape are multi-layered, overlapping three- to four-year cycles between elections, with changes of government and political parties leading to changes in the values shaping policy.

Alongside understandings of some of the values that shape policy, another way to understand policy conception is to consider constructions of childhood that underpin policy development (Mitchell, 2010). The values and beliefs about children that shape policy go some way to explaining an orientation towards education and/or care. For example, children constructed as 'participants in society and autonomous beings' (Mitchell, 2010, p. 330) challenges the notion of early childhood policy being about 'a service to support parental employment . . . and as a service to rescue disadvantaged children' (p. 330).

Policy shifts

As part of policy reform in Australia, the National Quality Standard (NQS) was established, coming into effect from January 2012 (ACECQA, 2014a). The National Quality Framework (NQF) was established under an applied law system, comprising the *Education and Care Services National Law* and the *Education and Care Services National Regulations* (Queensland Government, 2011). The NQF applies to long day care (child care), family day care, outside school hours care and kindergarten/preschools. The NQF and associated regulatory systems are enacted through the legislation that established a national system for early childhood. *The Education and Care Services National Regulations* support the legislation and provide detail on a range of operational requirements for education and care services.

With the complexity of ECEC and the rapid changes in policy have come challenges for the ECEC field, both to keep up to date with policy shifts and to implement the required changes. Key documents provide support to enact change in an informed and sustainable manner. *The Early Years Workforce Strategy: The early childhood education and care workforce strategy for Australia* (Standing Council on School Education and Early Childhood [SCSEEC], 2012) includes five key priority areas for ECEC, each with a focus on developing an ECEC workforce to enable the implementation of policies. Notable in this document is a diagram that visually represents the 'roll out' of ECEC policy in Australia. In the following, and final, section of this chapter, quality, as a concept and policy consideration, is explored.

Perspectives and practices in ECEC policy and provision

Quality

Quality has gained increased prominence in early childhood in recent years with claims that 'the better the quality of child care and early education, the better it is for the child's development' (DfES, 2005, in OECD, 2006, p. 165). Links between neuroscience/brain research and outcomes for children and quality have emerged and resulted in outcomes-based measures focused on quality. The appropriateness of ECEC for children is, to an extent, defined through quality.

There are many quality measures in ECEC. The Early Childhood Environmental Rating Scale (ECERS) (Harms, Cryer, & Clifford, 1998) and the Infant/Toddler Environment Rating Scale (ITERS) are two quality measurement tools to support research and program improvement in ECEC. In Australia, the ECERS was used as a basis for developing the Quality Improvement and Accreditation System (QIAS) (National Childcare Accreditation Council [NCAC], 2005) to consider and measure quality in child care. More recently, it was used to develop the NQF and NQS, the quality rating tools for all prior-to-school ECEC contexts.

Currently, prior-to-school early childhood contexts in Australia are rated against the seven quality areas in the NQS. This process involves the centre or service developing a Quality Improvement Plan (QIP) and the relevant regulatory authority in each state and territory (for example, Department of Families Resource Officer) undertaking the assessment and rating process. The centre is assigned a rating, from Excellent, Exceeding, Meeting, Working Towards to Significant Improvement Required. The rating is made publicly available via the ACECQA website. For further information see more at <www.acecqa.gov.au/assessments-and-ratings>.

The concept of quality has come under scrutiny, with its construction considered to be contingent on political, cultural and contextual features, and therefore complex to define and difficult to measure (Dahlberg & Moss, 2005). The ways in which quality may be understood in one country may vary considerably to the ways in which quality is contextualised in another (Penn, 2011). It is suggested that 'quality in early childhood education should be a process rather than a product, an ongoing conversation rather than a document' (Tobin, 2005, p. 435). Dahlberg and Moss (2005) also highlight the risk of quality being 'reduced to a set of criteria that constitutes a norm' and that is 'assessed using a technical instrument that measures the conformity of a service to the norm' (p. 9). There is a risk in assuming that quality is objective and is able to be measured and moderated.

Quality as a concept is widely contested. What may be considered 'quality' for one person may not be considered as 'quality' for another. A parent may think of quality in different ways to the ways in which an educator may think of quality. Likewise, what is considered quality by a parent or by an educator may be quite different again to what a child may consider as quality. Nonetheless, quality measures provide reassurances that the program offered may be safe— with particular attention to the physical environment and adequate numbers of staff with children; where children are afforded dignity and respect and their rights acknowledged; and where staff have knowledge about child development and therefore are able to provide an educational program that supports children's health and development.

CONCLUSION

ECEC provision is complex, with different contexts providing for both similar and disparate needs of children and families in Australia. The connections between policy and practice are understood more fully when there are shared conceptions of what constitutes different early childhood contexts—their origins, their purpose and their functions within and against the contemporary policy landscape. Through understandings of ECEC policy, both within Australia and the connected policies internationally, clearer insights into ECEC as a dynamic and complex field are made possible.

This chapter has explored a range of ECEC contexts that operate within Australia. Constructions of integrated ECEC models have provided insights into bringing care and education together, where professional cross-disciplinary teams work collaboratively to provide programs and services for children and their families. Exploration of the policy landscape was foregrounded by origins of ECEC, current research and the political climate, each of which shape policy agendas. Consideration of quality as a construct and ways that quality in ECEC is measured in Australia have provided both insights and challenges.

Perspectives and practices in ECEC policy and provision

FURTHER THINKING

1. *Contexts:* What are the key early childhood contexts? What are some of the complexities in the provision of ECEC in Australia? How do you see yourself as an early childhood educator working in one or more of these contexts?

2. *Policy:* How are policies developed in ECEC? What is the purpose of policy? What have been some of the key shifts in ECEC policy in recent years? What impact has the EYRA had on ECEC contexts?

3. *Quality:* Why is quality an area of interest in ECEC policy? What is the current system for measuring policy in Australia? Go the website for ACECQA and look at how this system works. Why is the measurement of quality contested?

REFERENCES

Australian Bureau of Statistics (ABS) (2011). 4402.0—Childhood Education and Care, Australia, June 2011. Retrieved 3 August 2015, <www.abs.gov.au/ausstats/abs@.nsf/Products/4402.0~June+2011~Main+Features~Main+features?OpenDocument>.

Australian Children's Education and Care Quality Authority (ACECQA) (2014a). National Quality Standard. Retrieved 3 May 2014, <www.acecqa.gov.au/national-quality-framework/the-national-quality-standard>.

—— (2014b). National Quality Framework. Retrieved 5 April 2014, <http://acecqa.gov.au/national-quality-framework/introducing-the-national-quality-framework>.

Australian Curriculum and Assessment Reporting Authority (ACARA) (2014). Curriculum. Retrieved 3 May 2014, <www.acara.edu.au/curriculum/curriculum.html>.

Australian National Audit Office (ANAO) (2010). *ANAO Audit Report No. 8, 2010–11. Multifunctional Aboriginal Children's Services (MACS) and Crèches.* Canberra: ANAO.

Berk, L.E. (2013). *Child Development,* 9th edn. Boston: Pearson International Edition.

Brennan, D. (2007). The ABC of child care politics, *Australian Journal of Social Issues,* 42(2), 213–25.

Council of Australian Governments (COAG) (2008). *A National Quality Framework for Early Childhood Education and Care: A discussion paper.* Canberra: COAG.

—— (2009). *Closing the Gap: National partnership agreement of Indigenous early childhood development.* Canberra: COAG.

Contexts, policy and frameworks of early childhood education and care

Dahlberg, G. & Moss, P. (2005). *Ethics and Politics in Early Childhood Education*. Abingdon: RoutledgeFalmer.

Department of Education, Employment and Workplace Relations (DEEWR) (2009a). Belonging, Being and Becoming: The early years learning framework for Australia. Barton, ACT: Australian Government.

—— (2009b). *National Early Years Workforce Strategy*. Canberra: DEEWR.

—— (2011). *My Time, Our Place: Framework for school age care in Australia*. Canberra: DEEWR.

English, R. (9 December 2014). Evidence of home schooling success erased from inquiry report, *The Conversation*. Retrieved March 2015, <http://theconversation.com/evidence-of-home-schooling-success-erased-from-inquiry-report-35087>.

Fenech, M., Sumsion, J. & Goodfellow, J. (2006). The regulatory environment in long day care: A 'double edged sword' for early childhood professional practice, *Australian Journal of Early Childhood*, 31(3), 49–58.

Goodfellow, J. (2001). Wise practice: The need to move beyond best practice in early childhood education, *Australian Journal of Early Childhood*, 26(3), 1–6.

Goodfellow, J. & Laverty, J. (2003). Grandparents supporting working families: Satisfaction and choice in the provision of child care, *Family Matters*, 66 (Spring/Summer), 14–19.

Harms, T., Cryer, D. & Clifford, R.M. (1998). *Early Childhood Environment Rating Scale*, revised edn. New York: Teacher's College Press.

Heckman, J. (2006). *The Economics of Investing in Early Childhood*. National Investment for the Early Years (NIFTeY) Conference. Retrieved 10 May 2007, <www.niftey.cyh.com/webpages/conferences/conferenceframe.htm>.

Mitchell, L. (2010). Constructions of childhood in early childhood education policy debate in New Zealand, *Contemporary Issues in Early Childhood*, 11(4), 328–41.

Moore, T. & Oberklaid, F. (2010). Investing in early childhood education and care: The health and wellbeing case, *Encyclopedia of education*, 3rd edn. Oxford: Elsevier.

National Childcare Accreditation Council (NCAC) (2005). *Quality Improvement and Accreditation System: Quality practices guide*. Surry Hills, NSW: NCAC.

Organisation for Economic Co-operation and Development (OECD) (2006). *Starting Strong II: Early childhood education and care policy*. Paris: OECD.

Penn, H. (2011). *Quality in Early Childhood Services: An international perspective*. Berkshire, UK: Open University Press.

Press, F. (2014). The state of play in early childhood policy: A note from Australia, *New Zealand Early Childhood Education Journal*, 17, 11–19.

Queensland Government (2011). *Education and Care Services National Law (Queensland) Act 2011*. Retrieved 3 August 2015, <www.legislation.qld.gov.au/LEGISLTN/ACTS/2011/11AC038.pdf>.

Shonkoff, J.P. & Phillips, D.A. (eds) (2000). *From Neurons to Neighbourhoods: The science of early childhood development*. Washington, DC: National Academy Press.

Standing Council on School Education and Early Childhood (SCSEEC) (2012). *Early Years Workforce Strategy: The early childhood education and care workforce strategy for Australia*. Canberra: SCSEEC.

Tayler, C. (2011). Changing policy, changing culture: Steps toward early learning quality improvement in Australia, *International Journal of Early Childhood*, 43(3), 211–25.

Tayler, C., Cloney, D., Farrell, A. & Muscat, T. (2008). *The Queensland Hubs Study: Child care and family services in rural and regional communities*. Brisbane: Queensland University of Technology.

Tobin, J. (2005). Quality in early childhood education: An anthropologist's perspective, *Early Education and Development*, 16(4), 421–34.

White, L.A. (2002). Ideas and the welfare state: Explaining child care policy development in Canada and the United States, *Comparative Political Studies*, 35(6), 713–43.

Chapter 7

Cultural safety for Indigenous children in early childhood education and care

Margot Ford

In this chapter you will find:
- demographics of Indigenous Peoples
- an outline of early childhood education and care services designed for Indigenous Peoples
- educational challenges facing Indigenous Peoples
- indigenous cultural safety in education.

This chapter discusses the social and educational context of Aboriginal and Torres Strait Islander children in Australia. It begins by providing demographics of Indigenous Peoples and the early childhood education and care (ECEC) services that are specifically designed to cater for an Aboriginal and Torres Strait Islander social and cultural worldview. It presents the educational context in which Indigenous students operate, before discussing strategies to ensure that early childhood education sites are culturally safe and supportive learning environments for Indigenous children.

In Australia a person can identify as Aboriginal and Torres Strait Islander by declaring his or her Aboriginality and by being accepted as Aboriginal by their community. There is continual debate about the most appropriate title for Aboriginal and Torres Strait Islanders. Some accept 'Indigenous People(s)' with initial capitals to afford the same respect for the naming of any nation of people, such as 'Australian' or 'English'. The addition of the 's' signals that there is more than one nation of Indigenous People in Australia. This became popular after the

Year of Indigenous People in the early 1990s. However, others would rather the full Aboriginal and Torres Strait Islander nomenclature be used (not abbreviated). This chapter uses all, depending on context. Furthermore there are more collective local names for Indigenous Peoples, such as Murri in Queensland and Koori in New South Wales. However, it has become the convention for Indigenous Peoples to refer to themselves by nation and/or clan group; for example, Noel Pearson is from the Guggu Yalanji Peoples in North Queensland and Aboriginal people from inner Sydney are from the Gadigal Clan of the Eora Nation. To show respect for local Aboriginal and Torres Strait Islander people it is worthwhile knowing the local nation or clan group. An interactive Indigenous language map is available at <www.abc.net.au/indigenous/map/>.

At the outset it is important to note that there is great diversity among Aboriginal and Torres Strait Islander families and children in Australia. There is cultural diversity with many different nations and language groups across widely different environments, including desert country, lush tropical northern Australia and the highly urbanised Eastern seaboard. Indigenous Peoples occupy seats in federal, state and territory parliaments and are lawyers, doctors and teachers. Their superb knowledge of the environment helps support natural resource management projects and they are well represented in the arts and in sport. While it is critical to recognise this social and economic diversity, it must be highlighted that there are considerable challenges facing the vast majority of Indigenous Peoples in Australia. The reasons for the challenges are myriad and complex. With unequal treatment, dispossession of land and outright violence against them, historically Indigenous Peoples in Australia were not accorded the same rights as everyone else; not the least was access to education—a situation that continued well into the last century and still resonates today.

THE SCOPE OF INDIGENOUS PEOPLES IN AUSTRALIA

At the last census in 2011 there were 548 400 Aboriginal and Torres Strait Islanders in Australia; 2.5 per cent of the total Australian population of 21 million. New South Wales has the highest number of Aboriginal and Torres Strait Islanders at 172 600 (32 per cent of the total Indigenous population) (Australian Bureau of Statistics [ABS], 2012). The Northern Territory has the highest proportion of Aboriginal and Torres Strait Islanders at 27 per cent of the total population

Cultural safety for Indigenous children in early childhood education and care

with approximately 57 000 people. What is important to note is that the median age of Aboriginal and Torres Strait Islanders is 21 years as against 38 years in the non-Indigenous population. Figure 7.1 illustrates the distribution of the Indigenous and non-Indigenous population in Australia (Australian Bureau of Statistics [ABS], 2012). It shows that nearly 13 per cent of the Indigenous population is between the ages of birth to four years, while it is below 7 per cent in the non-Indigenous population. The proportion of Aboriginal and Torres Strait Islander children between the ages of five and fifteen years is also much higher. However, less than 2 per cent of the Aboriginal and Torres Strait

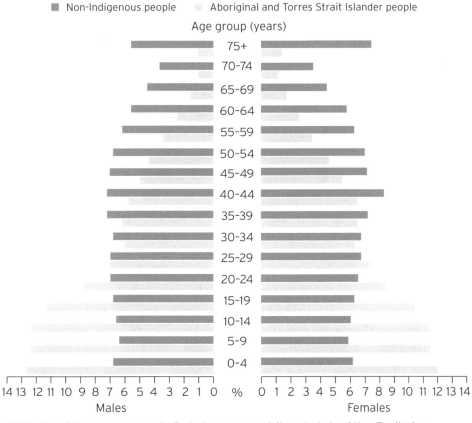

Figure 7.1: Population structure (a) by age in 2011 between Aboriginal and Torres Strait Islander and non-Indigenous people

(a) Usual residence census counts. Excludes oversees visitors. Includes Other Territories.

Source: Australian Bureau of Statistics, 2012

Perspectives and practices in ECEC policy and provision

Islander population are over 70 years old. Indeed, the population proportion compared to their non-Indigenous counterparts decreases after the age of 30 and is a reflection of poorer health and education outcomes in the Aboriginal and Torres Strait Islander population.

Reflection

For more information about 'Closing the Gap' see:
http://caepr.anu.edu.au/sites/default/files/Publications/topical/ClosingTheGaps.pdf

1. This report was written in 2008. Consider the conclusion and discuss if you believe there have been any changes in the situation of Indigenous families and students since then.

The 2015 prime minister's report 'Closing the Gap'can be found at:
http://www.dpmc.gov.au/sites/default/files/publications/Closing_the_Gap_2015_Report_0.pdf

2. In the prime minister's report of 2015 the then prime minister Tony Abbott noted he was 'profoundly disappointed' with the results of 'Closing the Gap' data. Discuss what could be done more effectively to close the gap from an early childhood education and care perspective.

Because increases in education outcomes are linked to better health outcomes and also directly related to increased chances of job opportunities, it is vital that Indigenous children receive a high-quality education at all levels: early childhood, primary, secondary and tertiary. In 2011 the census showed that 56 per cent of Aboriginal and Torres Strait Islander children between three and five years old attended preschool or primary school as compared to 63 per cent of non-Indigenous children; a gap of 7 percentage points. The Australian Early Development Census (AEDC) (previously known as Australian Early Development Index) indicates that five-year-old Aboriginal and Torres Strait Islander children are more than twice as likely to be developmentally vulnerable than their non-Indigenous counterparts (AEDC, 2012).

144

During primary and secondary school 85 per cent of Indigenous students between six and fourteen years attended school as opposed to 93 per cent of non-Indigenous students; a gap of 8 percentage points, although this is not uniform across the country. The same 2011 census shows that 25 per cent of the Indigenous population had Year 12 or equivalent as their highest educational achievement compared to 52 per cent of the non-Indigenous population (ABS, 2012). Later in the chapter the implications of educational inequality is discussed in more depth. What the statistics tell us is how critically important it is to offer a range of high-quality ECEC services with staff that are fully informed about Indigenous issues and are highly culturally competent. The aim is to offer services that are culturally safe for young Aboriginal and Torres Strait Islander children and their families in a setting that holds Indigenous culture and practice in high regard.

EARLY CHILDHOOD EDUCATION AND CARE SERVICES IN AUSTRALIA

In 2011 there were 268 children's services specifically for Aboriginal and Torres Strait Islander children across Australia at a cost federally of $44 million to operate these services. These include 33 Multifunctional Aboriginal Childcare Services (MACS) and 36 crèches costed at $20.7 million (Australian National Audit Office, 2011). By far the largest number of services are in the Northern Territory, with 34 services, because of requirements in remote and very remote areas and the fact that local funding is less available than to states. Furthermore, there was an increase in the numbers of MACS and crèches after the Northern Territory Emergency Response in 2007. There are nine MACS each in New South Wales and South Australia, six in Victoria and Western Australia, three in Queensland, and one in both the Australian Capital Territory and Tasmania. The states and territories have their own raft of services depending on the need to supplement the funding by the federal government.

MACS centres have the same regulatory requirements as all other early childhood centres, but they provide the opportunity to create centres specifically for Indigenous children. They usually support a long day care facility but also have other services attached to them, such as playgroups and other parent support groups. There are several benefits of MACS centres for Indigenous parents and their children (Kitson & Bowes, 2010), including an increased likelihood of Indigenous staff in the facilities and a commitment to an Indigenous approach to teaching and learning. MACS centres are best placed to respond to local community needs and indeed Indigenous parents and educators would like to see the model expanded (Kitson & Bowes, 2010).

The Aboriginal Playgroups and Enrichment Program is another federally funded initiative that provides access to affordable and culturally appropriate child care either as part of MACS centres or sometimes as a standalone program. This is a community-based service that is responsive to local needs. Like many other early childhood settings, these playgroups support parents to gain skills in parenting as well as providing a place for young Indigenous children to meet up and play. These ECEC services contribute to a positive beginning for young children. The next section will discuss the reasons why.

EDUCATIONAL CHALLENGES FACING INDIGENOUS FAMILIES

The challenges facing Indigenous families and their children are not dissimilar to those facing Indigenous families and children ten, twenty or even 30 years ago. According to Griffiths (2011):

> Factors such as adverse socioeconomic conditions, poor housing conditions, unemployment, family violence and child abuse all contribute to poorer outcomes for Indigenous students when compared to non-Indigenous students. (p. 70)

In more remote areas of Australia these factors are further compounded by requirements to be educated in a language other than a first language, the prevalence of otitis media (a conductive hearing loss brought on by ear infections that can lead to permanent ear damage and deafness) and the very fact of remoteness from larger centres where more services may be available.

While these factors in themselves appear overwhelming, further considerations need to be taken into account. As was established earlier in this chapter, the history of Indigenous Peoples in Australia is informed by injustices and unfair treatment that have left scars to this day, and can feel like a constant reminder in the face of daily poverty, struggle and ongoing racism.

An effective ECEC system with high-quality educators is critical for any marginalised group, but is especially the case for Indigenous Australians. In

Cultural safety for Indigenous children in early childhood education and care

order to understand just how important high-quality care and education is for Indigenous children birth to eight years old, first we need to examine the current educational context.

Some child care centres and schools in Australia are effectively responding to an Indigenous worldview with Aboriginal-focused educational sites leading the way. Some of these are showcased on the 'What Works' web site (see the box 'Resources for tackling prejudice', below, for further details). For example, Kura Yerlo Children's Centre in South Australia has a successful Indigenous Readers are Achievers program, whereby Indigenous 'Big Buddies' in Years 4 to 6 from local hub schools visit the children's centre to engage with a variety of literacy activities. The inclusion of 'Big Buddies' helps emphasise the community and family connections that are so important from an Indigenous perspective (Department of Education, Employment and Workplace Relations [DEEWR], 2011). Later in this chapter there are lots of suggestions for addressing Aboriginal

Figure 7.2: Reading at Years 3, 5 and 9 in New South Wales, Victoria, Western Australia and the Northern Territory and the national average for Indigenous and non-Indigenous students

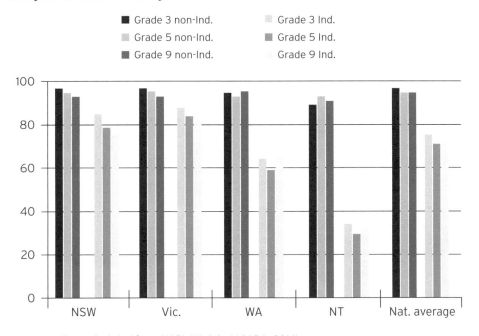

Source: Author calculated from NAPLAN data (ACARA, 2014)

147

Perspectives and practices in ECEC policy and provision

and Torres Strait Islander worldviews more effectively. The next section identifies inequality of educational outcomes for Indigenous learners.

Across Australia there is persistent educational inequality of achievement between Indigenous and non-Indigenous students. This is evident by examining the National Assessment Program—Literacy and Numeracy (NAPLAN) in the states and territories. Figure 7.2 illustrates the percentage of Indigenous and non-Indigenous students who attained the national minimum standard and above in reading for three states and the Northern Territory.

In each state and in the Northern Territory there is inequality of educational achievement for Indigenous students, with disparities at their worst in those states and territories with greater numbers of Indigenous students in rural and remote regions. The most serious disparity is in the Northern Territory.

The percentage point difference between Indigenous and non-Indigenous students for reading and numeracy across Years 3, 5 and 9 in Table 7.1 compares 2009 and 2014, demonstrating the inequality of achievement (sometimes referred to as the educational gap) in New South Wales and the Northern Territory. This state and territory were chosen as New South Wales is the state with the highest number of Aboriginal and Torres Strait Islander people and the Northern Territory has the highest proportion of Aboriginal and Torres Strait Islander people in

Table 7.1: The percentage point difference between Indigenous and non-Indigenous students in reading and numeracy in New South Wales and the Northern Territory between 2009 and 2014

	New South Wales		Northern Territory	
Reading	**2009**	**2014**	**2009**	**2014**
Year 3	10.5	12.2	50.0	55.0
Year 5	16.4	15.5	58.1	60.3
Year 9	16.1	16.2	58.4	57.2
Numeracy	**2009**	**2014**	**2009**	**2014**
Year 3	11.9	11.2	51.4	50.2
Year 5	13.6	15.6	47.4	56.1
Year 9	15.2	14.2	49.2	49.0

Source: Author calculated from NAPLAN (Australian Curriculum, Assessment and Reporting Authority [ACARA], 2014)

Australia. The table illustrates an increase in the achievement gap for Year 3 reading in New South Wales or the Northern Territory since NAPLAN began. The results for numeracy show a very small reduction in the achievement gap.

Table 7.1 also reveals the inequality of achievement increases as Indigenous students move through school, except for Year 9 numeracy in the Northern Territory. This means more Indigenous students have lower educational outcomes than their non-Indigenous counterparts the longer they stay in the schooling system. It is therefore critical that as much as possible is done in the early years to support Aboriginal and Torres Strait Islander children and their families in education. Sims (2011) is unequivocal about what is required:

> Services are more effective for Indigenous children and families when they are aware of and address cultural competence/cultural safety in their service delivery. (p. 1)

Coupled with this is the need for a high-quality teaching and learning environment with a focus on engaging early literacy and numeracy experiences. One of the best ways to ensure cultural safety and competence is to have Indigenous staff in a centre or school as there are in MACS centres. It is clear that a positive beginning in school will make all the difference and this begins with positive and educationally productive learning experiences in the birth to five settings.

So what does a culturally safe and supportive early childhood education environment look like for Indigenous children? The next section will describe seven strategies that contribute to cultural safety.

INDIGENOUS CULTURAL SAFETY IN EDUCATION

Whether an ECEC site has one Indigenous child or many, the cultural needs of those children require a different focus and it is our responsibility as early childhood educators to understand that difference. It is worth noting that the following list of strategies may be adapted to include the cultural and educational needs of a variety of different cultural groups.

1. Creating positive community relations.
2. Knowing the particular histories of Indigenous families and communities.
3. Connecting closely with families in a way that is understanding, non-judgemental and informed about Indigenous cultural practices.

Perspectives and practices in ECEC policy and provision

4. Comprehending an Indigenous pedagogical framework and ways of Indigenous learning.
5. Recognising and attending to the social, physical and educational needs of Indigenous children.
6. Recognising the social dynamics between Indigenous and non-Indigenous children in ECEC sites.
7. Being prepared to address the dynamics of social inclusion and exclusion in ECEC sites.

1. Creating positive community relations

Aboriginal and Torres Strait Islander communities are often tight-knit, with elders being held in high regard. Every early childhood site should make connections with elders and Indigenous community groups by accessing local Indigenous organisations; through Land Councils, Aboriginal art and sporting groups and local Indigenous environmental groups. The key here is relatedness. According to Karen Martin:

> As an Aboriginal educator, the role of the teacher has expanded to first be one as a learner in order to establish a physical, social, intellectual, emotional, cultural and spiritual environment where relatedness is the currency. (2007, p. 18)

The main task of all early childhood educators, then, is to show the utmost respect for elders, land and culture. The best way to achieve this is by quietly listening, watching and learning. It is possible for early childhood educators to play an important role in supporting Indigenous families and their children.

In the text box below is one such model—the SpICE model.

Special Integrated Community Engagement (SpICE) model
The aims of this model are to specifically address 'poor childhood development and learning outcomes; Indigenous, rural and remote community disadvantage; and rural and remote workforce challenges in a collaborative way.' This avoids what has come to be known as 'silos'—service provisions that are available from a range

Cultural safety for Indigenous children in early childhood education and care

of different government departments, but are not well coordinated and are in separate sections that may not have effective avenues for communication between the sections.

At the centre of the model is a 'community of learners', which acts as a conduit for social capital and capacity building to ensure culturally appropriate links with Indigenous communities and effective family health and wellbeing. In the words of one participant, 'Engagement and relationships are everything' (Clarke and Denton, 2013, p. 40).

In this model needs are articulated at the community level, and the linkages created are sustainable. The lessons for early childhood educators are to forge links with families and communities and the services available to them. Early childhood sites that have registers of available services and those members of communities are best placed to understand the needs and issues that will help target sometimes scarce resources most effectively. The early childhood educators can become part of a wider community of learners.

2. Knowing the particular histories of Indigenous families and communities

All social, cultural and ethnic groups are marked by their history, language and cultural practices. For Indigenous Australians, their history is troubled by injustices perpetrated against them but they have shown remarkable resilience and stoicism in the face of continued injustices. It is helpful to understand the local history of the Indigenous community and how this impacts upon current contexts. Indeed, educators can help in recording local histories. A great example of this is *Jackson's Track* by Daryl Tonkin and Carolyn Landon (1999). A primary school teacher in East Gippsland began talking to the mother of some Aboriginal children in her class and became intrigued with the story of Darly Tonkin, the children's white grandfather. They ended up writing together and produced a local history that is both poignant and informative of the treatment of Aboriginal people in that area since the 1920s. On many levels this is an important resource: as a model of teacher/family relations; as a record of injustice and exclusion; and as a great story of love and determination.

151

Perspectives and practices in ECEC policy and provision

3. Connecting closely with families in a way that is understanding, non-judgemental and informed about Indigenous cultural practices

All families are different and it is a central principle of the National Quality Standard (NQS) (Australian Children's Education and Care Quality Authority [ACECQA], 2013) and Belonging, Being and Becoming: The early years learning framework (EYLF) for Australia (DEEWR, 2009) that early childhood educators work closely with families in the best interests of their children.

A longitudinal study of Aboriginal children from preschool to their first year of school in Western Australia provides interesting insights (Taylor, 2010). Aboriginal children have lower rates of attendance at preschools and schools than non-Aboriginal children. This can be a source of complaint and frustration for educators, but what Taylor found were legitimate reasons:

> cultural maintenance (such as funerals), face-saving, family dysfunction, business commitments, changes in family circumstances and illness and/or illness-related factors. (p. 686)

Once it is understood that Indigenous People have some of the highest poverty rates of any social group in Australia and the poorest health outcomes these reasons make sense. Sometimes parents keep their children away because they cannot afford the fees and the historical (and contemporary) legacy of children being taken away by welfare means that some parents are fearful to send children to preschool and school if their clothes are not clean. It has been noted, however, that attendance alone will not necessarily increase effective educational outcomes (Guenther, 2013).

Developing positive relations with families is integral to developing trust. The act of an Indigenous parent handing over a child to a carer is a signifier of that trust and it comes with an expectation of the child being treated calmly and respectfully. Relationships are central in Aboriginal and Torres Strait Islander communities, with complex kinship rules guiding behaviour. Adult Indigenous educators often see themselves in the kinship position of 'grand-mother' or 'Aunty' with the commensurate obligations of those roles (Fasoli & Ford, 2001). Also, quite young children may have kinship obligations to other children, regardless of age. It is possible they are related as mothers, aunties,

152

fathers and uncles and will take their obligations seriously. These nuanced social dynamics will sometimes be missed or misunderstood by non-Indigenous educators, so it is important that efforts are made to understand local kinship relationships.

4. Comprehending ways of learning within an Aboriginal and Torres Strait Islander pedagogical framework

It is a given that Aboriginal and Torres Strait Islander children are as diverse in their learning styles as children in the wider community. However, there are ways of learning that may be better suited, but not exclusively so, to Indigenous children. Indeed, considering alternative learning styles and pedagogical frameworks helps us to understand how all children learn in different ways.

While educators need to be mindful of embedding Aboriginal content into their programs, it is more effective to recognise the processes of learning that take place and draw on these to inform practice. An eight-way interconnected Aboriginal Ways of Learning framework has been devised and can be seen in the figure below. This Eight Aboriginal Ways of Learning framework (www.8ways. wikispaces.com) reminds us how learning is intimately connected in a variety of ways to land and community, with symbol, image and metaphor playing a larger role than in the way the wider Australian community learns (Yunkaporta & Kirby, 2011).

The non-verbal symbols remind us that many Aboriginal children learn by watching and then doing. Long-winded verbal explanations do not work so well. In non-Aboriginal pedagogy information is often broken into small chunks, but sometimes the chunks are not explicitly reconnected, so understanding remains fragmented. The Eight Aboriginal Ways of Learning framework emphasises holistic connections and at some point these fragments need to be woven together again so full understanding can emerge. As a non-Aboriginal person, what I find striking about this framework is that these are effective pedagogical ways of learning for all children. The connection to land, for example, reminds us of our global responsibilities and reflects the underpinning theme of environmental sustainability that is a feature of the EYLF (DEEWR, 2009). Take time to visit the web address relating to Figure 7.3 and learn more about the Eight Ways pedagogical approach.

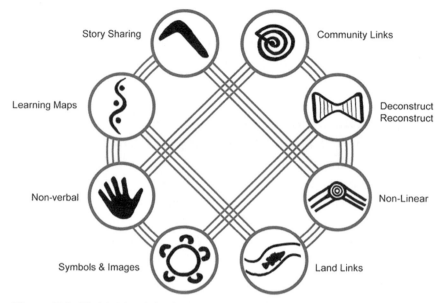

Figure 7.3: Eight Aboriginal Ways of Learning
Source: www.8ways.wikispaces.com

The 8ways or Aboriginal Pedagogy belongs to a place, not a person or organisation. They came from country in Western New South Wales. Baakindji, Ngiyampaa, Yuwaalaraay, Gamilaraay, Wiradjuri, Wangkumarra and other nations own the knowledges this framework came down from.

So we acknowledge the elders and peoples from these nations.

Story telling/story sharing is a fundamental way that knowledge is exchanged in an Aboriginal context. Stories are used as moral tales to illustrate correct ways to behave; stories are used to talk about the bush and the animals and plants that live there, and may include information about what animals and plants to avoid as well as the ones that can be used for food and medicine; stories speak about the past, lore and important events. Of course, story telling is an integral part of broader early childhood pedagogy, but can sometimes be lost among other curriculum requirements once children go to school. The Eight Aboriginal Ways of Learning framework demonstrates that story telling is a powerful pedagogical tool for Indigenous children, and arguably is effective for the learning styles of many other children as well.

Indigenous languages and Aboriginal English as an additional language/dialect

An aspect of Indigenous pedagogy that may be missed by non-Indigenous educators is that often Aboriginal and Torres Strait Islander children are taught in a language that is not their first language. It may be clear when an Indigenous child is speaking an Indigenous language as their first language, and as a consequence teaching English as another language techniques will form part of a teacher's repertoire. In some places Indigenous children are fortunate enough to have a bilingual curriculum that provides for teaching in both their first language and English. However, it is also the case that many Indigenous children speak a form of Aboriginal English.

There is now greater attention being given to Aboriginal English as a dialect of English as a result of a national initiative currently endorsed by New South Wales, the Northern Territory, Western Australia and Queensland. The Capability Framework for teaching Aboriginal and Torres Strait Islander English as an additional language or dialect (EAL/D) learners is mapping the ways teachers can relate their knowledge of Aboriginal English to the Australian Professional Standards for Teachers (Department of Education, Training and Employment [DETE], 2013). It clearly sets out the need for teachers to identify speakers of Aboriginal English, to plan and implement effective teaching for Aboriginal English speakers, and to engage in professional learning about Aboriginal English. A website is in development to support this initiative.

Sometimes in schools and early childhood settings the use of Aboriginal English has been denigrated, and consistently corrected as being 'bad' English. However, this is not the case as Aboriginal English has consistent and structured features associated with a dialect, if not a fully fledged different language. Educators need to be mindful to provide opportunities for children to use Aboriginal English without constant correction. Indeed, evidence suggests that Aboriginal English use can help build the foundations for Standard English (Siegel, 2005 in Harrison, 2011). The success of addressing the needs of Aboriginal English speakers can be found in Western Australia, and the WA Department of Education and Training (DET) website for Aboriginal education has excellent resources in the form of 'Ways of Being, Ways of Talk' (DET, 2007).

Perspectives and practices in ECEC policy and provision

5. Recognising and attending to the social, physical and educational needs of Aboriginal and Torres Strait Islander children

Footprints in Time: The longitudinal study of Indigenous children (LSIC) (Department of Families, Housing, Community Services and Indigenous Affairs [DFaHCSIA], 2009) has gathered evidence since 2008 from over 1500 Indigenous children and their families across eleven clusters. The clusters include most major urban centres throughout Australia, some regional centres and more remote locations. The purpose of the study is to collect evidence that can be used to develop policies in a bid to close the health, educational and economic gap between Indigenous and non-Indigenous Australians.

The inequality of educational achievement remains stubbornly high over time, but the LSIC does demonstrate there is an increasing awareness in schools of the diverse cultural requirements of Indigenous students. For example, in the study cohort of children now attending school, teacher responses showed that in over 65 per cent of schools, Indigenous elders were invited into or teach in schools, and 60 per cent of schools are involved in activities with local Aboriginal communities (Department of Social Services [DSS] 2013, p. 10). According to the teacher responses, 85 per cent understand the importance of identity and family (DSS, 2013, p. 10). This recognition is an important first step, but then it is necessary to translate such understanding into appropriate action resulting in better educational outcomes.

Taylor's (2010) study focused on issues of school attendance that reveals explanations for high rates of non-attendance. In Taylor's longitudinal study located in Western Australia, she found a number of reasons for Indigenous children not wanting to be in school. In mainstream schools there seemed a 'lack of relevance and appropriateness of the mainstream school in the children's lives' (Taylor, 2010, p. 681). This relates to the point about Aboriginal content— all children need to feel engaged with learning in ways that connect them with their own experiences, interests and understandings. Point four earlier in the chapter focused on the learning processes but here the emphasis is on *content* to ensure that there is relevant, recognisable, engaging and meaningful content that Indigenous students can relate to. This is provided in a context where Indigenous needs and perspectives are understood.

In early childhood sites birth to five, this is more easily achieved by providing a play-based emergent program where children have a large choice of what and how to engage in learning activities. But resources (including technological), artefacts, and visits by Aboriginal elders, artists, musicians and environmental experts will provide additional meaning not only for Aboriginal children but for all children in the centre. It is important to have these learning experiences peppered throughout the program, throughout the year. For example, restricting Aboriginal content to a one-week-only approach is tokenism and does not provide the rich set of experiences Indigenous and non-Indigenous children alike require.

Aboriginal independence and autonomy

It is worth noting that in Aboriginal families independence and autonomy are highly valued, and learned from a very early age. Children as young as six and seven may take care of their younger siblings and cousins, so they learn responsibilities very early on. The high level of autonomy means that schools with all their rules and constraints can be awkward places for Aboriginal children. Often Aboriginal children are not misbehaving – they are just making their own decisions and do not see the need to seek permission for their actions. Below is a story of early childhood independence.

Rosie is a two-year-old girl who lives in Ngaanyatjarra country, which is desert country in the middle of Australia. We are on a bush trip to collect honey ants and we are with Rosie's grandmother and some other elders. We climb down from the four-wheel drive and Rosie immediately sets off into the bush. Although she has bare feet, she strides off over the red sand. Rosie comes to a large log across her path. She carefully climbs over, checking where she puts her feet, and continues on her way.

A little while later her grandmother has lit a fire. Rosie picks up a stick and marches towards the fire. Her grandmother is watching but does not intervene. Rosie gets close and begins poking the fire, some sticks dislodge, but she competently takes a step back

Perspectives and practices in ECEC policy and provision

and continues her playing. Later Rosie picks up a large knife and begins to cut some damper.

When I comment that in my culture we would never let a two year old do the things Rosie does, her grandmother just smiles and explains that children will learn from their mistakes. That if they get too close to the fire, they will feel the heat. They practise with knives and they can use them well. Little children watch their elders and when they are ready they will try. They judge carefully when they try new things, because if they get it wrong they will be teased and this would be shameful for them.

6. Recognising social dynamics in early childhood education and care sites

Taylor's (2010) longitudinal study of non-attendance of Aboriginal students is useful to unpack what more can be done to create a safe and supportive educational environment. There were several explanations in the literature, including the acknowledgement that curriculum could be more relevant and culturally appropriate. Drawing on the work of Purdie and colleagues, Taylor also referred to, 'the racism, rejection and reproof many [Aboriginal] children report experiencing from other children and school staff' (2010, p. 681).

It is clear that while there are many teachers dedicated to supporting Indigenous children and who are providing high-quality learning experiences, there are also teachers who do not recognise the particular needs, background and challenges of Indigenous children. Indeed there are some who perpetuate stereotypes and myths about Aboriginal children and yet others who find it difficult to know what to do when there is racism in their education sites. Finally, there may be others who are not aware of the impact of their negative attitudes and behaviour.

In order to develop an anti-racist pedagogy (and one that will benefit all children of colour and those from diverse backgrounds) the first step is to recognise that we are all capable of racialised practices because we live in a racialised world. We are therefore all on a journey of critical reflection as we move through a world that can be discriminatory, to find out ways we can improve our own understanding and take responsibility to enact change.

158

Second, we must be prepared to watch, listen and learn from elders and other knowledgeable Aboriginal people. The more we can learn, the more we can understand and appreciate Indigenous cultures. Related to this, we must be prepared to acknowledge our mistakes, apologise and learn how to do things differently next time. When we are in intercultural contexts, it is likely we will transgress cultural norms. People from a diverse range of cultures understand mistakes will be made, but are more likely to act as cultural teachers if they see people willing to learn and take time to understand different ways of doing things.

Third, early childhood educators need to take it seriously when a parent or child tells us that there has been an incidence of racism or prejudice. Too often members of staff dismiss concerns—and in these cases the responsibility is often placed back on the shoulders of the child or parent as excuses are made. Staff can be reluctant to accept that prejudice or racism exists, partly because the task of tackling racism and prejudice seems too daunting. Educators should be aware that children can be vehicles for prejudice, however unwittingly, as they begin to navigate their social worlds.

The first step then is to recognise and understand the social dynamics that are at play. Educators can help each other and be supportive in the struggle to come to terms with dealing with difficult topics. Some strategies for how we might do this are found in the next section.

7. Being prepared to address the dynamics of social inclusion and exclusion in early childhood education and care sites

We need to tackle the dynamics of social inclusion and exclusion in the classroom by creating a space where all children feel they belong. This of course echoes the underpinning foci of the EYLF, that of 'Belonging, Being and Becoming' (DEEWR, 2009). We need to explicitly teach social rules around how to treat each other and this includes acceptable ways to explain to someone if they do not want to play. Even very young children understand the social hierarchies in our society. One way we can do this is by teaching all children that:

- We are the same in some ways and different in some ways.
- We all have feelings and we all feel sad when we do not belong.
- In the education setting everyone must be kind to each other.

Perspectives and practices in ECEC policy and provision

These simple strategies are a starting point as we try to instill in young children a sense of empathy and understanding of others. There are several nationally recognised resources available to help navigate these sensitive areas (see box).

> ### Resources for tackling prejudice
> The most effective resource for kindergarten to Year 3 is the Prejudice No Way site <www.prejudicenoway.com/>. The site is nationally endorsed by all education departments and contains a wealth of information about prejudice and racism and includes activities for teachers. The activities come under the topics of developing identity and self-esteem; being comfortable with difference; understanding prejudice; and taking action against prejudice. There are activities for each year group within each topic.
>
> For specifically Indigenous education the site What Works <www.whatworks.edu.au/> provides information on a range of success stories in schools. While not specifically for early childhood, it provides many ideas of how to bring communities together and many strategies that are culturally appropriate. Each state and territory Department of Education also has sites to access resources.
>
> Finally, there are several resources directly related to Indigenous early childhood settings. *Including Aboriginal Australia in your service* is a fact sheet providing contact details to help you connect with Aboriginal organisations, <www.earlychildhoodaustralia.org.au/nqsplp/wp-content/uploads/2012/05/including_aboriginal_australia.pdf>.

CONCLUSION

Aboriginal and Torres Strait Islanders come from a range of cultural backgrounds across Australia. There is no 'one size fits all' approach, but there are some commonalities that are worth taking into account in order to establish more culturally safe and appropriate Indigenous ways of belonging, being and becoming. Family and community are integral to understanding relationships and cultural practices. Inviting elders and Indigenous parents into an early childhood site will allow not only Indigenous children to feel more valued and at home, but will also provide non-Indigenous children with valuable experiences.

Early childhood educators can consider the processes of Indigenous learning and curriculum content as they cater for Indigenous children. They can embrace anti-racist pedagogy as a way to meaningfully engage with the wider implications of what it means to be an Aboriginal and Torres Strait Islander in today's Australia.

FURTHER THINKING

1. View the You Tube clip Putting cultural competency into practice <www.youtube.com/watch?v=7wdIvMsHY1Q&feature=relmfu>, *Examining cultural competence for Indigenous children* and the Educators' Guide *Belonging, Being and Becoming*, pages 77–85 and 103.

2. Consider how you could address cultural competence in an early childhood service.

3. Consider the Eight Aboriginal Ways of Learning framework and discuss how your programming and planning could reflect this approach.

4. Check out <www.prejudicenoway.com> and discuss the most appropriate activities to incorporate into your own practice.

REFERENCES

Abbott, T. (2015). Statement to the House of Representatives—Closing the Gap 2015. <www.indigenous.gov.au/news-and-media/announcements/prime-minister-abbott-statement-house-representatives-closing-gap-2015. Accessed 21 October 2015.

Altman, J., Biddle, N. & Hunter B. (2008) The Challenge of 'Closing the Gaps' in Indigenous Socioeconomic Outcomes. Centre for Aboriginal Economic Policy Research, No. 8/2008. The Australian National University.

Australian Bureau of Statistics (ABS) (2012). *2076.0 Census of Population and Housing: Characteristics of Aboriginal and Torres Strait Islander Australians*. Canberra: ABS.

Perspectives and practices in ECEC policy and provision

Australian Children's Education and Care Quality Authority (ACECQA) (2013). *Guide to the National Quality Standard*. Retrieved 9 February 2015, <http://files.acecqa.gov.au/files/National-Quality-Framework-Resources-Kit/NQF03-Guide-to-NQS-130902.pdf>.

Australian Curriculum, Assessment and Reporting Authority (ACARA) (2014). *National Assessment Program Literacy and Numeracy National Report for 2013.* Retrieved 3 August 2015, http://www.nap.edu.au/verve/_resources/naplan_2013_national_report.pdf

Australian Early Development Census (AEDC) (2012). Retrieved 20 November 2014, <www.aedc.gov.au/early-childhood/findings-from-the-aedc>.

Australian National Audit Office (ANAO) (2011). *Multifunctional Aboriginal Children's Services (MACS) and Crèches.* ANAO Audit Report No. 8, 2010–11. Retrieved 20 November 2014, <www.anao.gov.au/uploads/documents/2010-11_Audit_Report_No_8.pdf>.

Clarke, K. & Denton, M. (2013). Red dirt thinking on child wellbeing in Indigenous rural and remote Australian communities: The SpICE Model 'I just don't want my kids to struggle like I did at school', *Australian Journal of Indigenous Education*, 42(2), 136–44.

Commonwealth of Australia (2015), Closing the Gap, Prime Minister's Report, 2015. Australian Government.

Department of Education, Employment and Workplace Relations (DEEWR) (2009). Belonging, Being and Becoming: The early years learning framework for Australia. Canberra, ACT: Council of Australian Governments: Commonwealth of Australia.

—— (2011). *Improving Outcomes for Indigenous Students: Successful practice*, 2nd edn. Abbotsford, Vic.: National Curriculum Services. Retrieved 15 January 2015, <www.whatworks.edu.au/upload/1300931817872_file_SuccessPrac2.pdf>.

Department of Education, Training and Employment (DETE) (2013). *Capability Framework: Teaching Aboriginal and Torres Strait Islander English as an Additional Language/Dialect learners.* Brisbane: DETE.

Department of Education and Training (DET) (2007). *Ways of Being, Ways of Talk.* Perth, Western Australia: DET. Retrieved 29 November 2014, <www.det.wa.edu.au/aboriginaleducation/detcms/aboriginal-education/aboriginal-education/docs/ways-of-being-ways-of-talk.en?oid=com.arsdigita.cms.contenttypes.FileStorageItem-id-7146860>.

Department of Families, Housing, Community Services and Indigenous Affairs (DFaHCSIA) (2009). *Footprints in Time: The longitudinal study of Indigenous children. Key Summary Report Wave 1*. Retrieved 9 January 2015, <www.dss.gov.au/sites/default/files/documents/08_2014/lsic_wave_one_report.pdf>.

Department of Social Services (DSS) (2013). *Footprints in Time: The longitudinal study of Indigenous children. Report from Wave 4*. Retrieved 13 January 2015, <www.dss.gov.au/sites/default/files/documents/08_2014/footprints_in_time_wave4.pdf>.

Eight Aboriginal ways of learning (n.d.). Retrieved 4 August 2015, <https://intranet.ecu.edu.au/__data/assets/pdf_file/0016/510073/8-Aboriginal-ways-of-learning-factsheet.pdf>.

Fasoli, L. & Ford, M. (2001). Indigenous early childhood educators' narratives: relationships, not activities, *Australian Journal of Early Childhood*, 26(3), 18–22.

Griffiths, A. (2011). The components of best practice Indigenous education: A comparative review, *Australian Journal of Indigenous Education*, 40, 69–80.

Guenther, J. (2013). Are we making education count in remote Australian communities or just counting education? *Australian Journal of Indigenous Education*, 42(2), 157–70.

Harrison, N. (2011). *Teaching and Learning in Aboriginal Education*, 2nd edn. South Melbourne: Oxford University Press.

Kitson, R. & Bowes, J. (2010). Incorporating Indigenous ways of knowing in early education for Indigenous children, *Australasian Journal of Early Childhood*, 35(4), 81–9.

Martin, K. (2007). Ma(r)king tracks and reconceptualising Aboriginal early childhood education, *Childrenz Issues*, 11(1), 15–20.

Sims, M. (2011). *Early Childhood and Education services for Indigenous Children Prior to Starting School*. Resource Sheet No. 7, Closing the Gap Clearinghouse. Canberra: Australian Institute of Health and Welfare, Australian Institute of Family Studies.

Taylor, A. (2010). Here and now: The attendance issue in Indigenous early childhood education, *Journal of Education Policy*, 25(5), September, 677–99.

Tonkin, D. & Landon, C. (1999). *Jackson's Track: Memoir of a dreamtime place*. Camberwell, Vic.: Penguin.

Yunkaporta, T. & Kirby, M. (2011). Yarning up Indigenous Pedagogies: A dialogue about Eight Aboriginal Ways of Learning. In N. Purdie, G. Milgate and H.R. Bell (eds), *Two way Teaching and Learning: Toward culturally reflective and relevant education*. Camberwell, Vic.: ACER Press, pp. 205–13.

Chapter 8

Diversity and inclusion in early childhood education and care

Melinda G. Miller

In this chapter you will find:
- An overview of inclusion in Australia
- Educational responses to diversity
- Inclusive education practices
- Barriers to inclusion.

Contemporary views of inclusion encompass a broad range of factors that influence children's learning and development. Beyond traditional ideas of children with 'special needs' or 'additional needs', or groups identified as 'minority' or 'at risk', broad categories of diversity take into account differences such as cultural, linguistic, spiritual and religious, gender and sexuality, giftedness, and physical and mobility differences. Ever-increasing forms of diversity challenge traditional ideas or certainties about child development, parenting and early childhood education practices. For this reason, it is critical for educators to expand their definitions of what is considered 'normal' to include diverse understandings about people, ideas, values, behaviours and approaches to early education and care (Moore, Morcos & Robinson, 2009).

Questions about diversity and inclusion are sometimes connected only to individuals and groups who are positioned outside boundaries of who and what is considered 'normal' in a society. Labels and categories such as 'children with a disability' and 'culturally and linguistically diverse children' can be important to how children and families self-identify and position themselves (Giugni, 2011,

p. 10). Simultaneously, labels and categories can limit how children are viewed in terms of their unique capacities and the ways they can access and participate in early years programs and society more broadly (Giugni, 2011). Moore et al. (2009) challenge professionals working with young children to embrace changing ideas about social inclusion and exclusion, disadvantaged and vulnerable populations, cultural and ethnic diversity, and ability and disability. Embracing new ideas requires a shift from notions of deficit or dysfunction belonging to children and families to exclusion and unequal outcomes being seen as social injustices (Breen, 2009). A concern for early childhood services is how to *reduce* rather than *reinforce* injustices experienced by children and families who identify with broad and fluid concepts of diversity (Breen, 2009).

In this chapter, I begin with an overview of diversity and approaches to inclusion in Australia. This is followed by discussion about inclusive education, which examines a range of conditions (for example, educator attitude, resources and professional development) that support inclusive practices in educational contexts. Three case studies are presented to outline approaches and responses to inclusive practices related to Indigenous perspectives, same-sex parenting and the work of a special education program coordinator in a primary school setting. The chapter concludes with discussion about implications of socially just policy and provision for children and families accessing Australian early years services.

INCLUSION IN AUSTRALIA

Australia is characterised by a diverse population. In addition to Aboriginal and Torres Strait Islander peoples who comprise the Indigenous population, decades of immigration have produced a country where over one-quarter (26 per cent) of the population were born overseas and a further one-fifth (20 per cent) have at least one parent born overseas (Australian Bureau of Statistics [ABS], 2013a). Planned immigration programs by successive Australian governments, the humanitarian program for refugees, as well as temporary immigrants who fill gaps in the availability of skilled workers have transformed Australian society since colonisation. Patterns of migration are shaped by historical events and policies. For example, the White Australia policy, introduced with Federation in 1901 and dismantled progressively between 1949 and 1973, favoured immigration from North-West European countries, especially Britain. This was followed with large numbers of migrants born in Southern and Eastern Europe and, in the 1970s, from Southeast Asia (ABS, 2013a).

In relation to disability, the ABS's *Profiles of Disability* (2013b) showed that one in five people reported having a disability in 2012. In the birth to four years age range, this equated to 3.6 per cent of the population, and in the five to fourteen years age range, 8.8 per cent of the population. For those people with disability, most (88 per cent) had a specific limitation or restriction that limited activities (including self-care, mobility or communication) or that restricted schooling or employment in some way (ABS, 2013b). In Australia, there are three main options for the schooling of children with a disability: special schools, special classes and mainstream schools. Special schools base enrolment on a child exhibiting mental or physical disability, slow learning ability and/or social or emotional difficulties. Special classes operate within mainstream schools to provide additional support for children with diverse and complex learning needs. Mainstream schools refer to primary and secondary schooling classified as public, private or independent. In line with changing attitudes and approaches to inclusion over time, in 2009 most children with disability who attended school participated in classes in mainstream schools regardless of the severity of their disability (ABS, 2013b).

Broad definitions of inclusion will continue to influence the range of individuals and groups who require additional forms of support in educational systems. Hyde, Carpenter and Conway (2014) draw attention to the recent global financial crisis, which has impacted most heavily on individuals living within cycles of poverty. Children experiencing long-term poverty often have greater difficulties with access and participation in schools due to the correlation between poverty and social disadvantage, illness, poor literacies and emotional difficulties. These factors combine to produce ongoing social inequities that impact children and families long term and sometimes across generations. For this reason, Hyde et al. (2014) advocate:

> Education systems and schools will need to be able to see social inequity based on poverty as a priority within the implementation of inclusive education policies and strategies. (p. 387)

Poverty is often linked to particular groups in society, although cycles of poverty can impact any family dependent on personal circumstances and changes in social systems. Under broad definitions of inclusion, issues with poverty require ongoing attention in educational contexts alongside other forms of diversity.

EDUCATIONAL RESPONSES TO DIVERSITY

Educational responses to diversity are not static. In line with shifts in political and social agendas, responses to diversity have ranged from segregation and mainstreaming to integration and inclusion (see Table 8.1). Despite shifts towards more inclusive approaches, the portrayal of diversity in western education has centred mostly on notions of 'deficit'. This portrayal has enabled attitudes and practices that silence or assimilate individuals, languages and perspectives to persist within mainstream educational systems (Colbung et al., 2007). For example, movements such as multicultural education, prominent in the 1970s and 1980s, were, at the time, seen as progressive against the overtly racist White Australia policy that persisted until 1973. However, despite the rhetoric of harmony and celebration, multiculturalism achieved little in terms of addressing social inequities and related disadvantage (Gozdecka, Ercan & Kmak, 2014). Remnants of multiculturalism persist in some early years settings today, with the adoption of one-off approaches to diversity (for example, Indigenous Week or Italian Food Day) rather than embedded practices that are present in the curriculum at all times and that are responsive to local children, families and communities.

Table 8.1 Shifts in understandings of diversity and inclusion in Australia

Segregation → (1860s-1980)	Mainstreaming → (1940s-1980)	Integration → (1970-1995)	Inclusion (1990-Present)
Children with a disability or impairment are excluded from mainstream schools.	Children formerly excluded or placed in special schools are placed in local, regular schools.	Children 'fit in' to a regular school dependent on degree of ability rather than the school adapting to the child's needs.	It is assumed that all children are included in society, and education in particular. The focus is on conditions necessary for inclusion.

Perspectives and practices in ECEC policy and provision

More recently, notions of cultural competence and social inclusion have become popular in educational policy. For example, the recently introduced Belonging, Being and Becoming: The Early Years Learning Framework (EYLF) for Australia (Department of Education, Employment and Workplace Relations [DEEWR], 2009a) for children aged birth to five years and the Australian Curriculum (Australian Curriculum, Assessment and Reporting Authority [ACARA], 2011) for formal schooling contexts both foreground intercultural priorities, with particular reference to recognising and engaging with Aboriginal and Torres Strait Islanders' histories and cultures. In these two policies, cultural competence is linked explicitly with recognition of Aboriginal and Torres Strait Islander peoples as the First Australians. In the EYLF recommendations for practice include:

- value[ing] the continuity and richness of local knowledge shared by community members, including Aboriginal and Torres Strait Islander Elders, and
- respond[ing] to children's expertise, cultural traditions and ways of knowing, [and] the multiple languages spoken by some children, particularly Aboriginal and Torres Strait Islander children. (DEEWR, 2009a, pp. 13–14)

Such recommendations go some way to addressing a history of marginalisation and cultural displacement for Aboriginal children in Australian schooling and Aboriginal groups in Australian society. In the Australian context, it is critical for educators to acknowledge that 'Indigenous students have now had nearly 200 years of inadequate access, participation and success in education' (Andersen & Walter, 2014, p. 69). In line with approaches to inclusion outlined in Table 8.1, McConnochie and Russell (1982) explain that schooling for Aboriginal children has moved through three distinct phases beginning with the removal of Aboriginal children from their families to become 'civilised' and converted to Christianity (1770–1860s). This was followed by the assimilation of Aboriginal children in western society by way of training as labourers and domestics (1860s–1940s) and compensatory education focused on interventionist programs in early childhood services (1940s–1980s). All of these educational approaches relied on the marginalisation and cultural displacement of Aboriginal peoples and worldviews (Martin, 2007). While current early childhood education policy

168

foregrounds Aboriginal and Torres Strait Islanders' histories and cultures, Martin makes reference to the enactment of policy; specifically, the need for educators to be self-reflexive about their own race and positioning in society, and to examine related underlying values, beliefs and assumptions that inform their pedagogy.

Alongside early childhood education policies, legislation that frames inclusive education in Australia includes the United Nations Convention on the Rights of Persons with Disabilities (United Nations, 2006). Ratified by Australia in 2008, the Convention reflects a commitment to promoting and supporting the equal and active participation of people with disability in social life, including education. Specific to Australia, the *Disability Standards for Education 2005* (Commonwealth of Australia, 2006) apply to all education settings, including early childhood, and focus on areas including enrolment, participation, curriculum, student support, and harassment and victimisation. The United Nations Declaration on the Rights of Indigenous Peoples (United Nations, 2007) reflects the rights of Indigenous peoples to access the same standard of education as all other Australians, and the right to own and control schools and educational institutions. Initially, Australia voted against the Declaration but endorsed this landmark document in 2009. The Australian *Racial Discrimination Act 1975* (Commonwealth of Australia, 2009) also reflects rights of equal access to educational opportunities without discrimination. Legislation and policy influence approaches to inclusive education in Australia; although it is the role of early years settings and educators to enact inclusive education in daily practice. The section following considers conditions that support this aim.

INCLUSIVE EDUCATION PRACTICES

For inclusion to be realised in educational contexts, investment and action are needed to bring about conditions that support inclusive practices. Conditions that support inclusion include family/community connections, educator attitude, ongoing professional development, resources, curriculum and the environment. Combined, these elements provide opportunity to accommodate a child's abilities and needs and move towards inclusive education, defined by Hyde (2014a) as a process of responding to the uniqueness of individuals, increasing their sense of presence, access, participation and engagement in a learning society and . . . in schools. (p. 11)

Hyde (2014a) makes a further distinction between *engagement* (which refers to the degree to which a child experiences a sense of belonging or connectedness to the school emotionally, socially, cognitively and academically) and a general definition of inclusion focused on access and conditions. Achieving positive outcomes in these engagement areas requires attention to a range of conditions, as outlined below.

Inclusive education practices begin with recognition of the family as the constant in a child's life. Espe-Sherwindt (2008) describes a family-centred approach to inclusion as a model in which professionals view families as equal partners. Families are the critical decision-makers and it is the role of professionals in early years settings to support family functioning. The core of inclusive relationships with families is engagement and reciprocity rather than power and control (Miller & Petriwskyj, 2013). In this sense, guiding questions for practice shift from 'How do I direct the family to accept my professional judgement?' to 'How do we commit to working together?' and 'What evidence is there to show I am responding to families' perspectives in practice?' Productive ways of working with families require investment in relationships that recognise all parties as being 'capable of defining meaning and making choices' (Espe-Sherwindt, 2008, p. 140) around inclusive education practices.

Positive attitudes, values and relationships with families are further supported by conditions that promote participation in classrooms and engage educators in ongoing learning. Adequate resourcing is critical to inclusive education, both in terms of staffing and classroom resources (for example, communication aids, low-vision devices, visual aids, and technologies, such as iPads). Individual educators can also adapt the classroom environment to support the inclusion of children with particular needs. For example, children with a hearing impairment benefit from certain environmental accommodations, including reducing background noises by placing carpets on floors, using furniture to reduce echo and reverberations, and asking school administrators for a classroom located away from the music room or tuck-shop (Hyde, 2014b). Pedagogical adaptations could include the use of visual aids, locating the child near the front of the class to reduce educator–child distance, speaking clearly and monitoring the child's comprehension of content without attracting undue attention (Hyde, 2014b). Environmental and curriculum adaptations support the range of conditions necessary for inclusive education and are often easily adopted by individual educators with support from specialist colleagues and administration.

Professional education around inclusion is critical to building knowledge, skills and confidence. Ongoing learning about disability, complex learning and behavioural needs, and intercultural competence all require models of professional development that attend to intellectual as well as technical skills (Miller & Petriwskyj, 2013). Technical skills are vital for day-to-day tasks associated with the practice of teaching. Intellectual skills support educator integrity and critical reflection, and strengthen connections between practice and personal beliefs. Critical reflection is a learned skill that enables educators to go beyond practical considerations and gain insights into issues of power and control in educational decision-making. Professional development that incorporates time for critical reflection, including self-analysis, supports educators to learn not only about disability, behavioural needs and cultural groups, but also the attitudes and values that support respectful interactions between educators, children and their families.

The British Index for Inclusion (Booth & Ainscow, 2011) is one tool that provides a comprehensive list of criteria to support educational contexts to self-evaluate their approach to inclusion, produce a detailed improvement plan, empower adults and children to action ideas, and minimise barriers to learning and participation. Drawing on a broad framework of inclusion that encompasses values, rights, health promotion, restorative approaches and global citizenship, the Index for Inclusion provides educators with dimensions, indicators and questions for self-evaluative purposes. For example, Dimension A, 'Creating Inclusive Cultures', is focused on 'building community' and 'establishing inclusive values'. Related indicators include 'practitioners and parents/carers collaborate' and 'everyone involved in the setting shares a commitment to inclusion'. Questions posed to educators and schools include 'Are differences in family structure acknowledged and appreciated?' (Booth & Ainscow, 2011). The application of the Index for Inclusion in the Australian context has proved valuable, although numerous authors (Bourke, 2010; Carrington & Robinson, 2006; Deppeler & Harvey, 2004) cite a need to attend to contextual factors and local cultures, including the values and assumptions of school personnel, and broader socio-political agendas in Australia that influence industrial conditions, funding, policy and curriculum design.

Perspectives and practices in ECEC policy and provision

BARRIERS TO INCLUSION

Inclusive education can present challenges to educators who sometimes report a lack of knowledge and skills, a lack of resources, issues with time, and the lack of capacity to differentiate curriculum to meet the needs of a diverse class group (Bourke, 2010). Barriers to inclusive education require rethinking, with explicit training and support sometimes needed for educators and schools to address limitations and move towards inclusive practices. Barriers that can impede educators' efforts include:

- *Theoretical barriers*—Family/child practices are viewed as 'deficient' or in need of 'fixing' against (white) western models of child development and milestones (Lubeck, 1996).
- *Framing of family practices*—Family practices are positioned by individuals and society as too far from the 'norm' and viewed socially as 'deviant' rather than different (Goodwin, Cheruvu & Genishi, 2008).
- *Teacher education*—Inclusion content is isolated in individual units rather than embedded in the suite of units offered in a degree program (Conway, 2014).
- *Policy developments and reform agendas*—Transferring policy and reform agendas into practice is a complex process. Variables that impact this process include the ambiguous framing of inclusion in new policies, power relations in schools that impede educators' efforts, and unexamined personal theories and assumptions about broad categories of diversity (Bourke, 2010).
- *Environmental constraints*—Low staff–child ratios, the architectural design of buildings and classrooms that limit access or participation, a lack of resources that support inclusive practices, and limited access to ongoing professional development (Carrington & Robinson, 2006).

Inclusive education should be understood in relation to the broader socio-political context to understand influences on educators that can impede efforts despite the best of intentions. To show links between approaches to inclusion in early years settings and broader socio-political influences, I outline three case studies that reflect broader changes in attitudes towards inclusion for particular groups in Australia. Case Study 1 outlines the work of non-Indigenous educators embedding Indigenous perspectives in an urban child care setting.

172

Case Study 2 examines attitudes to same-sex parenting and responses to an Australian children's television program aired in 2004 that showed two mothers and their child at an amusement park. Case Study 3 presents the perspectives of a special education program coordinator from a Queensland primary school setting.

CASE STUDIES

Case study 1: Embedding Indigenous perspectives

In a non-Indigenous child care setting in inner-city Brisbane, educators undertook an action research project to embed Indigenous perspectives at a curriculum and operational level, and by forming connections with the local Indigenous community (see Miller, 2013). This whole-centre approach moved beyond tokenistic responses based on the inclusion of resources or a one-off focus, such as NAIDOC (National Aborigines and Islanders Day Observance Committee) week. Educators at the centre identify as non-Indigenous people who recognise the importance of embedding Indigenous perspectives within centre practices at all times, regardless of the demographic of children and families in attendance. In line with guidelines for embedding practices outlined by Dreise (2007) and the Department of Education and Training (2011), the educators focused on:

- being professionally and personally accountable (for example, critical awareness of one's attitudes and perceptions and that of colleagues, parents, community and children)
- understanding Indigenous perspectives and processes (for example, recognising the diversity of Indigenous peoples and the ways unique knowledge systems are embedded in community practices, relationships, rituals and institutions)
- understanding Indigenous protocol (for example, use of appropriate local protocols to make introductions and to build relationships)
- critically reviewing texts and resources (for example, evaluating appropriateness in terms of voice, imagery, terminology and authorship)
- planning appropriate learning experiences (for example,), and
- developing community partnerships (for example, building reciprocal partnerships with a diverse range of people and organisations).

Perspectives and practices in ECEC policy and provision

For non-Indigenous educators, embedding Indigenous perspectives in respectful and genuine ways can be challenging. This is due mostly to a lack of content knowledge, fear of causing offence, and issues with how non-Indigenous educators are socialised and carry their own education and related deficiencies in understanding into their teaching practices (Lampert, 2012). From the outset of the action research project, educators at the centre expressed such concerns, as in this comment by Jenny:

> For me, I would like to explore that more within [the centre], but it's really hard because we don't have any Indigenous families, and for me, I don't want to do the tokenistic thing of 'Let's do a dot painting and let's . . .' you know. I want it to be ingrained within, but I think the barrier is not having any [Indigenous] parents there to help and explore that with . . . [It's] also knowing what's culturally appropriate too. We do that whole project around NAIDOC and I know one of the staff was really looking into it because we do Aboriginal art, but art tells a story and we don't know the story. (p. x)

Here, Jenny identified barriers to embedding practices, described as difficulty in accessing Indigenous support, wishing to avoid tokenistic curriculum, and a lack of content knowledge. In one sense, these barriers provided Jenny with justification for inaction when considered against expectations for inclusive practice. In another sense, they paralysed action and the need for non-Indigenous educators to take an intellectual and emotional risk to embed Indigenous perspectives (Andersen & Walter, 2014). Jenny's point about consulting with Indigenous families is sound practice, but it is important to consider that in the relationship Jenny constructed, Indigenous parents were assumed to be cultural experts who could bring authority, ability and a willingness to impart culturally specific information (Santoro & Reid, 2006). A consequence of this positioning is that parental expertise is attached to matters of culture only. Despite her initial concerns, over the course of the project Jenny overcame perceived barriers to embedding processes by developing her knowledge base and 'having a go' at embedding Indigenous perspectives with a commitment to reflecting critically on her approach.

174

Positive changes in attitudes, classroom practices and operational procedures were achieved throughout the action research project and following its formal completion. For example, at the operational level, Indigenous protocols (for example, Acknowledgement of Traditional Owners and Welcome to Country) were introduced for formal gatherings, and an Indigenous Employment Strategy introduced to expedite the employment of Indigenous staff. The development of partnerships included a staff exchange with a local Indigenous child care centre and ongoing collaborations with a local Indigenous artist. At the curriculum level, educators conducted a critical review of resources showing representations of Indigenous peoples and cultures (most of which were historical) and monitored educator talk around resources and learning experiences, and some educators developed reflective journals that supported self-analysis about their positioning in society and the influence of their own cultural background on thinking and practices. One example is this journal entry by Meg, an educator in the kindergarten classroom:

> [In] terms of myself, I think it's the realisation that you, yourself, have a culture and that you're not the middle thing that everyone else revolves around and is different from. (p. x)

Meg's reflection is a form of identity work that is often challenging for white individuals who generally have low racial literacy and who are not often asked to question their race and positioning in Australian society (Moreton-Robinson, 2004).

Despite the positive outcomes achieved in the action research project, it is necessary for early childhood educators to acknowledge that subtle racialising practices are always present in their work, even when it is viewed as inclusive and high quality (Miller, 2013). Some authors, including Kitson and Bowes (2010) and Santoro and Reid (2006), outline examples of subtle racialising practices that include:

- trivialising the richness and diversity of Indigenous peoples through simplistic talk, images and resources
- romanticising aspects of Indigenous cultures and relying only on overt cultural symbols (for example, art, dance, music and food)

Perspectives and practices in ECEC policy and provision

- accessing support and engagement from Indigenous people as a reactive step, including making contact only when gaps in knowledge become apparent or in response to new policy directions, and
- failing to demonstrate preparedness (for example, listening, learning, unlearning and self-analysis) in partnerships with Indigenous people to support reciprocity and long-term engagement.

Commitment to ongoing learning and critical self-reflection supports educators to identify and reduce the impact of subtle racialising practices that are more common and less easily identifiable than overt forms of racism in contemporary educational contexts.

Reflection
1. Discuss why Indigenous perspectives should be embedded in curricula and operational procedures at all times in Australian early years settings.
2. Write a personal standpoint statement that reflects your commitment to embedding Indigenous perspectives and building relationships with Indigenous people and community in your role as a future educator.

Case study 2: Diversity in family structures—same-sex parenting

In 2004, the Australian children's television program *Play School* aired an episode in which a young girl told viewers, 'I'm Brenna. That's me in the blue. My mums are taking me and my friend Meryn to an amusement park.' The image accompanying the voiceover showed Brenna's two mothers standing together, smiling and waving at the children as they rode a carousel.

At the time, the 'two mums' *Play School* episode created international controversy. Institutional responses within Australia included comments from then Prime Minister, John Howard, and a senior columnist at *The Australian*, Janet Albrechtsen:

Diversity and inclusion in early childhood education and care

> This is just a very foolish thing for the ABC to do and to introduce that into a children's program is just being politically correct. (John Howard)

> It shouldn't have been shown ... [You] can reflect a lot of happy households, diverse households without getting involved in what is essentially still a very controversial subject. (Janet Albrechtsen)

From within the Australian early childhood field, responses from Newman (2004) and Dau et al. (2004) highlighted issues with misnaming diversity (to mean deviant) in family patterns and the importance of reflecting all children's and families' lived realities:

> What is normal and who decides this? If we cannot represent the vast range of real people's 'normalities' in family pattern and daily realities, what else can't we represent as normal to children? (Newman, 2004, p. 4)

> Young children are likely to meet lesbian and gay people among their parents, early childhood staff, family and friends ... Gays and lesbians face personal and social discrimination, including verbal and physical stereotyping, harassment and abuse and legal discrimination ... Young children need to know that some people face such discrimination ... From this perspective, *Play School* didn't go far enough! (Dau et al., 2004, pp. 1–2)

As early as 2002, Kerry Robinson, an early childhood educator and researcher, drew attention to the perpetuation of notions of irrelevance, invisibility, and exclusion of gay and lesbian issues by the Australian early childhood field. More recently, Kintner-Duffy et al. (2012) explain:

> Just as heterosexual families require child care to enable work and want high-quality early childhood education to enhance their children's development, lesbian, gay, bisexual or transgender (LGBT) families experience the same needs and desires for their children. (p. 208)

The Australian Raising Children Network (2011) reported that in the year 2011, there were 32 365 same-sex de facto relationships/couples in Australia, with approximately 12 per cent parenting a child. Families who identify as LGBT can and do access early years services, meaning educators are likely to engage with these families throughout their careers. As most LGBT families report experiences of discrimination, either against them or their children (Australian Raising Children Network, 2011), it is critical for early years services to recognise their capacity to reduce the impact of discrimination through strong, respectful connections with families, and inclusive practices.

Interestingly, in 2007, *Play School* aired an episode in which a family living in a two-storey 'box house' had the names John, Janette, Melanie and Richard. This family represented the Howard family, of then Prime Minister John Howard, his wife, Janette, and two of his three children, Melanie and Richard. An article in the *Sydney Morning Herald* (2007) reported: 'An ABC spokeswoman told us the program was happy to honour the Howards, because the PM had been a big supporter of *Play School* during its 40th-anniversary festivities last year, when he revealed that his children Melanie and Richard (and Tim) had grown up with Big Ted.'

This response provides an interesting comparison to the lack of support provided by key Australian political figures for the 'two mums' episode aired in 2004. What exactly is supported and why raises questions around boundaries for who is considered a 'normal' family in Australian society, and how different families are represented and perceived.

Reflection
1. How might your own views on diverse sexualities reduce or reinforce discrimination experienced by lesbian, gay, bisexual or transgender parents and children?
2. Discuss how silences around diverse sexualities and family structures in early years classrooms can be as damaging as overt forms of discrimination.

Case study 3: Perspectives of a special education program coordinator

Tracy Crombie is a special education program coordinator for a Queensland primary school. With seven years experience in primary settings and one year in high school, Tracy explains that her role is multifaceted and evolving, reflecting broader changes to inclusion and inclusive practices over time:

> My role has changed significantly over the past eight years, based on mine and others' attitudes and approaches to inclusion. When I commenced the role, I colour-shaded my timetable—the colour blue represented *in-class support* for children and the colour green represented *external or withdrawn support* whereby a child would be removed from the classroom to work one-on-one or in a small group with me and/or a teacher aide. At the time, there was far more green shading on the timetable than blue. Two years later the green shading was minimal, and in-class support remains the adopted approach across classrooms within the school.

When discussing her role, Tracy explained that changes in approach to inclusion at the school were a result of greater confidence in her own abilities to support and build relationships with classroom teachers, and to adopt a collaborative approach to developing inclusive in-class strategies that did not interrupt the integrity of a lesson. Positive results from in-class support resulted in greater acceptance of this approach by classroom teachers in place of external or withdrawn support. In-class strategies include visual cards with instruction steps for children, 'I need help' cards and positive reinforcement. The use of particular strategies in different classrooms align with the development of an Education Adjustment Profile to support the needs of children along a continua of learner diversity, as well as personalised goals developed for individual children through an Individualised Education Plan.

Early in her role, Tracy became aware of how overwhelmed some teachers felt in having students with very diverse capacities and diagnosed conditions in their classrooms. This was at times exacerbated by having an 'expert' on inclusion in the classroom, with some teachers feeling they were being judged, and others

Perspectives and practices in ECEC policy and provision

perceiving Tracy's role as the 'expert' who works with a child separately from the class group and regular classroom activities.

The shift from a specialist withdrawing a child to becoming a colleague in the classroom with some level of input and control is critical to inclusive education (Hyde, 2014c). Tracy explains how, through team-teaching, the specialist can provide support to the whole class group, act as an observer (another pair of eyes) who evaluates the environment, and assist with assessments of a child's behaviours to determine potential barriers and enablers to learning. This approach supports a specialist team member to develop student profiles with classroom teachers through collaborative data collection and analysis, and the development of related goals, strategies and processes of evaluation. At times, it is beneficial for the specialist to withdraw a child to receive one-on-one support in a quiet environment. For example, a child on the autism spectrum may require direct teaching of emotional regulation whereby coping strategies are developed with the child away from their peers, then practised (for example, role play), and eventually introduced and trialled in the classroom environment with adult guidance and support that is reduced gradually. While withdrawal is beneficial for individual children at times, the adoption of an in-class support approach across the whole school is ideal and centres on Tracy's role of building teacher capacity, as she explains:

> Building teacher capacity is critical to my role. With the support of the School Administration team, I facilitate on-site professional development sessions regularly for all staff, especially those who have a student with disabilities in their classroom, support staff who work with the children, and new teachers as part of their induction.

Tracy outlines further that the professional development sessions provide opportunities for her to explain and describe to colleagues the diversity of her role and how she can assist within and outside the classroom. With a wealth of knowledge and a specific skill set, Tracy assists classroom teachers to develop inclusive practices, provides information about particular conditions (for example, Down syndrome and autism spectrum disorders) and related resources

180

(for example, visual boards and sensory integration equipment), and connects teachers and families with community agencies and services, such as Autism Queensland and the Down Syndrome Association of Queensland. A whole-school approach to inclusion is also supported by facilitated sessions at assembly where many parents are present. Tracy describes this as a powerful discussion forum that invites questions and understanding about diversity and inclusion from children, parents and teachers.

IMPLICATIONS

While terminology and approaches to inclusion have shifted towards social justice frameworks, it is important to continually monitor the meanings that are attached to broad categories of diversity and how meanings translate to educational contexts. More contemporary thinking about inclusion is under-pinned by a rights-based approach that aims to support children to succeed within existing social structures and attitudes, but this relies on removing factors in policy and practice that can prevent children from participating fully in educational programs (Moore et al., 2009). Children and families benefit most from socially just policy and provision when educational contexts adopt a holistic approach to diversity and inclusion. This includes creating conditions for inclusion both inside and outside the early years setting and individual classrooms.

Inclusion policies do set minimum standards for practice and provide educators with important guidelines for ongoing skill development in their professional role. Importantly, they also establish a need to respect diversity at all levels of centre or school operation. How educators interpret and enact policy is dependent on a range of variables, including context, experience and attitude. Bourke (2010) argues that policies and reform agendas always require critical reading as some continue to 'label, isolate and segregate students within schools in the way in which segregated special education facilities did in the past' (p. 183). Further, classroom educators may not have the time and support needed to 'examine critically the underlying assumptions about disability, difference and inclusion that underpin their practices' (Bourke, 2010, p. 183). Teacher education plays an important role in developing critically reflective capacities for future educators, including examination of historical, social and political influences that have impacted approaches to inclusive education in

Australia over time. Combined with a commitment from educational contexts to provide sufficient and appropriate financial, physical and human resources (Hyde, 2014c), educators can be supported to develop skills and dispositions for inclusive education practices that meet the needs of all children.

CONCLUSION

Approaches to diversity and inclusion in Australian early childhood education have shifted significantly over past decades. From early approaches of segregation and integration to the current focus on engagement, inclusive education continues to evolve due to changes in policy, practices and attitudes. Broad conceptions of inclusion introduce the idea that exclusion and unequal outcomes are social injustices rather than a deficit or dysfunction belonging to children and families. Embracing broad conceptions of inclusion and advocating for investment and action enables early childhood educators, services and schools to reduce rather than reinforce injustices experienced by children and families who identify with broad and fluid categories of diversity.

Reflection
1. What issues can arise when educators view inclusion support staff (for example, special education teachers and coordinators, and teacher aides) as the 'experts' on inclusion in their classrooms?
2. Begin to develop a list of inclusion support agencies, key people and resources available to you to support inclusive practices in your future classroom.

REFERENCES

Andersen, C. & Walter, M. (2014). Indigenous perspectives and cultural identity. In M. Hyde, L. Carpenter & R. Conway (eds), *Diversity, Inclusion and Engagement*, 2nd edn. South Melbourne: Oxford University Press, pp. 68–89.

Australian Bureau of Statistics (ABS) (2013a). *Cultural Diversity in Australia: Reflecting a nation—Stories from the 2011 census*. Retrieved 14 April 2014, <www.abs.gov.au/ausstats/abs@.nsf/Lookup/2071.0main+features902012-2013>.

Diversity and inclusion in early childhood education and care

—— (2013b). *Profiles of Disability, Australia, 2009: Children at school with disability*. Retrieved 14 April 2014, <www.abs.gov.au/ausstats/abs@.nsf/Lookup/4429.0main+features100302009#>.

Australian Curriculum, Assessment and Reporting Authority (ACARA) (2011). *The Shape of the Australian Curriculum Version 3.0*. Retrieved 29 March 2012, <www.acara.edu.au/verve/_resources/The_Shape_of_the_Australian_Curriculum_V3.pdf>.

Australian Raising Children Network (2011). *Parenting in a Same-sex Relationship*. Retrieved 15 May 2014, <http://raisingchildren.net.au/articles/parenting_in_a_samesex_relationship.html/context/1000>.

Booth, T. & Ainscow, M. (2011). *Index for Inclusion: Developing learning and participation in schools*, 3rd edn. Bristol, UK: Centre for Studies on Inclusive Education.

Bourke, P.E. (2010). Inclusive education reform in Queensland: Implications for policy and practice, *International Journal of Inclusive Education*, 14(2), 183–93.

Breen, L.J. (2009). Early childhood service delivery for families living with childhood disability: Disabling families through problematic implicit ideology, *Australasian Journal of Early Childhood*, 34(4), 1421.

Carrington, S. & Robinson, R. (2006). Inclusive school community: Why is it so complex? *International Journal of Inclusive Education*, 10(4–5), 323–34.

Colbung, M., Glover, A., Rau, C. & Ritchie, J. (2007). Indigenous peoples and perspectives in early childhood education. In L. Keesing-Styles and H. Hedges (eds), *Theorising early childhood practice: Emerging dialogues*. Castle Hill, NSW: Pademelon Press, pp. 137–61.

Commonwealth of Australia (2006). *Disability Standards for Education 2005*. Retrieved 10 April 2014, <http://docs.education.gov.au/system/files/doc/other/disability_standards_for_education_2005_plus_guidance_notes.pdf>.

—— (2009). *Racial Discrimination Act 1975*. Retrieved 10 April 2014, <www.comlaw.gov.au/Details/C2009C00388>.

Conway, R. (2014). Australian schools, policy and legislation in perspective. In M. Hyde, L. Carpenter & R. Conway (eds), *Diversity, Inclusion and Engagement*, 2nd edn. South Melbourne: Oxford University Press, pp. 3–14.

Dau, E., Hughes, P., MacNaughton, G. & Coady, M. (2004). *Lesbian mothers on 'playschool': What's the fuss?* Centre for Equity and Innovation in Early Childhood, Issue Paper, July 2004.

Department of Education, Employment and Workplace Relations (DEEWR) (2009a). Belonging, Being and Becoming: The early years learning framework for Australia. Canberra: DEEWR.

Perspectives and practices in ECEC policy and provision

Department of Education and Training (DET) (2011). *Embedding Aboriginal and Torres Strait Islander Perspectives in Schools: A guide for school learning communities.* Retrieved 4 February 2014, <http://deta.qld.gov.au/indigenous/pdfs/eatsips_2011.pdf>.

Deppeler, J. & Harvey, D. (2004). Validating the British Index for inclusion for the Australian context: Stage one, *International Journal of Inclusive Education*, 8(2), 155–84.

Dreise, M. (2007). *My Country, My Mob: Embedding Indigenous perspectives in schools— An Arts framework.* Canberra: Department of Education, Training and the Arts.

Espe-Sherwindt, M. (2008). Family-centred practice: Collaboration, competency and evidence, *Support for Learning*, 23(3), 136–43.

Giugni, M. (2011). *Inclusion through Relatedness: Learning 'with'—Inclusion support facilitators encountering the early years learning framework.* Canberra: ACT Inclusion Support Agency in partnership with the ACT Professional Support Coordinator.

Goodwin, A.L., Cheruvu, R. & Genishi, C. (2008). Responding to multiple diversities in early childhood education: How far have we come? In C. Genishi and A.L. Goodwin (eds), *Diversities in Early Childhood Education: Rethinking and doing.* New York: Routledge, pp. 3–10.

Gozdecka, D.A., Ercan, S.A. & Kmak, M. (2014). From multiculturalism to post-multiculturalism: Trends and paradoxes, *Journal of Sociology*, 50(1), 51–64.

Hyde, M. (2014a). Understanding diversity, inclusion and engagement. In M. Hyde, L. Carpenter & R. Conway (eds), *Diversity, Inclusion and Engagement*, 2nd edn. South Melbourne: Oxford University Press, pp. 15–33.

—— (2014b). Understanding hearing impairment. In M. Hyde, L. Carpenter & R. Conway (eds), *Diversity, Inclusion and Engagement*, 2nd edn. South Melbourne: Oxford University Press, pp. 255–69.

—— (2014c). Creating inclusive schools. In M. Hyde, L. Carpenter and R. Conway (eds), *Diversity, Inclusion and Engagement*, 2nd edn. South Melbourne: Oxford University Press, pp. 351–61.

Hyde, M., Carpenter, L. & Conway, R. (2014). Inclusive education: In M. Hyde, L. Carpenter & R. Conway (eds), *Diversity, Inclusion and Engagement*, 2nd edn. South Melbourne: Oxford University Press, pp. 386–94.

Kintner-Duffy, V.L., Vardell, R., Lower, J.K. & Cassidy, D.J. (2012). The changers and the changed: Preparing early childhood teachers to work with lesbian, gay, bisexual and transgender families, *Journal of Early Childhood Education*, 33(3), 208–23.

Kitson, R. & Bowes, J. (2010). Incorporating Indigenous ways of knowing in early childhood education for Indigenous children, *Australasian Journal of Early Childhood*, 35(4), 81–9.

Lampert, J. (2012). Becoming a socially just teacher: Walking the talk. In J. Phillips & J. Lampert (eds), *Introductory Indigenous Studies in Education: Reflection and the importance of knowing*, 2nd edn. Frenchs Forest, NSW: Pearson Education Australia, pp. 81–96.

Lubeck, S. (1996). Deconstructing 'child development knowledge' and 'teacher preparation', *Early Childhood Research Quarterly*, 11(2), 147–67.

McConnochie, K. & Russell, A. (1982). *Early Childhood Services for Aboriginal Children*. Canberra: Australian Government Printing Service.

Martin, K. (2007). 'Here we go 'round the broombie tree': Aboriginal early childhood realities and experiences in early childhood services. In J. Ailwood (ed.), *Early Childhood in Australia: Historical and comparative contexts*. Frenchs Forest, NSW: Pearson Education Australia, pp. 18–34.

Miller, M.G. (2013). Action for change? Embedding Aboriginal and Torres Strait Islander perspectives in early childhood education curricula. PhD thesis, Brisbane: Queensland University of Technology. Retrieved 15 May 2014, <http://eprints.qut.edu.au/view/person/Miller,_Melinda.html>.

Miller, M.G. & Petriwskyj, A. (2013). New directions in intercultural early education in Australia, *International Journal of Early Childhood*, 45(2), 251–66.

Moore, T., Morcos, A. & Robinson, R. (2009). *Universal Access to Early Childhood Education: Inclusive practice—Kindergarten access and participation for children experiencing disadvantage*. Melbourne, Vic.: Centre for Community Child Health, Royal Children's Hospital.

Moreton-Robinson, A. (2004). Whiteness, epistemology and Indigenous representation. In A. Moreton-Robinson (ed.), *Whitening Race: Essays in social and cultural criticism*. Canberra, ACT: Aboriginal Studies Press, pp. 75–88.

Newman, L. (2004). Who is the boss of normal? *Every Child*, 10(3), 4–5.

Robinson, K.H. (2002). Making the invisible visible: Gay and lesbian issues in early childhood education, *Contemporary Issues in Early Childhood*, 3(3), 415–34.

Santoro, N. & Reid, J. (2006). 'All things to all people': Indigenous teachers in the Australian teaching profession, *European Journal of Teacher Education*, 29(3), 287–303.

Sydney Morning Herald (21 June 2007). Family life: There's no bare in there. Retrieved 13 April 2014, <http://blogs.smh.com.au/sit/archives/2007/06/family_life_theres_no_bare_in.html>.

Perspectives and practices in ECEC policy and provision

United Nations (2006). *United Nations Convention on the Rights of Persons with Disabilities*. Retrieved 10 April 2014, <www.un.org/disabilities/convention/conventionfull.shtml>.

—— (2007). *United Nations Declaration on the Rights of Indigenous Peoples*. Retrieved 10 April 2014, <www.un.org/esa/socdev/unpfii/documents/DRIPS_en.pdf>.

Chapter 9

Ethical responsibilities in early childhood education and care

Ann Farrell

In this chapter you will find:
- an overview of ethics in early childhood education and care
- research ethics
- professional ethics
- ethics of participation, power and partnerships.

Early childhood education and care (ECEC) is the focus of increasing international policy, legislative and research attention. Evidence demonstrating the importance of quality early years programs for children's lives today and their life chances tomorrow (Camilli et al., 2010) points to the work of early years educators and their everyday ethical practice in ensuring children's strongest start to life. Against a backdrop of policy and curriculum reform in ECEC in Australia, this chapter addresses the ethical work of early years educators working *in situ* with children, families, colleagues and the community. In particular, the chapter focuses on:
- the ethics of participation
- the ethics of power, and
- the ethics of partnerships.

Before considering these three aspects of ethical professional practice, we first consider the field of ethics and its historical antecedents, as this informs the ways in which professional ethics are now understood and practised in ECEC.

AN OVERVIEW OF ETHICS

The field of ethics is expansive. Dictionary definitions of ethics are characteristically broad. *The Macquarie Dictionary* (2014), for example, defines ethics as a 'system of moral principles by which human actions and proposals may be judged good or bad or right or wrong; the rules of conduct recognised in respect of a particular class of human actions, such as *medical ethics*'. In theoretical terms, ethics has been cast as a justificatory discourse concerned with human values and judgements, using rules of behaviour or conformity to a code or set of principles (Freakley & Burgh, 2000; Kimmel, 1988). Cribb (2004) argues that 'ethical behavior springs from a desire to act properly in all circumstances, not just those which have been identified by rule-makers. Ethics exists as a characteristic of humankind precisely because law is inadequate to the task of creating morally good behavior' (p. 55).

Second, the field of ethics has a long history. It can be traced back to the Hippocratic School of Ancient Greece (Smith, 1996), through to the eighteenth-century philosophical work of Immanuel Kant concerned with 'moral laws as categorical imperatives' (1781/2003, 1785/1995), and to the nineteenth-century work of Thomas Percival (1803/1997) with respect to medical practice and clinical research (Emmanuel et al., 2008; Newsom, 1990; Smith, 1996). These earlier ideas, combined with the medical advances and new forms of globalisation that appeared in the early twentieth century, gave rise to the fledgling field of *research ethics* that was to emerge in the mid-twentieth century.

RESEARCH ETHICS

The field of research ethics emerged as a discipline, in its own right, following the Second World War; a major catalyst being the Nuremberg Military Tribunal (NMT, 1949) and its commitment to the good of society, to avoid unnecessary physical or mental harm and to ensure voluntary consent of humans to participate in and withdraw from research without force, deceit or coercion (Farrell, 2005, 2013b; Weithorn & Scherer, 1994). Since then, we have witnessed the emergence of the field of *practitioner research* in a range of disciplines, including that of ECEC. So, too, there has been a proliferation of research resources for early years educators (Arnold 2012; Powell et al., 2012; Roberts-Holmes, 2005). While practitioner research and its practical resourcing have seen substantial growth, the early childhood practitioner research literature shows scant reference to specific ethical issues (such as informed voluntary consent). A meta-analysis of ten international early childhood journals, conducted by Mayne and Howitt (2014) (for the period 2009 to 2012) showed that ethical issues were considerably under-reported in research articles. Is it possible that scant attention to research ethics in early childhood journals is symptomatic of (1) scant attention to research ethics on the part of the researcher(s); and/or (2) scant attention to research ethics on the part of the journal?

Goodfellow (2005) defined practitioner research as 'systematic inquiry-based efforts directed towards creating and extending professional knowledge and associated understandings of professional practice' (p. 48) (see also Goodfellow & Hedges, 2007). So, too, early years practitioner research was featured in the *Research in Practice* series (Goodfellow, 2009) published by Australia's peak ECEC body, Early Childhood Australia (ECA). Beyond Australia practitioner research in 2012 became a named category in annual research awards sponsored by the British Educational Research Association and SAGE Publications (2012), and the European Early Childhood Education Research Association and Routledge (2012).

In time, practitioner research came to be regulated by codes of conduct (for research with humans). Australia's *National Statement on Ethical Conduct in Human Research* (National Health and Medical Research Council [NHMRC], 2007; revised 2014) (known as *The National Statement*), for example, became the prime vehicle for the regulation of Australian research conducted with children and adults in ECEC. *The National Statement* (2007) shares with numerous other codes (of research ethics) a commitment to research merit and integrity and to ensuring:

- justice
- respect, and
- beneficence (that is, the relative benefit versus the risk to those involved in the research).

These three elements resonate with key values that underpin professional ethics in a range of fields. In relation to the education sector in Australia, Forster's (2012) analysis of codes of ethics and conduct revealed the ways in which the codes position the teacher as a professional, as a moral agent and as a public servant. Forster (2012) argues that ethical standards for teachers fall into two distinct forms of code: the 'regulatory' and the 'aspirational', with the latter aligned to teachers making autonomous ethical judgements based on integrity and capacity for respect, as core to the teaching profession.

PROFESSIONAL ETHICS IN EARLY CHILDHOOD EDUCATION AND CARE

What do we mean by ethics in professional practice in the early years? Australia's Guide to the National Quality Standard (NQS) (Australian Children's Education and Care Quality Authority [ACECQA], 2013) specifies that:

> It is the role of the approved provider, nominated superviser, educators and co-ordinators to establish effective and ethical practices in the service. A sound philosophy guides decision making, including decisions about the appropriate number and deployment of suitably qualified and experienced educators, coordinators and staff members. (p. 106)

Further, the NQS (2013) defines 'a code of conduct/code of ethics as an agreed code that applies to management, educators, coordinators and staff members . . . [and] clearly explains the responsibilities of all parties in relation to one another and to children and families using the service' (p. 106). The NQS (2013, p. 8) features the following guiding principles:

*   The rights and best interests of the child are paramount.
*   Children are successful, competent and capable learners.
*   Equity, inclusion and diversity underpin the framework.
*   Australia's Aboriginal and Torres Strait Islander cultures are valued.
*   The role of parents and families is respected and supported.
*   Best practice is expected in the provision of education and care services.

Taking a critical stance, Moss (2005) and Dahlberg and Moss (2005) define professional ethics as 'encounters' within the everyday contexts of early childhood, encounters that are reflective of its dominant discourses (such as managerialism). Ethics includes the decision-making, practice and reflection of professionals as they interact with children, colleagues, families and communities.

Ethical responsibilities in early childhood education and care

In the last twenty years, professional associations, such as ECA, have formulated their own codes of professional ethics as related to, yet distinct from, research ethics (Coady, 1991; Coady & Bloch, 1996; Farrell, 2013b; Hydon, 2007; Powell et al., 2011) (see Table 9.1 for a sample of Codes of Ethics for professional practice in ECEC).

Forster (2012) notes that the ECA *Code of Ethics* is Australia's only national code of ethics. That said, the Australian Institute for Teaching and School Leadership (AITSL) Australian Professional Standards for Teachers (2014) is a national standard applicable to the work of early childhood teachers and articulates 'professional standards and responsibility' (Standard 7.1, 2014) as part of the educator's professional engagement with colleagues, parents/carers and the community.

The ECA *Code of Ethics*—with its specific focus on children, families, colleagues and communities—articulates a commitment to:

- respect
- democracy
- honesty
- integrity, and
- justice.

As Table 9.1 shows, the ECA *Code of Ethics* (2006) has been drawn upon and/ or cited by other leading bodies, such as ACECQA and the British Association for Early Childhood Education (2014). Such information-sharing and cross-fertilisation of ideas are emblematic of collaboration across organisations and jurisdictions, such that specific bodies are able to distil and customise shared knowledge to their own contexts and challenges. Researchers such as Thomas (2009) have critiqued codes such as ECA's, as shaping and expressing professional identities (see also Lasky, 2005; Moss & Petrie, 2002), particularly when practitioners face uncertainty in their professional relationships with children, families, community, colleagues and employers.

In addition, in particular jurisdictions, codes of ethics such as that of the Queensland College of Teachers (QCT) (2014) or the Victorian Department of Education and Early Childhood Development (DEECD) (2014) govern the work of educators. For early years educators working in primary schools, AITSL's Australian Professional Standards for Teachers usually combine with the relevant state-based code (for example, that of QCT or DEECD) to guide the ethical practice of teachers. Where there is a breach of the code, jurisdictions

191

Perspectives and practices in ECEC policy and provision

Table 9.1: A sample of Codes of Ethics related to professional practice in ECEC

Year	Organisation	Name of Code	Key features
2006	Early Childhood Australia (see ACECQA below)	*Code of Ethics*	Values: respect, democracy, honesty, integrity and justice In relation to: children, families, colleagues and communities
2011	National Association for the Education of Young Children, USA	*Code of Ethical Conduct* and *Statement of Commitment*	Ideals and principles in relation to: children, families, co-workers, employers and community and society
2013	My Early Childhood Education (ECE) New Zealand	*Code of Ethical Conduct for Early Childhood Services*	An ethic of care Compliance with the law and maintenance of social cohesion Being well informed and professionally connected Accountability, honesty and openness Socially and professionally responsible
2014	British Association for Early Childhood Education, UK	*Code of Ethics*	Values: protection and wellbeing of children and families In relation to: children, families, communities, employers, colleagues, students, profession and conduct of research
2014	Australian Institute for Teaching and School Leadership (AITSL)	Australian Professional Standards for Teachers	Standard 7—Engage professionally with colleagues, parents/carers and the community 7.1—Meet professional ethics and responsibilities
2014	Australian Children's Education and Care Quality Authority (ACECQA)—National Quality Framework	Refers to *ECA Code of Ethics*	

192

Ethical responsibilities in early childhood education and care

(typically) do not enforce teacher registration disciplinary proceedings or action for misconduct or unsatisfactory performance. Rather, they have their own policies and processes to deal with conduct, performance and disciplinary issues (for example, DEECD, 2013). Forster (2012) notes that:

> Control of teachers' behavior by static values embedded in disciplinary processes may lead to perfunctory action up the chain of command rather than grounded ethical decision making and that an individual may be more likely to be motivated by external factors such as fear of litigation or punishment rather than internally by their highest ideals in a context of dynamic and supported professional dialogue around ethical values in teaching. (p. 14)

In short, the ethical practice of early years educators, whether in school-based contexts or prior-to-school contexts, is framed by published codes of ethics and by prevailing frameworks, legislation, regulations and policies, such as the Australian Professional Standards for Teachers and/or the National Quality Framework (NQF) (ACECQA, 2012). The *Guide to the Education and Care Services National Law* and the *Education and Care Services National Regulations* (ACECQA, 2011) now accompanies the NQF. The *Guide to the National Law and National Regulations* (ACECQA, 2011) specifies that 'policies should be informed by the service's philosophy statement, the ECA *Code of Ethics* and current advice from recognized authorities' (p. 109). Guides such as these stress the importance of the *Code of Ethics* in everyday practice, at both the grass-roots and the systems levels of an ECEC service. In turn, the NQF's National Quality Standard (NQS) comprises seven quality areas in which ethical practice is enacted.

Belonging, Being and Becoming: The early years learning framework (EYLF) for Australia (Department of Education, Employment and Workplace Relations [DEEWR], 2009) highlights the educator's reflective practice in building professional knowledge and learning communities, as co-learners with children, families and community. The EYLF does not explicitly deal with 'ethics', although it mentions the word 'ethics' (only once) in the context of reflective practice as 'a form of ongoing learning that involves engaging with questions of philosophy, ethics and practice' (DEEWR, 2009, p. 13). While this is the single mention of the term 'ethics', the EYLF is undergirded by understandings of ethics contained in the ECA *Code of Ethics*. The EYLF asks these overarching questions that guide reflective practice:

- What are my understandings of each child?
- What theories, philosophies and understanding shape and assist my work?
- Who is advantaged when I work in this way? Who is disadvantaged?
- What questions do I have about my work? What am I challenged by? What am I curious about? What am I confronted by?
- What aspects of my work are not helped by the theories and guidance that I usually draw on to make sense of what I do?
- Are there other theories and knowledge that could help me to understand what I have observed and experienced What are they? How might those theories and that knowledge affect my practice? (p. 13)

These questions lead us to consider three key aspects of professional ethics in ECEC:

- the ethics of participation
- the ethics of power, and
- the ethics of partnerships.

Following are sections on each of these aspects. Each section will be introduced by a scenario and related question, followed by a discussion of a key aspect of ethical practice, and finished with a set of questions for discussion and/or follow-up.

Ethics of participation

Scenario

Xian is new to the area and this is his first day in the early years service. The other children have been attending the service for some months and are well established in their daily routines and their peer groups. Xian has just arrived and is introduced to Simon, whose locker adjoins his.

In operating as an ethical professional, what might the educator say and do?

Participation is theorised as children's active and competent engagement in matters that affect them. It involves children speaking, engaging and making decisions about their everyday lives and involves adults listening and/or consulting with children about children's lives (Alderson & Morrow, 2011; Clark, 2013; Tisdall, Davis & Gallagher, 2009). Within this set of sociological understandings, childhood is seen as socially constructed within particular times, places and contexts, rather than as universal and generalisable (Alanen & Mayall, 2002; Corsaro, 1985, 1997; Danby, 2002; James, Jenks & Prout, 1998; Jenks 1996; Mackay 1991; Qvortrup, 1994, 2000). These understandings can be seen to fly in the face of earlier developmental notions of children, where children tended to be seen as precompetent (Danby, 2002; Mackay, 1991); 'underdeveloped . . . thus *not something* rather than *something*' (Waksler, 1991, p. 63); or 'human becomings' (Phillips & Alderson, 2002, p. 6), that is, as one day becoming adult humans.

Participation is enacted and made visible through children's play-based social interactions, their co-production of ideas and artefacts. While play and its affordances for children's inclusion, participation, learning and wellbeing are articulated in curriculum frameworks and resources (for example, EYLF), the affordances of play for conflict and exclusion are less often discussed. Grieshaber and McArdle (2010) argue that play is 'not always innocent and fun; it is also political and involves morals and ethics' (p. 1). So, too, Punch (2002) challenges the claim that play is uniformly good and urges practitioners to seek greater reflexivity and criticality in providing children with opportunities that may be touted as participatory. There is also the question of adult participation in matters that affect adults and children. This question will be picked up later in the chapter when considering the 'ethics of partnership'.

Child participation also draws upon conceptual understandings of children's rights and agency (Archard, 1993; Babbie, 1998; Kimmel, 1988) from the social sciences (Franklin, 1995), the health sciences (Salek & Edgar, 2002), philosophy (Archard, 1993; Ekman Ladd, 1996), legal theory (Eekelaar, 1994; Freeman, 1996; Freeman & Veerman, 1992) and political science (O'Neill, 1995). Over 40 years ago, John Stuart Mill (1972) argued that human rights have corresponding duties or responsibilities and include positive rights that require actions from others and negative rights that require the individual to be permitted to act in certain ways without unnecessary restrictions imposed by others. While the

Perspectives and practices in ECEC policy and provision

rhetoric of children's rights is applauded in ECEC (Alderson & Morrow, 2011; Mayall, 2013), there is a counter-stance that decisions affecting children are the responsibility of the family and that children's rights, in effect, subordinate parental rights (Maley, 1998; Muehlenberg, 1994; Myers, 1994). In either case, the values underpinning each stance shed light on the nature and degree of children's participation and how participation is negotiated by children and adults, be they educators, parents and/or community members.

The **ethics of participation** evokes question such as:
1. Who participates? Children? Adults? Children and adults together? Who initiates participation?
2. What does participation look like? How is participation documented and used in reflective practice?
3. Are there peak times (during the course of the day/week/year) that afford greater/fewer opportunities for participation?
4. How might participation make a difference to children's everyday lives and their life chance?
5. What if children choose to not participate or to resist participation?

Ethics of power

Scenario

Peta is engrossed in sandplay outdoors. Most of the other children are outdoors, and are tidying up in preparation for lunch indoors. The educator reminds the children that it is time to tidy up. Peta continues to play in the sand and appears to ignore the educator and the other children.

In operating as an ethical professional, what might the educator say and do?

Professional ethics is also concerned with the ethics of power. Educators hold positions of responsibility, exercising varying degrees of power in their

Ethical responsibilities in early childhood education and care

interactions with children, families, colleagues and communities. What is power and how is it used? And what are the broader agendas framing the ethical use of power?

In terms of professional ethics, power denotes authority and the responsible exercise of one's authority. A pedagogical challenge for early years educators, with respect to the ethics of power, is to ensure that young children are seen to be competent while, at the same, recognising their potential vulnerability to adverse experiences and potential power imbalances that may undermine their competence and capacity to participate in their own learning and development.

The ethics of power is also concerned with the possibility of status and power differentials between children and adults (as well as between children and between adults). In relation to contexts that espouse participation and partnership yet feature power differentials, Woodhead and Faulkner (2002) call for adults to 'structure children's environments, guide their behaviour and enable their social participation in ways consistent with their understanding, interests and ways of communication, especially in the issues that most directly affect their lives' (pp. 31–2).

Some authors refer to 'symmetrical' and 'asymmetrical' uses of power in contexts in adult–child interactions (Christensen & Prout, 2002; Speier, 1973, 1976). In the context of child and/or adult conversations, the early work of Speier (1973, 1976) identified the ways in which power was used and shared, and showed evidence of children having restricted conversational rights to those of adults; that is, asymmetrical rights, by virtue of their position within the adult-oriented interactional order (Busch, 2011). With respect to children's asymmetrical rights, Speier (1976) argued:

> The manner in which they can participate in conversations with adults is controlled by an asymmetrical distribution of speaker's rights, when adults claim rights of local control over conversations with children and children are obliged to allow them that control. (p. 101)

In relation to research contexts, Christensen and Prout (2002) recognise power differentials and explore the conditions for 'ethical symmetry' (p. 477) as a dialogic relationship between the child and adult researcher. With regards to

Perspectives and practices in ECEC policy and provision

child research, Barker and Smith (2002) discuss the notion of the gendered 'positionality' of the researcher and child participant.

Professional ethics are enacted within institutional and interactional practices, whether in prior-to-school or school-based early years contexts. David, Edwards and Alldred (2001) refer to school-based pedagogical approaches that are 'inscribed with differential power relations' (p. 347). In turn, Theobald and Kultti (2012) showed child participation to be constrained by the institutional contexts and the institutional categories of 'teacher' and 'student'. They noted teachers seeking to balance the pedagogical intent of their 'teaching' with institutional expectations of the site (see also Theobald, Danby & Ailwood, 2011).

Such power relations are not necessarily confined to school or 'schoolified' contexts (Cohen et al., 2003) and may be seen in the categories of educator, child, parent and colleague inherent in early years contexts. In short, they can be seen to be part of broader social and institutional processes, some of which may need to be challenged if not dismantled. Kincheloe (2003) argues that considering such processes can 'move us to uncover the genesis of the assumptions that shape our lives and institutions and to ask how they can be altered'.

The ethics of power also concerns how children and adults get to make decisions and how they engage in knowledge (co-)production. Is the production a focus for reflection and/or further action? Understandings from the field of research ethics are helpful here and can shed light on professional ethics in contexts that may not be classified as 'research' contexts—they are concerned with child consent to participate or to not participate. In the broader context, consent requires interactive dialogue, negotiation and renegotiation over time (see also Alderson & Morrow, 2011). Roberts (2000) argues that listening to children, hearing children and acting on what children say are 'central to recognizing and respecting their worth as human beings. Children are not simply objects, either of concern, of research or of a media story' (p. 238).

> The **ethics of power** evokes questions such as:
> 1. What are the evidences of power in ECEC (for example, in relationships and interactions?

Ethical responsibilities in early childhood education and care

2. How do educators use power? What times/activities during the day/week/year exemplify the use of power by children, by educators and by families?
3. How do educators share power? With children? With families?
4. How might some people, ideas and practices be privileged over others?
5. What conditions support the ethical use of power?

3. Ethics of partnerships

Scenario
Mardu and her younger brother, Sae, attend the early years program. They are fluent English speakers and speak Urdu at home with their mother. Their mother is learning English at the community centre adjoining the site.

In operating as an ethical professional, what might the educator say and do?

By operating in participatory partnership with children and adults and while recognising possible power differentials, educators are in a prime position to transform the lives of young children and those around them. Australia's NQS (ACECQA, 2013) Quality Areas 6 and 7 (concerned with collaborative partnerships with families and communities; and leadership and service management) speak directly to the importance of leadership in developing collaborative partnerships and achieving quality outcomes for children. The NQF refers to respectful and supportive relationships with families: supporting families in their parenting; respecting families' values and beliefs about child-rearing; and collaborating with other organisations and service providers to enhance children's learning and wellbeing. But what if parents or community members do not hold a common language or if their child-rearing values run counter to those of the service? Here, again, the balance of children's rights to participation and their rights to protection is invoked, as educators enact their legislative and professional responsibilities (for example, in the area of

199

child protection from abuse and neglect). Their responsibilities may also mean tackling injustice.

Fraser's (2008) theoretical perspectives on social justice and tackling injustice include consideration of (1) redistribution (economic), (2) recognition (cultural) and (3) representation (political). Redistribution involves public resources being directed towards the least advantaged; recognition seeks to redress social *mis*recognition by identifying historically marginalised groups; and representation involves the rights of individuals and groups to participate in decision-making. Early years educators are well positioned to recognise and address redistribution, recognition and representation given their daily interactions with families. Moreover, their professional communities are pivotal to tackling the injustice that educators themselves, as well as families and communities, may face in relation to economic structures, social resources and governance structures that may limit their democratic participation and/or institutional practices that deny equitable participation (Fraser, 2008).

> The **ethic of partnerships** evokes questions such as:
> 1. What conditions enhance partnerships? What conditions work against partnerships?
> 2. How is information about and from the service and information about and from the family shared?
> 3. How are wider community resources used and shared?
> 4. What if the parenting practices of families are at odds with those of the ECEC service?
> 5. What happens if families resist involvement in the service and its decisions?

CONCLUSION

Early years educators working ethically with children, families, colleagues and communities are at the frontline of ethical professional leadership. In enacting the ethics of participation, power and partnership, they, along with children and adults in their services, are well positioned to lead and to learn. Early years educators are well placed to identify and tackle the assumptions that circumscribe children's lives and to provide opportunities for transformative learning and development. Sumsion (2003) calls for ethical educators to do so within relationships of humility, reciprocity and community.

The work of early years educators , however, is set squarely within the realities of real-world ECEC contexts. As Merriam (2002) reminds us: 'We must learn to live in the middle of things, in the tension of conflict, confusion and possibility; and we must become adept at making do with the messiness of that condition' (p. 401).

FURTHER THINKING

1. What agendas are shaping and producing ethical practice in ECEC?

2. What does ethical practice look like in ECEC?

3. How might young children and their families contribute to the educator's ethical practice?

4. What is the role of Codes of Ethics and/or regulations in ensuring ethical practice?

5. What are the major challenges to ethical practice in ECEC into the future?

REFERENCES

Alanen, L. & Mayall, B. (eds) (2002). *Conceptualising Child–Adult Relations*. London: RoutledgeFalmer.

Alderson, P. & Morrow, V. (2011). *The Ethics of Research with Children and Young People: A practical handbook*. London: SAGE Publications.

Archard, D. (1993). *Children, Rights and Childhood*. London: Routledge.

Arnold, C. (ed.) (2012). *Improving your Reflective Practice Through Stories of Practitioner Research*. London: Routledge.

Australian Children's Education and Care Quality Authority (ACECQA) (2011). *Guide to the Education and Care Services National Law and the Education and Care Services National Regulation*. Canberra: ACECQA. Retrieved 10 August 2014, <http://files. acecqa.gov.au/files/National-Quality-Framework-Resources-Kit/NQF02-Guide-to-ECS-Law-and-Regs-130902.pdf>.

Perspectives and practices in ECEC policy and provision

—— (2012). *National Quality Framework*. Canberra: ACECQA. Retrieved 4 August 2014, <http://files.acecqa.gov.au/files/National-Quality-Framework-Resources-Kit/NQF03-Guide-to-NQS-130902.pdf>.

—— (2013). *Guide to the National Quality Standard*. Canberra: ACECQA. Retrieved 4 August 2014, <http://files.acecqa.gov.au/files/National-Quality-Framework-Resources-Kit/NQF03-Guide-to-NQS-130902.pdf>.

Australian Institute for Teaching and School Leadership (AITSL) (2014). Australian Professional Standards for Teachers. Retrieved 10 August 2014, <www.teacherstandards.aitsl.edu.au/DomainOfTeaching/ProfessionalEngagement/Standards/7>.

Babbie, E. (1998). *The practice of social research*. Belmont, CA: Wadsworth.

Barker, J. & Smith, F. (2001). Power, positionality and practicality: Carrying out fieldwork with children. *Ethics, Place & Environment*, 4, 142-147.

British Association for Early Childhood Education (2014). *Code of Ethics*. Retrieved 10 August 2014, <https://early-education.org.uk/sites/default/files/Code%20of%20Ethics.pdf>.

Busch, G. (2011). The Social Orders of Family Mealtime. Unpublished PhD dissertation. Brisbane: Queensland University of Technology.

Camilli, G., Vargas, S., Ryan, S. & Barnett, S.W. (2010). Meta-analysis of the effects of early education interventions on cognitive and social development, *Teachers College Record*, 112(3), 579–620.

Christensen, P. & Prout, A. (2002). Working with ethical symmetry in social research with children, *Childhood*, 21(3), 477–97.

Creche and Kindergarten Association of Queensland (C&K) (2012). *C&K Building Waterfalls Teaching and Learning Guidelines*, 2nd edn. Brisbane: C&K.

Clark, A. (2013). Understanding research with children. In T. Maynard & S. Powell (eds), *An Introduction to Early Childhood Studies*, 3rd edn. London: SAGE Publications.

Coady, M. (1991). Ethics, laws, and codes, *Australian Journal of Early Childhood*, 16(1), 17–20.

Coady, M. & Bloch, S. (eds) (1996). *Codes of Ethics and the Professions*. Melbourne: Melbourne University Press.

Cohen, B., Wallace, J., Moss, P. & Petrie, P. (2003). Re-forming education and care in England, Scotland and Sweden, *UNESCO Policy Briefs on Early Childhood, 12*. Retrieved 1 March 2015 <www.waece.org/ingles/notes_unesco/brief12en.pdf>.

Corsaro, W.A. (1985). *Friendship and Peer Culture in the Early Years*. Norwood, NJ: Ablex.

—— (1997). *The Sociology of Childhood*. Thousand Oaks, CA: Pine Forge Press.

Cribb, R. (2004). Ethical regulation and humanities research in Australia: Problems and consequences, *Monash Bioethics Review*, 23(3), 39–57.

Dahlberg, G. & Moss, P. (2005). *Ethics and Politics in Early Childhood Education: Contesting early childhood*. Hove, UK: Psychology Press/Taylor & Francis.

Danby, S. (2002). The communicative competence of young children, *Australian Journal of Early Childhood*, 27(3): 25–30.

David, M., Edwards, R. & Alldred, P. (2001). Children and young people's views of social research: The case of research on home-school relations, *Childhood*, 6(2), 26181.

Early Childhood Australia (ECA) (2006). *Code of Ethics*. Retrieved 10 August 2014, <www.earlychildhoodaustralia.org.au/our-publications/eca-code-ethics/>.

Early Childhood Education, New Zealand (2013). *Code of Ethical Conduct for Early Childhood Services*. Porirua, NZ: My ECE (Early Childhood Education). Retrieved 10 August 2014, <www.myece.org.nz/code-of-ethical-conduct>.

Eekelaar, J. (1994). The interest of the child and the child's wishes: The role of dynamic self-determinism. In P. Alston (ed.), *The Best Interests of the Child: Reconciling culture and human rights*). Oxford: Clarendon Press, pp. 42–61.

Ekman Ladd, R. (1996). *Children's Rights Revisioned: Philosophical readings*. Belmont, CA: Wadsworth Publishing.

Emmanuel, E., Grady, C., Crouch, R., Lie, R., Miller, F. & Wendler, D. (2008). *The Oxford Textbook of Clinical Research Ethics*. Oxford: Oxford University Press.

Farrell, A. (2005). New times in ethical research with children. In A. Farrell (ed.), *Ethical Research with Children*. Milton Keynes, UK: Open University Press/McGraw-Hill, pp. 166–75.

—— (2013b). Ethics in research with children. In H. Montgomery (ed.), *Oxford Bibliographies in Childhood Studies*. New York: Oxford University Press.

Forster, D. (2012). Codes of ethics in Australian education: Towards a national perspective, *Australian Journal of Teacher Education*, 37(9), 1–16.

Franklin, B. (1995). *Handbook of Children's Rights: Comparative policy and practice*. London: Routledge.

Fraser, N. (2008). *Scales of Justice: Reimagining political space in a globalising world*. Cambridge: Polity Press.

Freakley & Burgh (2000). *Engaging with ethics. Ethical inquiry for teachers*. Katoomba, NSW: Social Science Press.

Freeman, M. (ed.) (1996). *Children's Rights: A comparative perspective*. Brookfield, VT: Dartmouth.

Freeman, M. & Veerman, P. (eds) (1992). *Ideologies of Children's Rights*. Dordrecht: Kluwer.

Goodfellow (2005) Researching with/for whom? Stepping in and out of practitioner research. *Australian Journal of Early Childhood*, 30(43), 48–57.

—— (2009). *Early Years Learning Framework: Getting started*. Canberra: Early Childhood Australia.

Goodfellow, J. & Hedges, M. (2007). 'Practitioner research "centre stage": Contexts, contributions and challenges'. In L. Keesing-Styles & H. Hedges (eds), *Theorising Early Childhood Practice: Emerging dialogues*. Castle Hill, NSW: Pademelon Press, pp. 187–210.

Grieshaber, S. & McArdle, F. (2010). *The Trouble with Play*. Maidenhead, UK: McGraw-Hill/Open University Press.

Hydon, C. (2007). A way of travelling: The environment and our code of ethics, *Every Child*, 13(1), 7.

James, A., Jenks, C. & Prout, A. (1998). *Theorising Childhood*. Cambridge: Polity Press.

Jenks, C. (1996). *Childhood*. London: Routledge.

Kant, I. (2003) [1781]. *Critique of Pure Reason*, trans. N. Kemp-Smith. Basingstoke: Palgrave Macmillan.

—— (1995) [1785]. *Foundations of the Metaphysics of Morals and What is Enlightenment* (trans. L.W. Beck). Upper Saddle River, NJ: Prentice Hall.

Kimmel (1988). *Ethics and values in applied social research*. Newbury Park, CA: SAGE Publications.

Kincheloe, J. (2003). *Teachers as Researchers: Qualitative inquiry as a path to empowerment*. London: SAGE Publications.

Lasky, S. (2005). A sociocultural approach to understanding teacher identity, agency and professional vulnerability in a context of secondary school reform. *Teaching and Teacher Education*, 21(8), 899–916.

Mackay, R.W. (1991). Conceptions of children and models of socialisation. In F.C. Waksler, (ed.), *Studying the Social Worlds of Children: Sociological readings*. London: Falmer Press, pp. 23–37.

Macquarie Dictionary (2014). Retrieved 10 August 2014, <www.macquariedictionary.com.au/features/word/search/?word=ethics&search_word_type=Dictionary>.

Maley, B. (1998). Children's rights ascendent, *Quadrant*, 42(6), 32–6.

Mayall, B. (2013). *A History of the Sociology of Childhood*. London: Institute of Education.

Mayne, F. & Howitt, C. (2014). Reporting of ethics in early childhood journals: A meta-analysis of 10 journals from 2009 to 2012, *Australasian Journal of Early Childhood*, 2(2), 71–9.

Merriam, S.B. (2002). *Qualitative Research in Practice*. San Francisco, CA: Jossey-Bass.

Mill, J.S. (1972) On moral obligation and justice. In H.B. Acton (ed.), *Utilitarianism*. London: J.M. Dent, pp. 40–2.

Moss, P. (2005). Making space for ethics, *Australian Journal of Early Childhood*, 26, 1–6.

Moss, P. & Petrie, P. (2002). *From Children's Services to Children's Spaces: Public policy, children and childhood*. London: RoutledgeFalmer.

Muehlenberg, B. (1994). *In Defence of the Family*. Melbourne: Australian Family Association.

Myers, J. (1994). *The Backlash: Child protection under fire*. London: SAGE Publications.

National Association for the Education of Young Children (NAEYC) (2011). *Code of Ethical Conduct* and *Statement of Commitment*. Washington DC: NAEYC. Retrieved 10 August 2014, <www.naeyc.org/positionstatements/ethical_conduct>.

National Health and Medical Research Council (NHMRC) (2007, revised 2014). *National Statement on Ethical Conduct in Human Research*. Canberra: NHMRC. Retrieved 10 August 2014, <www.nhmrc.gov.au/guidelines/publications/e72>.

Newsom, B. (1990). Medical ethics: Thomas Percival, *JSCV Medical Association Journal*, 86(3): 175.

O'Neill, J. (1995). On the liberal culture of child risk: A covenant critique of contractarian theory. In A.M Ambert (ed.), *Sociological studies of children (7)*. Greenwich, CT: JAI Press.

Percival, T. (1997) [1803]. *Medical Ethics*. New York: Classics of Surgery Library.

Phillips, B. & Alderson, P. (2002). *Beyond 'Anti-smacking': Challenging violence and coercion in parent–child relations*. London: The Children's Society.

Powell, M., Fitzgerald, R., Taylor, N. & Graham, A. (2012). *International Literature Review: Ethical issues in undertaking research with children and young people*. Dunedin, New Zealand: University of Otago, Centre for Research on Children and Families.

Powell, M., Graham, A., Taylor, N., Newell, S. & Fitzgerald, R. (2011). *Building Capacity for Ethical Research with Children and Young People: An international research project to examine the ethical issues and challenges in undertaking research with and for children in different majority and minority world contexts*. Dunedin, New Zealand: University of Otago, Centre for Research on Children and Families.

Punch, S. (2002). Research with children: The same or different from research with adults? *Childhood*, 9(3), 321–41.

Queensland College of Teachers (QCT) (2014). *Code of Ethics for Teachers in Queensland*. Brisbane: QCT. Retrieved 10 August 2014, <www.qct.edu.au/conduct/codeofethics. html>.

Qvortrup, J. (1994). Childhood and modern society: A paradoxical relationship? In J. Branner & M. Brien (eds), *Childhood and Parenthood: Proceedings of ISA Committee for Family Research Conference on Children and Families*. London: Institute of Education, University of London, pp. 189–98.

—— (2000). Macroanalysis of childhood. In P. Christensen & A. James (eds), *Research with Children: Perspectives and practices*. London: Falmer Press, pp. 77–97.

Roberts, H. (2000). Listening to children: And hearing them. In P. Christensen & A. James (eds), *Research with Children: Perspectives and practices*. London: Falmer Press, pp. 225–40.

Roberts-Holmes, G. (2005). *Doing your Early Years Research Project: A step-by-step guide*. London: SAGE Publications.

Salek, S. & Edgar, A. (2002). *Pharmaceutical Ethics*. Chichester: John Wiley & Sons Ltd.

Secretariat of the International Military Tribunal (1949). *Trials of War Criminals before the Nuremberg Military Tribunals under Control Council Law*, 10(2), 181–2. Washington, DC: US Government Printing Office.

Smith, D.C. (1996). The Hippocratic Oath and modern medicine, *Journal of History and Medicine: Allied Sciences*, 51(4), 484–500.

Speier, M. (1973). *How to Observe Face-to-face Communication: A sociological introduction*. Pacific Palisades, CA: Goodyear Publishing Company Inc.

—— (1976). The child as conversationalist: Some cultural contact features of conversational interactions between adults and children. In M. Hammersley & P. Woods (eds), *The Process of Schooling: A sociological reader*. London: Routledge and Kegan Paul Ltd/Open University Press, pp. 98–103.

Sumsion, J. (2003). Researching with children: Lessons in humility, reciprocity and community, *Australasian Journal of Early Childhood*, 28(1), 18–23.

Theobald, M., Danby, S. & Ailwood, J. (2011). Child participation in the early years: Challenges for education, *Australasian Journal of Early Childhood*, 36(3), 19–26.

Theobald, M. & Kultti, A. (2012). Investigating child participation in the everyday talk of teacher and children in a preparatory year, *Contemporary Issues in Early Childhood*, 13(3), 210–25.

Thomas, L. (2009). Certainties and Uncertainties: Ethics and professional identities of early childhood educators. Unpublished PhD thesis. Brisbane: Queensland University of Technology.

Tisdall, K., Davis, J. & Gallagher, M. (2009). *Researching with Children and Young People: Research design, methods and analysis*. Los Angeles, CA: SAGE Publications.

Victoria Department of Education and Early Childhood Development (DEECD) (2014). *Victoria Teaching Profession Code of Conduct*. Melbourne: DEECD. Retrieved 10 August 2014, <www.vit.vic.edu.au/conduct/victorian-teaching-profession-code-of-conduct/Pages/default.aspx>.

Waksler, F. (1991). Studying children: Phenomenological insights. In F. Waksler (ed.), *Studying the Social Worlds of Children: Sociological readings*. London: Falmer Press, pp. 60–9.

Weithorn, L.A. & Scherer, D.G. (1994). Children's involvement in research participation decisions: Psychological considerations. In M.A. Grodin & L. Glanz (eds), *Children as Research Subjects: Science, ethics and law*. New York: Oxford University Press, pp. 133–79.

Woodhead, M. & Faulkner, D. (2000). Subjects, objects or participants? Dilemmas of psychological research with children. In P. Christensen & A. James (eds), *Research with Children: Perspectives and practice*. London: RoutlegeFalmer, pp. 9–35.

PART THREE

Perspectives and practices in teaching and leadership

Chapter 10

Planning for children's learning: curriculum, pedagogy and assessment

Sandra Cheeseman

In this chapter you will find:
- approaches to curriculum
- the early childhood curriculum context in Australia
- the early years learning framework
- the National Quality Framework (NQF) and National Quality Standard (NQS) for Australia
- the Australian Curriculum
- understanding pedagogy
- assessment.

The terms 'curriculum', 'pedagogy' and 'assessment' are relatively recent additions to the language of early childhood education and care (ECEC). Although the principles of these ideas have long existed within the ideologies of early childhood teaching and learning, the terms have not always sat comfortably within the informality of play-based approaches to the education and care of very young children. In recent years, the growth of knowledge about young children and their learning along with the expanding interest of governments in investing in the early years, has seen an increase in the formalisation of curricula documents. This brings a need to clarify educational terms as they relate to the unique educational settings that are identified as ECEC programs. Further to this is a need to identify the role of educators in working with ideas of curriculum, pedagogy and assessment with young children—identifying both the regulatory and legislative responsibilities of curriculum— but to also make space to consider the broader possibilities and indeed the joys of planning for and facilitating children's learning. Any discussion of early childhood curriculum, pedagogy and assessment must acknowledge the significant change that takes place for children in the years birth to eight. In the Australian context, educators work with multiple and varied curricula documents, each requiring interpretation and thoughtfulness to ensure they contribute to best learning outcomes for young children. Curriculum in this sense is a lived experience; that is, curriculum is enacted, interpreted and responsive to the diversity of children, communities and early childhood settings.

DEFINING KEY TERMS

The three terms that form the focus of this chapter—curriculum, pedagogy and assessment—can be viewed as a trilogy, or three related notions. The concepts interconnect in all stages of planning for children's learning and it is difficult to talk about one without reference to the others. All can be variously defined but for the purposes of this book the definitions chosen reflect ideas that fit with broad philosophical understandings of ECEC.

The term 'curriculum' has perhaps sat more comfortably within the discourse of school and higher education. Stemming from the Latin, meaning 'life course' the notion of curriculum has traditionally implied that there is a predetermined course or path to learning. While this intent of curriculum for young children may not always be acknowledged as predetermined, it is important to be aware that increasingly early childhood curriculum has become the business and priority of government education policy. In recent times curricula or learning frameworks have been closely linked to government productivity ambitions and as a strategy to ensure equity and social justice. Curriculum as a lived experience calls for educators to interpret the documents or frameworks and make decisions about how they can best facilitate learning that is responsive to children, families and community contexts, while still holding onto the importance of equity, social justice and outcomes for learning.

The term 'pedagogy', comes from the Greek, meaning 'to lead the child'. It traditionally referred to child-rearing practices, but, borrowing from the European tradition of the term, it has more recently become synonymous with the education of children more broadly. The term moves beyond the classic

Planning for children's learning: curriculum, pedagogy and assessment

notion of teacher or teaching and has been defined as a holistic, personal approach to working with children and young people (Petrie et al., 2009). It is a useful term in the early childhood context because it helps to frame the work of early childhood educators beyond the limitations of thinking purely about academic education. Pedagogy invites educators to think about their work with children in a broader sense, as being influenced by more than a set of outcomes to be achieved, but mindful of the importance of relationships, contexts and responsiveness to individuals.

The term 'assessment' stems from the Latin 'to sit beside'. While this notion may seem in contrast to ideas of assessment that promote testing or checking performance against a set standard, the origins of assessment remind us that we can work alongside children to monitor and consider their progression in learning and development. Put simply, assessment can be seen as the evidence of children's participation in learning. Belonging, Being and Becoming: The early years learning framework (EYLF) for Australia reminds us that assessment of children's learning is 'the process of gathering and analysing information as evidence of what children know, can do and understand' (DEEWR, 2009, p. 17). With this is mind, assessment is more than just the final summing up of children's learning, but is a part of the way educators observe, plan for and take note of children's responses to all experiences that contribute to their learning.

APPROACHES TO CURRICULUM

Over the last two decades, there has been increasing global interest in the role of curriculum in the lives of young children. The Organisation for Economic Cooperation and Development (OECD) has undertaken a number of international comparative studies that identify the role of curricula in young children's learning. Its *Starting Strong* reports of 2001, 2006 and 2012 have highlighted the importance of identified curriculum goals, appropriate pedagogies, and monitoring and assessment of children's learning as key contributors to both the quality of the program offered as well as the educational benefits and outcomes for children. The *Starting Strong III* report (OECD, 2012) notes that the approach to curricula by different countries varies greatly and is an expression of many factors, including:

- a society's values
- research findings about children and learning that are relevant to that country

213

Perspectives and practices in teaching and leadership

- community expectations for learning throughout life
- the degree to which standards and assessment are valued
- the qualifications and experience of educators, and
- the culture and languages of the country.

Although these factors are highly variable from country to country, there is now general agreement across much of the world that a coordinated and high-quality approach to articulating curriculum guidelines for young children provides direction for their learning and leads to positive child outcomes (Frede, 1998, cited in OECD, 2012).

The early childhood curriculum context in Australia

A key question relating to notions of curriculum, pedagogy and assessment in early childhood programs is perhaps 'what are we aiming for'? Within the Australian context answers can be found in the policy documents of both the National Quality Framework (NQF) for Early Childhood and in the Australian Curriculum for schools. Both of these documents reflect the position adopted by each of Australia's state and territory governments along with the Australian government in what is known as the Melbourne Declaration on Educational Goals for Young Australians (Ministerial Council on Education, Employment, Training and Youth Affairs, 2008). The Declaration set the direction for education in Australia and was broadly premised on a commitment by all governments that all young Australians become:

- successful learners
- confident and creative individuals, and
- active and informed citizens.

These broad goals can be readily identified in the development goals of the Australian Curriculum for schools and are easily recognisable in the five learning outcomes that form part of the EYLF. In this context, curriculum is both a strategy to ensure individual children have opportunities for full participation in Australian society and also to realise the long-term aspirations for a successful and globally competitive nation.

Within Australia, children in their early years might experience a number of different approaches to curriculum. Most Australian early childhood settings are now required to work with the EYLF or another approved framework. In the middle school years, children who attend school-aged care, such as outside school hours care programs or vacation care, will have experience of the My Time, Our Place: Framework for School Age Care in Australia. Essentially a framework emphasising play and leisure, My Time, Our Place aligns closely with the EYLF and provides continuity of learning through Pedagogical Principles, Practice and Learning Outcomes that are common to both documents. During the compulsory school years from foundation to Year 12, children across Australia will experience the Australian Curriculum, or an approved state/territory interpretation.

Belonging, Being and Becoming: The early years learning framework for Australia

In 2009 the Australian government launched the EYLF as part of a broad early childhood reform agenda. The EYLF was developed as a guide for educators to support them in planning for children's learning. While previously many of the states and territories of Australia had developed their own curriculum documents, this was Australia's first national learning framework designed for children from birth to five years, including the transition to school. As the title 'Learning Framework' suggests, this is not a prescriptive curriculum, but rather is intended as a framework guide. It supports educators 'in their curriculum decision-making and assists in planning, implementing and evaluating quality . . . It also underpins the implementation of a more specific curriculum relevant to each local community and early childhood setting' (DEEWR, 2009, p. 8).

The EYLF is an example of what the OECD (2012) refers to as a comprehensive or holistic approach to early childhood curriculum. Such an approach attempts to balance academic goals with a focus on child interest, creativity and wellbeing. It also places emphasis on the inputs to the educational program—in other words what educators do and how they teach. This is in contrast to more outputs-oriented curricula models that emphasise predetermined outcomes, often of an academic nature, and place importance on specifying the content that is to be learned rather than the pedagogies of teaching and learning.

The EYLF is underpinned by three broad notions that guide the work of educators—belonging, being and becoming—and provide a vision for children's experiences in early childhood settings. This vision emphasises the importance of all three notions being in balance and that no one concept is more important than the others.

Belonging—acknowledges that human connection is essential to wellbeing and development. Belonging builds confidence, reliance and trust. The notion of belonging provides educators with the opportunity to place significant emphasis in their curriculum planning on building relationships, emphasising the importance of partnerships and making space for many views and voices.

Being—celebrates children for who they are right now—not only on what they might become. This notion enables educators to take the time to get to know individual children, and to listen with all of their senses to better understand the social, cultural and spiritual life of children. It celebrates the joys of being a baby, toddler or preschooler without feeling the pressure to 'get ready' for the next stage.

Becoming—acknowledges that the early years are foundational to life. Much learning and development takes place in the early years and children increasingly take on new capabilities and understandings. Becoming promotes a curriculum that is suitably challenging, yet not frustrating. It requires educators to be responsive to children's ideas, thinking and theories, but to also extend and introduce new concepts and have high expectations for each child's learning.

Drawing on widely accepted philosophical and theoretical understandings of children and their learning, the EYLF reflects approaches to teaching and learning that are considered important in the Australian context. Practices like cultural competence, high expectations and equity reflect the diversity of Australian society, while learning through play, the significance of the learning environment and an educator's responsiveness to children articulate some of the key understandings from research about how young children learn. Table 10.1 summarises the key components of the EYLF and shows the emphasis that is placed on pedagogies and practice along with the learning outcomes.

The National Quality Framework and National Quality Standard

As part of the Australian Early Childhood Reform Agenda, the National Quality Framework (NQF) was developed following agreement by all state and territory

Planning for children's learning: curriculum, pedagogy and assessment

Table 10.1: Components of the Early Years Learning Framework and My Time, Our Place Framework

Principles	Practice	Learning outcomes
• Secure, respectful and reciprocal relationships • Partnerships with families • High expectations and equity • Respect for diversity • Ongoing learning and reflective practice	• Holistic approaches • Responsiveness to children • Learning through play • Intentional teaching • Learning environments • Cultural competence • Continuity of learning and transitions • Assessment for learning	• Children have a strong sense of identity • Children are connected with and contribute to their world • Children have a strong sense of wellbeing • Children are confident and involved learners • Children are effective communicators

Sources: Curriculum documents cited in the title, DEEWR, 2009

governments along with the Australian government to provide a framework for quality for early childhood settings across the country. The NQF calls for nationally consistent standards that contribute to better educational and development outcomes for all Australian children. A key component of the NQF is the National Quality Standard (NQS). You can find out more about the NQS at: <www.acecqa.gov.au/quality-areas#sthash.RnGfuQJn.dpuf>.

The NQS includes a ratings system that requires early childhood settings in Australia to demonstrate ongoing improvement and meet or exceed the benchmarks of the NQS. State and territory assessors visit early childhood settings to monitor and rate centres on each of the quality areas. The Pedagogical Principles and Practice of the EYLF are woven throughout each Quality Area of the NQS. In particular, Quality Area 1 (Educational Program and Practice) has an emphasis on curriculum, pedagogy and assessment with guidance for educators in how they might show evidence of their intent for children's learning. Within this standard, early childhood educators are required to be familiar with all aspects of the EYLF and able to articulate their understandings of the principles, practice and learning outcomes as they relate to their work with young children.

The Australian Curriculum

The Australian Curriculum describes what young Australians should learn as they progress through school from the foundation year to the end of compulsory schooling in Year 12. Within this broad span, the early years of school generally refer to children from five to eight years of age and are covered within the Australian Curriculum in the foundation year, Year 1 and Year 2. The Australian Curriculum, Assessment and Reporting Authority (ACARA) is responsible for the development, monitoring and reviewing of the curriculum; however, implementation of the Australian Curriculum sits with the state and territory governments who have policy responsibility for schools. The following table outlines the seven core learning areas, seven general capabilities and three cross-curriculum priorities that make up the Australian Curriculum.

The core learning areas identify the broad curriculum areas that will be covered in the lessons and learning experiences planned for children in each grade or year. Each of the learning areas contain content descriptions that specify what children will be taught. They also establish the achievement standards, which set out the depth of understanding and sophistication of skill expected of students at different points in their schooling. These achievement standards form the assessment criteria that teachers use to determine the level of achievement of each child against each standard.

Table 10.2: Components of the Australian Curriculum: foundation to Year 10

Core learning areas	General capabilities	Cross-curriculum priorities
English	Literacy	Aboriginal and Torres Strait Islander histories and cultures
Mathematics	Numeracy	Asia and Australia's engagement with Asia
Science	Information and communication technology	Sustainability
Humanities and social science	Critical and creative thinking	
The arts	Personal and social capability	
Technologies	Ethical understanding	
Health and physical education	Intercultural understanding	

Source: www.australiancurriculum.edu.au

The general capabilities refer to the dispositions, skills, understandings and capabilities that will assist children to contribute successfully throughout their life. These capabilities are woven throughout the core learning areas so that children encounter them within the context of other learning. You will notice that the general capabilities align closely with the Learning Outcomes of the EYLF (DEEWR, 2009) (see Table 10.1). This provides a clear link between the various curricula documents that children will encounter and promotes continuity for children's learning throughout their early and middle childhood education experiences.

The cross-curriculum priorities reflect the broader goals pertinent to contemporary Australian society and are designed to equip children to engage effectively in a globalised world. The focus of these priorities is to assist children to make sense of the world in which they live and make an important contribution to building the social, intellectual and creative capital of the nation. They are:

- *Aboriginal and Torres Strait Islander histories and cultures*—to ensure that all young Australians are given the opportunity to gain a deeper understanding and appreciation of Aboriginal and Torres Strait Islander histories and cultures, their significance for Australia and the impact these have had and continue to have on our world.
- *Asia and Australia's engagement with Asia*—to reflect the importance of young people knowing about Australia's engagement with Asia as a regional neighbour. As they develop a better understanding of the countries and cultures of the Asia region they will appreciate the economic, political and cultural interconnections that Australia has with the region.
- *Sustainability*—to allow young people to develop an appreciation of the need for more sustainable patterns of living, and to build capacities for thinking, valuing and acting necessary to create a more sustainable future. (from Connor, 2011)

The Australian Curriculum represents a content-oriented or academic approach to curriculum. It gives significant focus to the content of curriculum areas and is explicit about what should be taught and the standards of the learning that are expected by children at each year level. The focus of this style of curriculum is on the outputs—or the outcomes of learning. There is

Perspectives and practices in teaching and leadership

little guidance as to the inputs—or the pedagogies, principles or practices that underpin the learning.

The different styles of curriculum that are evident between the Australian Curriculum and the EYLF reflect different philosophical positions about the role and purpose of curriculum. They also reflect understandings of children's learning and how it changes as children mature and develop. As a learning framework, the EYLF promotes the importance of pedagogical relationships in the lives of young children and their families while articulating broad learning outcomes for educators to be mindful of as they plan for and assess children's learning. The Australian Curriculum gives focus to the content and outcomes of learning and articulates more specific direction for what should be taught.

There is emerging work showing links between the EYLF and the Australian Curriculum. A joint paper titled *Foundations for Learning: Relationships between the Early Years Learning Framework and the Australian Curriculum* was released by Early Childhood Australia (ECA) and the Australian Curriculum, Assessment and Reporting Authority (ACARA) in 2011 (Connor 2011). This paper makes clear links between the Learning Outcomes of the EYLF and the Core Learning Areas of the Australian Curriculum and will be a useful tool for early childhood teachers as they seek ways to promote continuity of learning and transitions for children. As early childhood teachers may work with each of the EYLF, My Time, Our Place and the Australian Curriculum they are encouraged to look for alignments and links among the documents and find ways to use the strengths of each approach to inform their teaching and curriculum decisions. No matter the style of a curriculum document, early childhood educators are charged with the responsibility to demonstrate professional judgement, reflective practice and analytic thinking. No curriculum document is intended as a prescription that a teacher merely implements without thought. Each document requires a high level of interpretation and adaptation to meet the unique needs of individual children, to various groups and communities and to changing circumstances and priorities for learning.

Thinking critically about curriculum

Understanding and working with learning frameworks and curriculum documents may be a high priority for early childhood educators, but there are other aspects of curriculum that may not be as explicit yet can still be powerful in the learning experiences of young children. If considering the definition of curriculum from the EYLF as 'all the interactions, experiences, activities, routines and events, planned and unplanned, that occur in an environment designed to foster children's learning and development' (DEEWR, 2009, p. 45), the notion of curriculum is far more expansive than the written documents. Blaise and Nuttall (2010) have summarised the complexity of curriculum using five key concepts.

- *The intended curriculum*—refers to planned and anticipated learning that takes place when an educator is guided by a curriculum document or specific learning outcome.
- *The enacted curriculum*—refers to the variation in curriculum depending on the individual educator, or his/her personality, style and knowledge of the children he/she is working with. The educator's core beliefs about children or the 'gaze' or lens that he/she interprets children through is also significant to the enacted curriculum.
- *The hidden curriculum*—refers to the learning that is often unintended and can pass by unnoticed. It often occurs when practices are assumed or uncritically accepted as views about gender, justice, fairness and power become embedded in the educator's actions and words. Hidden learning also takes place when educators shy away from confronting tough issues, such as bias and discrimination, or feel that such concepts are beyond children's capacity or are inappropriate to discuss with them.
- *The null curriculum*—refers to the deliberate omission of certain topics and experiences that are often based on an educator's own level of discomfort with issues he/she finds challenging. Sexuality, death or domestic violence, for example, are part of the world of young children and they may wish to explore these issues to better understand them.
- *The lived curriculum*—refers to the combination of the intended, enacted, hidden and null curriculum to view curriculum as the experience of the child rather than simply the intention of the educator. This concept invites us to view children as protagonists in curriculum rather than the passive recipients of a government-endorsed document.

Perspectives and practices in teaching and leadership

Early childhood teachers are charged with the responsibility to be critical curriculum thinkers and to use ongoing reflection and critical conversations to challenge their assumptions and beliefs. The potential of curriculum can only be realised when educators engage in thoughtful and reflective practice and view curriculum as a tool that they can influence and adapt to promote the highest expectations for their own teaching and for children's learning.

UNDERSTANDING PEDAGOGY

No matter how well written or comprehensive a curriculum document, the very essence of teaching and learning is found in the thinking and practice of educators and the artful way they apply knowledge to their teaching. Pedagogy in an early childhood context refers to the actions and decision of educators that affect children's learning. The term is relatively new to early childhood contexts in Australia. Perhaps previously referred to as teaching strategies or techniques, these terms alone do not capture the significance of responsive, caring and reciprocal relationships in working with very young children. Rather than being responsible for the transmission of content and ideas through direct instruction, the term 'pedagogy' lends itself to practices that might involve watching and waiting, suggesting, questioning, revisiting, extending and indeed playing. The term also suggests that the teacher might not always be in the lead or always know what the outcome might be. It provides scope to respond in many different ways and, in keeping with the European traditions of the term 'pedagogy', the child is encouraged to be empowered—to demonstrate agency and influence his/her own and others' learning.

The EYLF highlights a number of pedagogical principles and practices that underpin approaches to teaching and learning. There is not scope within this chapter to examine all pedagogical possibilities thoroughly. What follows is a more general discussion of some of the pedagogical approaches that have been shown to positively influence learning outcomes for children across the birth to eight years age range.

Each of the pedagogical approaches discussed below has been found to contribute positively to children's learning trajectories. They are thoughtful, evidence-based and intentional pedagogies that educators are encouraged to work with to bring curriculum to life and enhance the learning potential of children's early childhood experiences. They reflect the educational goals for

Australian children to be ambitious, emphasising high expectations for every child, but they also promote thoughtful and appropriate practices that respond to individual differences and the significant learning and developmental progression that children experience in the early years.

Interest-based learning

Often promoted as the basis for learning in early childhood, interest-based learning is perhaps a largely misunderstood concept. Premised on ideas emerging from the Project Approach and Emergent Curriculum (Jones & Nimmo, 1994; Katz & Chard, 1992), interest-based learning has its origins in the theoretical perspectives of John Dewey, an American education theorist who promoted progressive, real-life experience as learning. Children's interests and life experiences form the basis of what content will be explored, with a focus on children's knowledge, questions and theories. The pedagogies involved in promoting interest-based learning include listening carefully and thoughtfully to children's ideas and questions, watching intently to pick up on subtle cues and conceptions and engaging in extended conversations and investigations of ideas to draw out potential learning possibilities. It is not the case that educators take a passive, back-seat role in interest-based learning. Responsive educators are integral to rich and meaningful interest-based learning. The Researching Effective Pedagogies in the Early Years (REPEY) study (Siraj-Blatchford et al., 2002) found that in the highest quality settings there was a balance of educator-led and child-led learning. This suggests that interest-based learning should not be conceptualised as only about children's interests. Educator-introduced ideas can lead to an expanded range of interests that can challenge children to think in more complex ways. Educators who work with interest-based approaches look for the learning possibilities and are mindful of the learning outcomes that might be explored through a range of different interests and ideas.

Intentional teaching

A complex and challenging term in an early childhood context, intentional teaching involves educators being 'deliberate, purposeful and thoughtful in their decisions and actions . . . the opposite of teaching by rote' (DEEWR, 2009, p. 45). The notion of intentional teaching emerged from the HighScope and Creative

Curriculum approaches (see Epstein, 2007) that were developed as part of two influential studies of young children in the United States: the Perry Preschool Project and the Abecedarian Project. Intentional teaching in these contexts was designed to encourage early childhood educators to plan, implement and reflect with children about their learning and ensure that children gained the most from their play experiences.

In the Australian context, intentional teaching is a focus of the EYLF as it encourages educators to use intentional strategies, such as modelling, demonstrating, explaining, shared thinking and problem solving to extend children's thinking and learning. It promotes opportunities for teachers to make intentional provisions and to be actively involved in children's play and investigations. Intentional teaching can take place in the midst of play experiences when an educator chooses to extend the play through adding new resources, inspiring more complex thinking through questioning or provocation, or even by inviting children to contribute different perspectives or ideas. It can also mean that an educator draws children's attention to particular learning or exposes them to ideas and thinking that might open up new possibilities for thinking. It does not require educators to withdraw children for specific learning or to set aside a special time to teach a particular concept or skill. Intentional teaching is about deciding how it might be best to draw children's attention to new information or ideas that might not necessarily happen through play alone.

Content knowledge

An emerging area of research in early childhood is highlighting the benefits of educators' knowledge of curriculum content and concepts. The REPEY study (Siraj-Blatchford et al., 2002) identified that educators' knowledge of content about curriculum (for example, science and phonologic knowledge) was a vital component of early years teaching and just as important as it is in later stages of education. While much emphasis has traditionally been given to play-based pedagogies and interest-based investigations, there has been less attention to promoting the value of the educator's own knowledge of curriculum content. In-depth knowledge of the content of curriculum enables educators to expand children's thinking and problem solving. Having a grasp of mathematical concepts and the appropriate language to describe and explain concepts to children will expose children to deeper understandings of their initial ideas and questions. In the same way educators' knowledge of the arts and their skill in working with various tools and technologies can enhance children's experience and encourage new and emerging interests in innovation and creativity. Educators who are themselves inquisitive and thirsty for knowledge bring greater depth and richness to the curriculum that stems from the confidence they have in their own content knowledge.

Pedagogical relationships

Relationships and partnerships are widely understood to be the foundations of sound early childhood pedagogy. For young children, partnerships between educators and families are seen as essential in creating a secure and trusting bridge between home and the early childhood setting. Such relationships establish possibilities for sharing in curriculum decisions and embedding the knowledge and experiences of families into the learning experiences at the early childhood setting. Sharing in the child's world of culture, religion, family life and special events can offer an authentic richness to the curriculum and, as a community of learners, all children and families within the early childhood setting are exposed to expanded knowledge and experience. In the same way, trusting relationships with families can bring to light difficulties and challenges for children. When considered from the perspective of pedagogical relationships, educators make key decisions about how to support a child who is experiencing challenging circumstances and identify ways to sensitively respond to a child's concerns or fears.

Relationships with children within an early childhood setting demand a comprehensive skill set for early childhood educators. Cultural competence, responsiveness, reflectiveness and respectfulness are just some of the qualities suggested as contributing to best learning outcomes for young children (DEEWR, 2009). While these might appear as a list of natural dispositions, they are in fact intentional pedagogies that early childhood educators demonstrate when they work with young children in education and care settings. Such approaches to pedagogy reflect a particular image of a competent and capable child who is a partner in their learning experience rather than the recipient of a more powerful adult's knowledge. Educators recognise each child's agency and capacity to contribute to decisions that affect them, including their learning.

Perspectives and practices in teaching and leadership

WHAT ABOUT ASSESSMENT?

As the third component of this learning trilogy, assessment is an equally important aspect in contributing to high-quality curriculum decision-making. As previously discussed, the notion of assessment in an early childhood context can be quite different to the way that assessment is conceptualised in later grades of school. If understood as 'the ways in which, in our everyday practice, we observe children's learning, strive to understand it, and then put our understanding to good use' (Drummond, 2012, p. 12), we can view this approach to authentic assessment as an integral component of curriculum and pedagogy, not something that is done only at the end of a learning sequence. As the EYLF suggests, 'assessment is part of an ongoing cycle that includes planning, documenting and evaluating children's learning' (DEEWR, 2009, p. 17).

The notion of *authentic assessment* is important in early childhood as it involves observing children's abilities, theories and questions in their everyday play and learning experiences (Mueller, 2006). Importantly, authentic assessment illuminates the possibilities for curriculum by focusing on what children know and can do, rather than highlighting their deficits. It does not predetermine a standard or benchmark and does not require setting up experiences to test children's knowledge or skills. Authentic assessment involves documenting or recording observations that enable educators to track children's progression and show evidence of their learning journey, or, as the EYLF describes it, the 'distance travelled' (DEEWR, 2009, p. 17). In this way authentic assessment is about gathering information and insights about the small and often quiet steps in learning as well as the more obvious or significant events. Importantly, authentic assessment should focus the educator's attention on children's holistic learning and development and can be sensitive to the cultural, linguistic and developmental abilities of each child (Flottman, Stewart and Tayler, 2011). This holistic view acknowledges that children learn many things through each experience and enables educators to capture the complexity of children's learning rather than measuring children's achievement in discrete areas. For example, a child playing with unit blocks will be learning about problem solving, patterning, shape, balance and creativity but will also be engaged in learning about him/herself, including his/her confidence, persistence and ability to represent his/her ideas through blocks. The child may engage with others and negotiate ideas and

226

Planning for children's learning: curriculum, pedagogy and assessment

solutions, persuade others to follow his/her lead, be exposed to new thinking and need to articulate his/her ideas. There are multiple possibilities for learning in this play experience. If we focus attention on only the child's ability to use the blocks, we miss so much about all of the other learning.

The educational theorist John Dewey said, 'Observation alone is not enough. We have to understand the significance of what we see, hear, and touch. This significance consists of the consequences that will result when what is seen is acted upon' (Dewey, 1938, p. 68). Making sense of what we observe or analysing what we see is essential in making observation data useful and meaningful. It enables us to assess what we observe using knowledge of children's development and understandings about how children learn, and assists us to plan future experiences that will extend and enrich children's experience. Without analysis, observation data are just interesting stories.

The National Quality Standard (NQS) requires educators to show evidence of their assessment of children's learning. The NQS suggests using a variety of strategies to collect, document, organise, synthesise and interpret the information that they gather to assess children's learning (Australian Children's Education and Care Quality Authority [ACECQA], 2011). Including both formative and summative assessement records can help to thoroughly analyse observations and create meaningful records of children's learning journeys.

Formative assessments are observations of children's everyday experiences. They might include jottings, annotated photographs, work samples, anecdotes, running records or transcripts of conversations. Formative assessments help to build a picture of the complexity of children's learning and should include observations across the range of experiences that children engage in, including play, investigations, routines, more specific learning tasks and conversations. They will be most useful when they include observations of both individual and group experiences that reflect how a child works in a range of play and learning situations.

Summative assessments are about bringing together a range of observations to create a summary of children's learning. They often include a direct reference to the relevant learning outcomes from the learning framework or curriculum document. Often completed at the end of term or perhaps twice each year, they represent the accumulated knowledge about a child's learning journey over a period of time. Summative assessments can be a good way of communicating with families about a child's strengths and interests as well as documenting any concerns or challenges a child might be facing.

Both forms of assessment contribute essential insights into what children are gaining from their experiences in early childhood settings. They help educators to ensure that the curriculum they plan for children is rich and challenging and select pedagogies that will extend children's learning towards the relevant learning outcomes.

CONCLUSION

This chapter has explored the interconnections between curriculum, pedagogy and assessment. It suggests the importance of the educator's role in making thoughtful connections between each of these concepts and actively reflecting on how they inform each other. Curriculum not only represents the written texts that come in the form of curricula documents or learning frameworks, but the actions and decisions of educators as they interpret and adapt the documents to meet the diverse learning contexts and individual children with whom they will work. Educators' pedagogies will be most effective when they are evidence-based and responsive to learning opportunities and the age of children, and give a focus to building authentic relationships with both children and their families. Authentic assessment informs both curriculum and pedagogies as it provides the reflective data that indicates whether interpretations and actions are effective. Assessment provides an insight into the children's responses to curriculum decisions and enables meaningful communication with families and other colleagues about ways to best support children's learning. Together these three key components require knowledgeable, thoughtful and reflective action on behalf of all educators to ensure that their work contributes to positive learning trajectories for all children.

FURTHER THINKING

1. How might educators show evidence of their curriculum and pedagogic decisions that contribute to children's learning? There are many ways of recording the educational program but how might we find efficient and effective methods that capture essential information without becoming an unnecessary regulatory burden?

2. What theories underpin my approach to curriculum, pedagogy and assessment? Am I able to explain to others why I do things the way I do?

3. How might educators be able to see beyond a narrow interpretation of learning outcomes? If we want to ensure a truly rich learning environment what strategies might help educators to reflect on how meaningful their approaches are?

4. How might educators provide smooth links and transitions for children who are moving from one curriculum approach to another? For example, when children are moving from a broadly based learning framework, such as the EYLF, onto the more outcomes- and content-oriented Australian Curriculum, how might we support the connections across settings?

5. How are the terms 'curriculum', 'pedagogy' and 'assessment' defined in other parts of the world or in other arenas of education? Why is it necessary to have clear understandings of these terms in relation to early childhood contexts in Australia?

REFERENCES

Australian Children's Education and Care Quality Authority (ACECQA) (2011). *Guide to the National Quality Standard*. Retrieved 10 October 2014, <http://files.acecqa.gov.au/files/National-Quality-Framework-Resources-Kit/NQF03-Guide-to-NQS-130902.pdf>.

Blaise, M. & Nuttall, J. (2010). *Learning to Teach in the Early Years Classroom*. South Melbourne: Oxford University Press.

Connor, J. (2011). *Foundations for Learning: Relationships between the Early Years Learning Framework and the Australian Curriculum*. Retrieved 10 October 2014, <www.earlychildhoodaustralia.org.au/pdf/ECA_ACARA_Foundations_Paper/ECA_ACARA_Foundations_Paper_FINAL.pdf>.

Department of Education, Employment and Workplace Relations (DEEWR) (2009). Belonging, Being and Becoming: The early years learning framework for Australia. Canberra: Australian Government Department of Education, Employment and Workplace Relations for COAG. Retrieved 10 October 2014, <www.coag.gov.au/sites/default/files/early_years_learning_framework.pdf>.

Dewey, J. (1938). *Experience and Education*. New York: Macmillan Publishing Company.

Drummond, M.J. (2012). *Assessing Children's Learning*. Abingdon, UK: Routledge.

Epstein, A.S. (2007). *The Intentional Teacher: Choosing the best strategies for young children's learning*. Washington DC: National Association for the Education of Young Children (NAEYC).

Flottman, R., Stewart, L. & Tayler, C. (2011). *Victorian Early Years Learning and Development Framework. Evidence Paper Practice Principle 7: Assessment for learning and development*. Department of Education and Early Childhood Development and the University of Melbourne. Retrieved 10 October 2014, <www.education.vic.gov.au/Documents/childhood/providers/edcare/pracassess.pdf>.

Jones, E. & Nimmo, J. (1994). *Emergent Curriculum*. Washington DC: NAEYC.

Katz, L. & Chard, S. (1992). *Engaging Children's Minds: The project approach*. Norwood NJ: Ablex Publishing Corporation.

Ministerial Council on Education, Employment, Training and Youth Affairs (MCEETYA) (2008). Melbourne Declaration on Educational Goals for Young Australians. Melbourne: MCEETYA.

Mueller, J. (2006). Authentic assessment toolbox. Retrieved 10 October 2014 <http://jonathan.mueller.faculty.noctrl.edu/toolbox/whatisit.htm#looklike>.

Organisation for Economic Co-operation and Development (OECD) (2006). *Starting Strong II*. Paris: OECD.

—— (2012). *Starting Strong III: A Quality Toolbox for Early Childhood Education and Care—Designing and implementing curriculum and standards*. DOI 10.1787/9789264123564-5-en.

Petrie, P., Boddy, J., Cameron, C., Heptinstall, E., McQuail, S., Simon, A. & Wigfall. V. (2009). *Pedagogy: A holistic, personal approach to work with children and young people, across services—European models for practice, training, education and qualification*. London: Thomas Coram Research Institute.

Siraj-Blatchford, I., Sylva, K., Muttock, S., Gilden, R. & Bell, D. (2002). *Researching Effective Pedagogy in the Early Years*. DfES Research Report 365. London: HMSO Queens Printer.

Chapter 11

Relationships between staff, children and families

Karen Hawkins

In this chapter you will find:
- an outline of the importance of relationships in early childhood settings
- listening pedagogy
- creating quality interactions
- building relationships with parents, families and the community
- developing relationships among educators, staff and para professionals.

This chapter explores the practice of relationships in early childhood settings, identifying why relationships are important for children's learning and development. It is not possible to teach without having relationships with children, and this chapter therefore highlights research investigating responsive and respectful relationships between educators and children in order to support children's learning and development (National Scientific Council on the Developing Child, 2009). As the quality and responsiveness of relationships between educators and families are of importance for children's learning and development (Redding, Murphy & Sheley, 2011; Thornton & Brunton, 2010), this chapter also highlights the importance of working collaboratively with families and the broader community. Teamwork and working collaboratively with other early childhood educators is a key part of relationship building. This chapter also explores the significance of building positive relationships among educators in early childhood settings.

To assist with this chapter, and to explore if what the research tells us is of

Perspectives and practices in teaching and leadership

significance to contemporary Australian early childhood education, the author held conversations with a number of stakeholders regarding the importance of relationship building and how their early childhood centres went about this. The stakeholders included directors, early childhood educators and parents from four early childhood centres on the Far North Coast of New South Wales. All stakeholders highlighted relationship building as a significant aspect of early childhood education and a major component of the work of early childhood educators. The children in the settings were identified as the focal point for these relationships. Every conversation highlighted that it was also vital that early childhood educators build strong, respectful and reciprocal relationships with parents/families, staff and the wider community.

PRACTISING RELATIONSHIPS WITH CHILDREN

Children are the core of what early childhood educators do. It stands to reason, therefore, that early childhood educators and children have relationships. Linda and Nicki from Centre A summed up what all other conversations highlighted:

> **Linda:** Our relationships with the children form the basis of our work.

> **Nicki:** Absolutely, we're here for the children first and foremost; and you must earn their trust and respect by forging those respectful relationships . . . That's the most important aspect of our work and the only place to start.

Clearly the educators in the above conversation have positive relationships with the children in their centre. However, relationships can be good/bad, trusting/ untrusting, respectful/disrespectful, harmonious/discordant, warm/cold or equal/unequal. It is usually how educators view children that determines how they build relationships with them. If an educator views children as powerless, passive, weak and dependent the relationship will be adult-centred and unequal. If, however, the educator views children as active agents, the relationship will be quite different.

Relationships between staff, children and families

> **Sophie (Educator, Centre B):** The base that supports my relationships with children is that I see them as capable learners and I want them to have agency in their learning. I'm learning with the children . . . This week the children wanted to build a fairy garden. I don't know how to build a fairy garden; so we researched together through iPads and books. I actually learned a lot about fairies and fairy gardens. That's bonding and coming together for a common goal. That builds relationships with children.

Recent developments in sociology, developmental psychology, feminist poststructural theories and child rights have helped produce a model of young children as a social actor constructing their identity, generating and articulating their ideas and with a right to contribute to and participate in society (Corsaro, 2005; Department of Education, Employment and Workplace Relations [DEEWR], 2009; United Nations, 1989). With these understandings in mind, early childhood educators should forge authentic, respectful, reciprocal relationships with children, to ensure their participation and contributions are valued.

> **Misty (Parent, Centre A):** I know that Ellie is valued and respected here. She just loves it . . . And they have things like the Gold Box; where families can write about something that's important, that's happening or happened and the teachers read it out to the class, then it goes into the children's portfolio. They have the Birth Story, where the family writes about the day the child was born, and it's read out on their birthday. It all just shows respect for the child and the family. It's important for me that Ellie is respected and listened to . . . I see it not just with Ellie but with all the children. They're respected, listened to and understood.

Developing a listening pedagogy

To develop relationships with children, early childhood educators can develop a *listening pedagogy* whereby they pay close attention to the constructs, concerns and interests that engross the children in their settings (Dahlberg & Moss, 2005; Rinaldi, 2005). Egan (2009) suggests, 'a listening pedagogy that both respects children's capabilities and rights and supports their learning in the most effective

Perspectives and practices in teaching and leadership

and beneficial manner is being increasingly recognized as fundamental to good practice in early years education' (p. 55). Developing a listening pedagogy that supports relationship building with young children is not an easy task and requires effort, attention and awareness over time.

> **Noni (Educator, Centre C):** If there's no relationship then learning can't take place; it's as simple as that. So, if you have a good relationship with children then they're prepared to invest in you, spend time with you and learn with you . . . You have to be an active listener . . . they know that you've listened to them and understand them and know what's going on in their lives; so they feel a sense of belonging. This active listening drives the planning; acting on the children's interests.

To complement this listening pedagogy and further assist relationship building with children, educators may also engage in what Sylva et al. (2003) refer to as *shared sustained thinking*. Siraj-Blatchford and Sylva (2004) describe this as *sustained cognitive engagements* between the adult and the child and suggest that 'the cognitive construction in this case would be mutual where each party engages with the understanding of the other and learning is achieved through a process of reflexive co-construction' (p. 720). What is highlighted here is that not only are relationships being built but co-constructed learning is also taking place. Clearly learning is a social endeavour and communication is essential to its success (Vygotsky, 1978).

> **Jenna (Director, Centre D):** It's through the environment that we build strong relationships with our children. We spend time with them in, say, the veggie patch, and we talk one-on-one with them about their likes and dislikes and interests and home. Meaningful conversations. It's a natural way to communicate; not forced or coerced.

From birth infants engage in communicative practices (crying, smiling, gurgling, laughing) and these encourage social interactions with those around them, which, in turn, encourages language, learning and development. Very young children often depend on older members of the family or adults to sustain communication and interactions. These communications and interactions are more meaningful if the relationship with the older member of the family or the adult is warm, strong and respectful. The infant or young child will *want* to engage with someone with whom they feel comfortable and with whom they have a connection and attachment. Indeed, infants and young children have an attachment to their early childhood educators in that they offer emotional and physical care, and they are consistent and predictable in children's lives (Bowman, Donovan & Burns, 2001). Therefore, the quality of the relationship between the infant and the educator is of great significance. Educators promote Learning Outcome 1 of the Early Years Learning Framework (EYLF) (DEEWR, 2009) 'when they support children's secure attachment through consistent and warm, nurturing relationships' (p. 21).

> **Casey (Director, Centre B):** To build relationships with children is just getting to know them and being with them. Know what they like, their interests, their family, know their siblings' names. Little things to us; big things to them. Greet them in the morning and give them a cuddle. Be at their level and make them feel welcome. Make this their second home; it's their place. So they feel safe and supported and enjoy the journey of their early childhood. It's a place to feel loved. It's a place for families to feel loved, valued and supported. And for educators to feel supported, valued and loved.

Creating quality interactions

The quality of the interactions and relationships between educators and children has a huge influence, not only on what children learn while in the early childhood setting, but also on their future interactions and relationships with educators in different settings, including formal school settings (Arthur et al., 2015). Children are likely to have more positive and constructive interactions with their peers, and consider their early childhood/school setting in a positive light, when their relationships with their educators are warm, authentic, respectful and reciprocal. This leads to productive learning where children connect with and extend on the educational opportunities they meet (Bowman et al., 2001).

> **Sophie (Educator, B):** We have a strong relationship with the school next door that most of our children will transition to. We visit the school every Thursday morning. We go to the Library and then they have morning tea and go to the canteen. So the children get an idea of what it's like at Big School . . . so it's a really good transition for them.

Early childhood educators must provide educational opportunities and create a social environment conducive to relationship building and learning. This type of climate is characterised by respectful adult–child relationships, pro-social behaviours, complex and intricate learning-through-play opportunities and should be co-constructed with the children in the setting. When children's opinions are listened to, valued and acted upon they have feelings of self-efficacy and are more likely to engage with learning opportunities, take risks and articulate their ideas and feelings. Children feel more confident, competent and supported when educators are caring, emotionally warm and approachable and engage in reciprocal relationships. Within these reciprocal relationships clear and appropriate expectations are discussed, which, in turn, supports children to develop social competence and build meaningful and respectful relationships with other adults and their peers.

From infancy children display a range of skills when developing and maintaining friendships, communicating, playing and resolving conflicts. These relationships and interactions influence children's development and learning. The role of the early childhood educator is to not only model relationship building and pro-social behaviour, but also provide some guidance and offer suggestions and perhaps intervention in order to help children to forge positive relationships and engage successfully in social interactions.

> **Linda (Director, Centre A):** We're [the staff] continually modelling how to be respectful and how to treat one another. And the children know exactly what we expect of them when they play and interact with one another. That's been discussed from the get go.

> **Paul (Director, Centre C):** As the director I get out and play and interact with children. Respecting their play and becoming involved

Relationships between staff, children and families

in their play, and listening to children's concerns. Every single child. You need to be actively listening and acting on their concerns not dismissing them. Especially for a child who might be a bit timid or shy; becoming interested and involved in their play helps boost their confidence to feel part of the group. That they belong. And other children see that and so you're role modelling for the children, and for the teachers.

Additionally, early childhood educators provide educational opportunities and build social environments conducive to relationship building through the physical learning environments that they create.

> **Linda (Director, Centre A):** We put a lot of effort into our environment to make it welcoming and aesthetically appealing.

> **Nicki (Educator, Centre A):** I think a beautiful environment helps build relationships, not only with educators and the children but among the children themselves. There's lots of areas for big groups but also for small groups of twos and threes to chat and play. We have the fairy garden, the sensory garden, the water area behind the sand pit. And the children add to and change these areas all the time. Through the children they evolve. And there's lots of nooks and crannies that encourage fantasy play. And our library area, with the big tree, is comfortable, intriguing and inviting.

PRACTISING RELATIONSHIPS WITH PARENTS, FAMILIES AND COMMUNITY

'Educators' practices and the relationships they form with children and families have a significant effect on children's involvement and success in learning. Children thrive when families and educators work together in partnership to support young children's learning' (DEEWR, 2009, p. 9). Building relationships with families can be complex and different perspectives on certain topics (for example, toilet training, feeding and sleep practices, and managing behaviour) can contribute to the complexity and tension (Hand & Wise, 2006). Both the EYLF (DEEWR, 2009) and the Australian Children's Education and Care

Quality Authority (ACECQA) (2014) state that parents and families must be respected and acknowledged as the child's first educator and that the funds of knowledge that children bring with them to the early childhood setting are first and foremost acquired by the children through the family. Building effective, collaborative partnerships with families is the sixth quality area of the National Quality Framework (NQF) (ACECQA, 2014).

> **Jenna (Director, Centre D):** The EYLF, ACECQA and the Rights of the Child underpin our work here and heavily impact on our dealings and relationships with our stakeholders in that they mandate respect for our stakeholders: children, families, staff and community. I mean we have always been respectful and built warm relationships but it was never really mandated that we do that. The Code of Ethics says that we should have respectful relationships but now it's actually mandated. That's powerful.

Partnership versus involvement

It should be noted here that *involvement* and *partnership* are two distinct ideas. Parent/family involvement includes the activities that parents/families undertake in the early childhood setting; for example, participating in working bees, supervising a stall at the centre's/school's fete or attending a committee meeting. While these activities are very important and contribute to building relationships they do not constitute a *partnership*. A partnership is a deeper, more meaningful relationship 'characterized by mutual trust, respect and recognition, sensitivity to another's perspective, shared decision-making and shared goals' (Lindon & Rouse, 2012, p. 1). Such a partnership seeks to acknowledge the parents/families as the child's first educator and honours their knowledge and expertise to develop mutual understandings that will positively impact on the child's development and learning.

> **Nicki (Educator, Centre A):** Our committee and our parents and families share their expertise, skills, hobbies and talents with us. It's a real partnership. We have an open door policy and families contribute to the portfolios and the centre's program.

238

> **Linda (Director, Centre A):** There can be difficult times; let's face it no family is the same. But we're always respectful. And we always remember that parents are their children's first and foremost teacher and need to value and respect that.

Family diversity

Families in Australia are diverse and vary according to many aspects, such as culture, religion, economic status, structure (for example, blended, extended and single-parent families) and sexuality (for example, gay, lesbian and trans-gendered families). Some of these families fall outside of what society views as the 'norm' and, therefore, these families may not see themselves depicted in the literature read, the images displayed and the play resources available in the centre/school.

Kitson and Bowes (2010) suggest that early childhood education must incorporate Indigenous ways of knowing 'to make early learning attractive and accessible to Indigenous families' (p. 81). It is also suggested that educators from the diverse backgrounds that reflect those of the families and community in which the setting is situated should be employed. Not only should educators form positive relationships with parents, but also extended family members (such as grandparents) and friends who are significant in the lives of the children and may be the person who drops off and collects the child or who may be the emergency contact. It is of great importance that educators are inclusive and respectful in their interactions with those people identified as significant to the child by the parents/family.

> **Sophie (Educator, Centre B):** Families and extended families, like grandparents and uncles and aunts, are important to our centre and we build warm happy relationships with them from the beginning of the year. I don't think relationships just happen, it takes time and you have to work at it and spend time talking and listening. Communication is very important. You need to listen a lot. And each family is different and we respect that; and we respect their ideas. When children see this, they begin to trust us as real people.

Perspectives and practices in teaching and leadership

Cultural competence

Highlighted in the above discussion is the need for cultural competence. Educators who are culturally competent respect, support and promote the three Ds (difference, diversity and dignity) and the numerous ways of knowing, seeing and living (Hawkins, 2014). They see value and benefit in celebrating diversity and have the ability to appreciate and respect differences. 'This is evident in everyday practice when educators demonstrate an ongoing commitment to developing their own cultural competence in a two way process with families and communities . . . developing skills for communication and interaction across cultures' (DEEWR, 2009, p. 16). While open communication is of significance it is more important to have respectful, friendly and helpful communication at a level that all parties understand and where they are positioned equally. When educators understand that *all* families have valuable knowledge that they can share, they initiate interactions and forge relationships with every family in their setting, and not just the ones with whom they feel comfortable. Therefore, educators need to reflect on their interactions with all the families in their setting and resolve any power differential and reposition the families as experts, allowing there to be a two-way exchange of knowledge between each party. Blaise and Nuttall (2011) refer to these types of interactions and relationships as *transformative relationships*. When educators value the diversity of families and communities, and the articulated hopes of the families that are held for their children, educators are able to motivate children to learn and reinforce their perception of themselves as having a strong sense of identity and as capable learners (DEEWR, 2009).

> **Jenna (Director, Centre D):** It can't be tokenistic when it comes to respecting Aboriginal and Torres Strait Islander culture and all cultures for that matter. So, it is not just during NAIDOC week that we show respect . . . cultural competence is important to us; so we ask as a staff: How do we connect with the diverse cultures that are in our community? So, yes, posters, puppets, stories, we invite the local Bundjalung people in to talk with the kids and share their knowledge.

Incorporated into valuing the diversity of families is an understanding of contemporary Australian families. A major factor that affects parental involvement

240

Relationships between staff, children and families

and partnerships is employment. It is now commonplace for both parents to work. Often parents work long hours and/or engage in shift work. Hughes and MacNaughton (2002) challenge early childhood education to consider how they can encourage parental partnerships while accommodating such diverse work patterns. For example, meetings and social functions will need to be scheduled according to these work patterns. It should be noted that there is no right way to create partnerships with families. Some families will be very involved with the setting while others are not. Additionally, the depth of engagement may ebb and wane according to what is going on in the family at any given time. For example, a new baby may cause the parents to be not as visible at the setting as previously. Educators should accept that families can participate in different ways and that participation alone is not a partnership; families have the right to choose how they involve themselves in the setting. Hadley (2012) argues that partnership building should be treated as an equity issue with each family treated individually. This requires educators to know each family and to be aware of any critical issues families may be facing (for example, a new baby or an ill family member) and provide opportunities to privately discuss these issues in a participatory, non-judgemental and mutually respectful manner (Rodd, 2013).

> **Danielle (Parent, Centre B):** Parents, anyone can stay as long as they want. They can be part of the morning program or they can leave. And conversation is always offered to you. It's very respectful, you never feel judged. As a parent I feel that you're always listened to and action taken if it's needed.

Strategies for relationship building

Educators support and enhance collaborative partnerships between themselves and parents/families when they:

- Involve parents/families in the development and/or evaluation of the setting's philosophy, vision, and mission statements, goals, policies and procedures and program.

> **Sophie (Educator, Centre B):** When Casey (new director) came we reviewed our philosophy and we re-wrote it as a team with staff and families. Children are at the centre of our philosophy, and families

Perspectives and practices in teaching and leadership

very important and community, education, play . . . all important. Our philosophy stresses the importance of teamwork and we work a lot on helping each other throughout the day.

- Engage in conversation with parents/families about their values and expectations for their child.

Jenna (Director, Centre D): I make sure that I connect with each family or parent; if not on a daily basis, I make sure that I have a meaningful chat with them before the end of the week. And we have 57 families. You know something more than 'Hi, nice day' and keep walking. It gets so busy here; but you just have to make the time to connect in meaningful ways. Having a good relationship with each family is important because you get to know the child better.

- Include parents/families in the documentation of their child's learning.

Misty (Parent, Centre A): In the very first week we were given the kids' portfolios to take home and make them just how we wanted. I thought that was wonderful. Ellie was so involved and we all (the whole family) found photos to glue onto the front and back. It's so beautiful. And now you can see all these gorgeous portfolios that the kids and families have created themselves. And we can add to them whenever we like, not just the teachers. It feels like we're really included in the learning.

- Connect the curriculum to the child's interests, home and community experiences.

Sara (Parent, Centre B): They listened to me about my concerns and took everything that I said on board. Patrick and a group of boys are right into dinosaurs and they (the educators) go out of their way to make their play with dinosaurs deep and complex and meaningful. All the staff have a respect for the children's interests and their play.

Relationships between staff, children and families

- Build a sense of community within the setting by providing many and varied ways for parents/families to become part of the centre's/school's community.

Danielle (Parent, Centre B): We have a great community spirit here. We're having a Bunnings barbeque in a few weeks, and we've got a list as long as your arm with people volunteering time and materials. Parents and families just all pitch in. And if we're fundraising for resources, well we see the resources in the centre as soon as the funds have been raised. Families know that whatever is raised directly benefits the children.

- Involve the broader community in the setting by invitations to events (for example, fetes) or as resources (for example, fire brigade visits).

Linda (Director, Centre A): I'm a local girl and I know an Aboriginal man who came in and spoke to the children about bush tucker and he painted our rainbow serpent mural. The local Lions Club have been good to us and donated funds so that we could paint our fence. We often get involved with 'Clean Up Australia Day' and we have visits from the fire brigade and police, and someone from the community comes in to instruct the children in yoga. So, yes, I think we have a pretty good connection with the [local] community.

- Exchange information with the parents/family regarding the child's interests, dispositions, experiences.

Paul (Director, Centre C): I meet with parents fairly regularly, often on a daily basis; so relationships have to be strong. As a director or educator you really need to know the child and then you can go to the parent with some information about the child. It could be something positive that the child has shared with you or that you observed during the day. Then the parents realise that their child is noticed and does matter and you're showing respect for their child.

243

Perspectives and practices in teaching and leadership

- Link families with relevant and appropriate community organisations and networks.

Jan (**Educator, Centre C**): As an educator you need to listen, and try to help and support and advise about where parents could go for help. I'm not a specialist (you know Occupational Therapist or Speech Therapist) but I can point parents in the right direction to get that help.

PRACTISING RELATIONSHIPS: EDUCATORS, STAFF AND PARA PROFESSIONALS

The foundation of effective early childhood education is positive, respectful and caring relationships among the adults that care for and educate children (Arthur et al., 2015). These adults are not only parents and family members but also, and very importantly, educators. Indeed, the National Quality Standard (NQS), in Quality Area 4, promotes respectful and ethical relationships and interactions among staff working in an early childhood setting (ACECQA, 2014). Positive relationships among staff (such as educators, assistants, cooks, cleaners and gardeners) and visiting para professionals (such as speech therapists) promote many benefits. These benefits include:

- When someone feels they are valued as a team member they tend to treat others (including children) in the same way.
- Workloads and responsibilities are shared among team members. Children see this team effort and feel a sense of belonging in a safe and secure environment (Baker & Manfredi/Petitt, 2004).
- When children witness the adults in the setting working as a team and engaging in respectful, positive, supportive and cooperative relationships they observe positive role models and strategies for getting along with others, managing conflict and enjoying being a team member.
- Warm, respectful, strong relationships among staff demonstrate to parents/families that the wellbeing of their children is the focus of the setting. Parents/families feel a connection with the staff and feel included.

Relationships between staff, children and families

- Being a valued member of a successful and effective team helps individual members enjoy their work. This provides staff with a strong incentive to engage in their work in meaningful ways and stay in the workplace.

To achieve the above, the early childhood setting should have a sound and collaboratively compiled vision that outlines high-quality outcomes for children and families, while also providing a space where staff are valued and respected as skilful and knowledgeable professionals (Waniganayake et al., 2012). The onus falls on the team leader to begin to create this collegial, inclusive and ethical workplace where all staff feel comfortable, valued and respected and actively contribute (Waniganayake et al., 2012).

> **Jenna (Director, Centre D):** We have a collaboratively written philosophy. When Sharon [the new owner] came to us she had a lot of beautiful ideas like using the natural environment and using natural materials. We went back to basics and developed our new philosophy that would give us renewed hope and energy . . . That was four years ago . . . Now our philosophy reflects the service: homey, warm, calm, respectful . . . Each year as a staff we review the philosophy and we work with the parents. It's on a pedestal in the foyer for all to read and have input.

Collegiality, respect and teamwork are extremely important. However, at times, these are put to the test. Often through times of adversity an early childhood centre can change and grow. It is through forging positive and collegial relationships that this can occur. The vignette below explains how one community centre, through respectful leadership and relationship building, traversed an extremely difficult time to become an exceptional centre valued by children, families, staff and the community.

> **Danielle (Parent, Centre B):** Staff morale was an issue after Shelbie [the previous director] passed away. Casey came in at a very difficult time; where there was resistance because . . . well they [the educators and staff] just wanted Shelbie back. But Casey's nature is very

composed and considerate and she just sat back and let it happen, and let people grieve. She supported people though their grief in very real and practical ways like always being on the floor and getting involved. She's also an amazing communicator and I believe, even when she's telling staff 'no' she does it in such a professional and considered manner that they end up coming on board. She doesn't manipulate, but she explains everything so well. She also listens to everyone and lets everyone have a voice. Any decision is made in consultation with children, families and staff. She has an open door policy and she's always available. Now . . . the morale is high, it's tangible. It's very collaborative now.

Teamwork

Working together in a collaborative partnership that forms a cohesive, respectful team is a key strategy and resource for the provision of quality in an early childhood setting. The setting that promotes teamwork exudes a workplace culture that values collaboration and collective responsibility. According to Rodd (2013) a collaborative team displays the following features:

- shared values, vision and personal experiences
- diverse yet complementary skills, knowledge and experiences
- open communication and respect for others' perspectives
- respect, empathy, friendliness, consideration and emotional intelligence
- honest, tactful and constructive feedback about the achievement of agreed common goals and performance standards, and
- inclusion, mutual accountability and collective responsibility.

Most early childhood educators understand that effective teamwork is fundamental to the quality of service that they provide, and that 'synergistic teams generate momentum, enabling them to achieve more than would be possible for one individual' (Rodd, 2013, p. 146). Teamwork is considered such an important aspect of early childhood education that the ability to work as an effective team member is specified as an employment criterion in most job descriptions.

Linda (Director, Centre A): We work well together because we trust each other and that's important. At the start of each year we sit down as a staff and go through each child's enrolment. As a team we talk about each child and what their interests might be and their experiences; what their strengths might be and then their family.

Nicki (Educator, Centre A): And we went through accreditation together as a team. It was huge for us and does make you have a really critical look at your service.

Linda (Director, Centre A): Yes and our philosophy was written collaboratively and we re-visit and update it regularly. We did this just before we got together as a team to discuss our quality improvement plan (QIP) because that's the basis of the QIP.

Indeed, teamwork and retention of staff in an early childhood setting is of critical importance to the feelings of safety, security and wellbeing for children, families and staff. Instability in an early childhood setting 'has detrimental effects on children's development and learning' (Rodd, 2013, p. 145). With high staff turn-over it is difficult to get a sense of *belonging* in an early childhood setting. Retention is linked to aspects such as job satisfaction, feeling valued as a team member, connectedness and feeling supported (Whitebrook & Sakai, 2003). Clearly, it is vital for staff to forge warm, respectful, supportive relationships to promote positive outcomes, not only for the children and families in the setting, but also for themselves.

Mitch (Parent, Centre C): Most of the staff have been here a long time and get along really well . . . that says a lot.

CONCLUSION

This chapter has explored the imperative for early childhood educators to build strong, respectful and empathetic relationships with all stakeholders: children, parent, families, staff, para professionals and the community. However, this is not always an easy task. In this chapter a number of directors, educators and parents from prior-to-school settings on the Far North Coast of New

Perspectives and practices in teaching and leadership

South Wales discussed their understandings of the importance of relationship building and highlighted strategies that worked to support relationship building in their centres.

As highlighted, early years educators are mindful not to make assumptions about children and families and ensure that they view each child and family and their circumstances as unique. This builds respectful, trusting and empathetic relationships with children and families. Strong links between the home and the early years setting are extremely important to support not only each child's outcomes while at the centre, but also later life outcomes. This chapter also discussed the importance of building a sense of community within the early learning centre and wider community. Additionally, it was emphasised that strong, respectful relationships among educators must be forged to support a peaceful, harmonious and enjoyable workplace. Such warm workplace relationships are not only beneficial to staff but also to children and their families. When children see this team effort and observe the significant adults in their lives (that is, parents, educators, other staff and para professionals) engaging in respectful, supportive, cooperative relationships, they feel safe and secure and have a sense of belonging. As Casey (Director, Centre B) so eloquently explains:

> Relationship building is the cornerstone of my philosophy and my leadership style. Building relationships with everyone: children first, families, committee, community, staff, all the educators on the team. I respect everyone and what they bring to our centre. Everyone deserves to be respected and valued.

FURTHER THINKING

1. What is your philosophy regarding relationship building? Think of all the stakeholders. Does an understanding and respect for the three Ds (difference, diversity and dignity) have a place in your philosophy when it comes to relationship building? If so, why/how? If no, why not?

2. What strategies could you use to discover children's and families' backgrounds, interests and experiences?

248

3. If you were a director of an early childhood setting what strategies would you use to build a warm, respectful and collaborative workplace?

4. Think of your own community. If you were (or are) involved with an early childhood setting in your community, how would you go about building relationships with your community? Does the community have an annual event? How could your setting become involved in this?

REFERENCES

Arthur, L., Beecher, B., Death, E., Dockett, S. & Farmer, S. (2015). *Programming and Planning in Early Childhood settings*, (6th edn.) South Melbourne: Cengage Learning.

Australian Children's Education and Care Quality Authority (ACECQA) (2014). *National Quality Framework*. Retrieved 20 October 2014, <http://acecqa.gov.au/national-quality-framework>.

Baker, A.C. & Manfredi/Petitt, M. (2004). *Relationships, the Heart of Quality Care: Creating community among adults in early care settings*. Washington, DC: National Association for the Education of Young Children.

Blaise, M. & Nuttall, J. (2011). *Learning to Teach in the Early Years Classroom*. South Melbourne: Oxford University Press.

Bowman, B., Donovan, S. & Burns, S. (eds) (2001). *Eager to Learn: Educating our preschoolers*. Washington, DC: National Academy Press.

Corsaro, W.A. (2005). *The Sociology of Childhood*, 2nd edn. Thousand Oaks, CA: Pine Forge Press.

Dahlberg, G. & Moss, P. (2005). *Ethics and Politics in Early Childhood Education*. London: RoutledgeFalmer.

Department of Education, Employment and Workplace Relations (DEEWR) (2009). Belonging, Being and Becoming: The early years learning framework for Australia. Canberra: Author.

Egan, B.A. (2009). Learning conversations and listening pedagogy: The relationship in student teachers' developing professional identities, *European Early Childhood Education Research Journal*, 17(1), 43–56.

Hadley. F. (2012). Early childhood staff and families' perceptions: Diverse views about important experiences for children aged 3–5 years in early childhood settings, *Contemporary Issues in Early Childhood*, 3(1), 38–50.

Hand, K. & Wise, S. (2006). *Parenting Partnerships in Culturally Diverse Child Care Settings: A care provider perspective*. Research Paper No. 36. Melbourne: Australian Institute of Family Studies. Retrieved 20 October 2014, <www.aifs.gov.au/institute/pubs/rp36/rp36.html>.

Hawkins, K. (2014). Teaching for social justice: A pedagogy for 21st century early childhood education, *European Early Childhood Education Research Journal*, 22(5), 723–38.

Hughes, P. & MacNaughton, G. (2002). Preparing early childhood professionals to work with parents: The challenges of diversity and dissensus, *Australian Journal of Early Childhood*, 28(2), 14–20.

Kitson, R. & Bowes, J. (2010). Incorporating Indigenous ways of knowing in early education for Indigenous children, *Australasian Journal of Early Childhood*, 35(4), 81–9.

Lindon, J. & Rouse, L. (2012). *Positive Relationships in the Early Years: Parents as partners*. Albert Park, Melbourne: Teaching Solutions.

National Scientific Council on the Developing Child (2009). *Young Children Develop in an Environment of Relationships*. Working Paper No. 1. Retrieved 20 October 2014, <www.developingchild.harvard.edu/index.php/activities/council/>.

Redding, S., Murphy, M. & Sheley, P. (eds) (2011). *Handbook on Family and Community Engagement*. Lincoln, IL: Academic Development Institute.

Rinaldi, C. (2005). *In Dialogue with Reggio Emilia*. London: RoutledgeFalmer.

Rodd, J. (2013). *Leadership in Early Childhood: The pathway to professionalism*, 4th edn. Sydney : Allen & Unwin.

Siraj-Blatchford, I. & Sylva, K. (2004). Researching pedagogy in English preschools, *British Educational Research Journal*, 30(5), 691–712.

Sylva, K., Melhuish, E., Sammons, P., Siraj-Blatchford, I., Taggart, B. & Elliot, K. (2003). *The Effective Provision for Pre-school Education (EPPE) Project: Findings from the pre-school period*. Research Brief RBX15–03. London: DfES Publications.

Thornton, K. & Brunton, P. (2010). *The Parent Partnership Toolkit for Early Years*. London: Optimus Education.

United Nations (1989). United Nations Convention on the Rights of the Child. Retrieved 20 October 2014, <www.ohchr.org/en/professionalinterest/pages/crc.aspx>.

Vygotsky, L. (1978). *Mind in society*, Cambridge, MA: Harvard University Press.

Waniganayake, M., Cheeseman, S., Fenech, M., Hadley, F. & Shepherd, W. (2012). *Leadership: Contexts and complexities in early childhood education*. South Melbourne: Oxford University Press.

Whitebrook, M. & Sakai, L. (2003). Turnover begets turnover: An examination of job and occupational instability among child care centre staff, *Early Childhood Research Quarterly*, 18(3), 273–93.

Chapter 12

Understanding babies: promoting young children's learning and development

Wendy Boyd

In this chapter you will find:
- an outline of the importance of the early years
- infant brain development, the importance of responsiveness and the effect of our image of infants
- forming attachments in an inclusive learning environment
- contemporary views of learning—learning throughout the day's routines, literacy and musical experiences and the physical and human environment.

So you are going to care for babies. What does this entail? What do you need to know about infants before you begin this work? This chapter provides an introduction to the importance of the first two years of life in the early childhood setting. Early years educators are pivotal in shaping experiences for infants in early childhood settings. The term 'infants' in this chapter refers to children up to two years of age. Of key importance in working with infants is the establishment of positive relationships with children, and their families. Developing trusting and nurturing relationships with an infant and their family is stimulating and exciting. Educators have a significant impact upon each infant's learning and development. Therefore, the learning environment needs to be welcoming, safe and stimulating for each child.

Each child comes to an early childhood setting with diverse interests, dispositions and backgrounds that require sensitive, responsive approaches by educators. Knowing each child well supports children being able to assert and build upon their identity, and is closely aligned with the formation of respectful partnerships with families. The early childhood educator's knowledge about brain research, how children learn and develop, and attachment theory informs decisions grounded in ethical and professional conduct, and aligned with families' aspirations for their children. Educators ensure holistic practices are implemented in sensitive and appropriate ways to support children's learning and development. Infants' practical care routines (such as feeding, sleeping and toileting) are informed by parents, and provide excellent opportunities to support children's learning, as does the opportunity to play and interact with peers and adults.

THE IMPORTANCE OF THE EARLY YEARS

During early childhood the most number of neural pathways, which pass on information in the brain, are produced for the entire lifespan. The opportunity for brain development is at its peak in early childhood and then continues to diminish over adolescence and into adulthood. The brain at six years has more neuron pathways than at any other period in life. Stimulation and interactions foster increased synapses in the brain. Less used pathways are pared down over time to the most used synapses (Shore, 1997).

RESPONSIVENESS AFFECTS CHILDREN'S LEARNING AND DEVELOPMENT

The ways early childhood educators respond to children affects the formation of neural pathways. Relationships with children need to be warm, nurturing and responsive to each infant, and demonstrate high levels of goodness of fit, meaning that the caregiving is shaped according to the child's temperament and disposition (Shonkoff & Phillips, 2000). Warm, responsive care has a protective function. For example, holding an upset infant close and comforting them soothes the child, which in turn supports the child to feel relaxed and interested in the environment. When a child is stressed and cortisol (the stress hormone) levels rise, this causes the brain to be vulnerable to processes that destroy neurons and synapses, thus interfering with learning and development. Children with high levels of cortisol can have more developmental delays in cognition, motor and social development (National Scientific Council on the Developing Child, 2014).

The way the child responds to the environment influences the child's learning. Temperament is described as the tendency to respond in predictable ways to environmental events, and is thought to be a biological foundation for individual differences in behaviour (Berk, 2013). Temperament characteristics emerge early in life, and show some stability over time. Temperament is pervasive across a range of situations and shows some evidence of heritability. Both heredity and environment influence temperament (Berk, 2013); however, it is known that the environment influences the expression of temperament. In 1977 Thomas and Chess (cited in Berk, 2013) identified three types of children: children with 'easy' temperaments have more positive relationships with friends and peers, and are more easy-going; children with 'difficult' temperaments are more likely to react negatively and appear to have more problematic relationships with their peers and friends; and children who are 'slow to warm up' are passive and take a while to adjust to new experiences. Research shows that 'difficult' infants with patient and sensitive caregivers are no longer classified as 'difficult' later in childhood or adolescence (Sanson, Hemphill, & Smart, 2004). Conversely, if infants with difficult temperaments elicit irritation, and early childhood educators are impatient and do not support the child's behaviour, then the child has their temperamental disposition reinforced.

The ability to self-regulate is a predictor of future life success and develops rapidly in early childhood. The role of the early childhood educator in providing responsive and nurturing caregiving is important to support infants to develop self-regulation, which refers to the capacity to regulate behaviour, thinking and emotions (Williams, 2014). Children require assistance to learn to self-regulate. This can be done, for example, by soothing a crying child when they are frightened by a loud noise, which assists the child to manage their emotions in a similar situation in the future. Or children may need support to go to sleep as they may not have the skills to settle themselves. In this case early childhood educators support children to sleep in the same manner used by their parents. The child may have a special sleep routine or object such as a teddy bear that they have when going to sleep at home; having this at the early childhood centre assists the child to self-settle and, in turn, self-regulate. Williams (2014) asserts that children do not learn to self-regulate immediately and require practice at these skills, supported by a responsive and nurturing educator. As the child responds to the educator so too the educator responds to the child and there develops a dynamic interplay between child and educator. The educator learns about the child and vice-versa, and this takes time. Initially, settling in to an early childhood setting can be traumatic for both the child and the family, and may evoke feelings of uncertainty. Knowing the infant's habits around feeding, sleeping and toileting is a good place to commence building the relationship with the child, and the family. The child will have a sense of familiarity regarding the educator's habits, and the parents will be reassured that their child is being cared for in the manner that they desire. Knowing theories of learning and development, and providing a warm, responsive environment, educators create the essential components to provide quality early childhood education and care.

OUR IMAGE OF INFANTS

The way that educators view infants influences the way educators work. Your philosophical approach to working with infants sends a clear message about your pedagogy, the way you structure the learning environment, how you view children and their families, your approach to diversity and your professional and ethical approaches, all of which influence your teaching, and consequently children's learning. If you have not worked with infants previously you may feel uncertain about whether you will be able to pacify infants if they cry, or how you will communicate with infants and know what they are 'saying'. Understanding that infants are both capable and vulnerable (Lally, 2007) is critical to understanding your role as an educator. Vulnerability relates to infants' dependence on adults— for survival, safety, security and learning; while infants are quite capable at trying to make meaning and at initiating communication and are curious and motivated to learn (Lally, 2007). Not all children have had a positive beginning to life, and some may have experienced stressful situations. Educators need to respond ethically and professionally, especially when signs of abuse are apparent.

Speaking in general terms, many people undervalue working with infants, and do not appreciate the significance of these early years of life. They view working with infants as 'just caring for' or 'babysitting' young children. Research into the brain has demonstrated the early years are critical to lifelong learning (Shonkoff & Phillips, 2000). Learning is often only valued when it is explicit, such as when children begin to read and write, and recite numbers up to ten. This is when parents often get excited about their child's abilities. However, deep learning occurs from birth onwards, and infants express themselves in ways that communicate their intent, so long as they have adults who respond to their expressiveness. Infants' communication can be through the tone of the infants' utterances, and body movements. As an early childhood educator sharing the child's interests, by watching their eyes and responding to their interests (joint attention), and being aware of other body language (such as whether they appear relaxed) will assist you to learn how to 'read' the children in your care. This takes time and informs educators in creating experiences for children based on these observations. As the adult responds to the child's interests, desires and needs, the infant comes to learn that this person can be trusted. The relationship develops bi-directionally and educators develop appreciation for children's capacities. Infants have influence over relationships with their parents and other important adults in their lives, who in turn influence the child. By developing strong attachments to adults children are then in a position to learn about the environment. As early childhood educators work with infants each of the Quality Areas from the National Quality Standard (NQS) (Australian Children's Education and Care Quality Authority [ACECQA], 2011) are upheld.

Reflection

Reflect on your teaching philosophy with respect to infants by thinking about the following questions:

- What is your personal philosophy about how infants learn and develop?
- What are the key factors that influence the way you teach?
- How do you view parents and your role in forming a partnership with them?
- How do you view infants? Capable and competent? Vulnerable? How will these views influence your practice?
- How can infants have agency and make their own decisions?
- What is important in the environment for infants?
- How will you approach pedagogy for infants?
- What is your approach to each family?

Understanding babies: promoting young children's learning and development

- What are important experiences for infants and toddlers in the environment? How will you implement learning experiences for this age group?
- How will you include young children with disabilities in early childhood settings? (Adapted from Arthur et al., 2015)

FORMING ATTACHMENTS IN AN INCLUSIVE LEARNING ENVIRONMENT

It is essential that children feel secure in the ECEC environment, so establishing a safe and secure environment where children know the staff, and know what to expect, will enhance children's sense of belonging and identity formation. If the child does not feel safe and secure in the environment then how can learning be achieved? A safe and secure environment requires staff to know the children, and understand each child's interests, disposition and background. Providing an environment that is inviting yet flexible enhances learning through promoting children's curiosity and exploration. Environments for infants include sensory experiences stimulated by sounds, textures and visual elements.

Children's sense of belonging will be enhanced when they form attachment with and trust educators who are familiar and know the child. To have familiar educators requires ongoing continuity of care. Ideally, educators meet the children and families at the commencement of the day, and the same educators farewell the child and family at the end of the day. Practically, it is usually not possible for the same people to meet and farewell the child, so procedures need to be enacted that inform families about their child's day. Families need to know what their child has done throughout the day to ensure the continuity of care as they go home for the evening.

The staffing arrangements (Quality Area 4, ACECQA, 2011) influence the environment of an early childhood setting. Ultimately, staffing arrangements should be such that children's learning and development is enhanced (ACECQA, 2011). Ensuring continuity of care by educators means that children and educators are able to form meaningful relationships. The relationship is long lasting and, as the educators and children know each other well, children feel secure in the setting. However, this long-term arrangement may not be possible. What is important is that the staff roster is done so that educators become well known to families and children, and they are rostered on at consistent times; for example, in the morning and afternoons to make smooth transitions from home to the centre and back.

Young children are able to form meaningful relationships with many people, not just one person as previously asserted by Bowlby (Berk, 2013), and it is advisable that the infant gradually forms relationships with all of the educators working with the babies. This is an arrangement that works well in early childhood settings that are open for long periods of time (for example, twelve hours a day) when educators only work eight hours per day. The child thus will be cared for by more than one educator, making having only one 'primary caregiving' arrangement impractical. Arranging staff may mean that services adopt a 'primary caregiver' approach where one educator; is with the same children each day. Or children may be family-grouped with one educator; that is, one educator has responsibility for four children aged from infancy to five years. Whatever staffing arrangements are chosen in an early childhood setting they will be closely aligned to the early childhood setting's philosophical approach as to how children are viewed to best learn.

Unhurried time ensures infants are able to develop attachments and not feel rushed in their day. Educators sometimes prioritise routines of the day over children. For example, they may attend to cleaning instead of sitting with and chatting to a child while they are eating. When this happens children are not listened to, and the quality of relationships suffer, as does children's learning. In particular Kolbe (2007) emphasises the need to be unhurried in being with children—to take time for discovery, looking, listening and engaging. Educators need to find the balance between ensuring that children's routines are met and that there is a sense of flexibility and joy in the setting. Early childhood educators reported feeling always rushed in a study by Wien and Kirby-Smith (1998). The educators were clock watching, feeding the infants according to the clock, putting children to bed according to the clock, and feeling that they had no time to be with the children. So after much discussion it was decided to take away the clocks, and encourage the educators to be responsive to infants' communications. The educators initially found no clocks very challenging but after a few weeks found that they were more responsive to the children, and felt like they had more time to play with the children. They had identified the need to practise 'unhurried time' (Wien & Kirby-Smith, 1998).

To forge attachments with children whose abilities and backgrounds are diverse involves staff in learning ways to work with children to enrich their learning. For children with a disability considerations may be required for accommodating in the physical environment, planning for behaviour learning, planning for differential steps in progress and working with professionals to develop individual support programs.

Cultural diversity includes both macro issues (for example, language, festivals and religious ideals) and micro issues (for example, daily care practices). Parents will tend to follow care practices that they are familiar with and are likely to hold very strong beliefs about routines, such as eating, sleeping and toileting. Educators' ideas may be challenged as parents' approaches may appear inappropriate. Communication with families requires sensitive approaches by educators who need to review the family's cultural practices as the starting point for being inclusive.

Reflection

Consider the following care practices. How will you work with parents around these approaches?

- toileting approaches include holding an infant over a potty at three months old
- a child sleeps in the arms of an adult or in an infant hammock
- children are dressed in a lot of clothing even in hot weather, in case the children become chilled
- infant exploration is not encouraged owing to unacceptable health and safety risks
- parents may be accustomed to hand-feeding babies solids to create interdependence

To achieve genuine partnerships with families as advocated in the National Quality Standard, Quality Area 6 (ACECQA, 2011), we need to develop respectful reciprocal relationships (Department of Education, Employment and Workplace Relations [DEEWR], 2009) based on effective communication. What does this entail? Being an effective communicator with parents of infants requires sensitivity to diverse perspectives about children's routines and child-rearing.

Perspectives and practices in teaching and leadership

Challenges to your beliefs and approaches may arise from contemporary ideas about any number of practices in working with infants. You may feel that infants should be cared for in the home; how will you think about this if you can see that families need to engage in paid work? Mostly the purpose of ECEC for infants and toddlers centres around parents' work. What will you do to ensure that the children have the best possible learning experiences? An ongoing challenge for early childhood teachers is to advocate and be accountable for the choice of programs for children. For infants it is likely families will be keen to hear about their child's day: the child's state of mind; the child's play and behaviour; and their feeding, sleeping and toileting. This then ensures a good transition home so the child is cared for consistently.

When a family arrives at the ECEC service to enrol their infant they should be provided with an orientation to the environment for both infant and family. Time is of the essence in developing partnerships with families, and at the initial contact stage is no exception. Families are able to discuss the centre's philosophy, procedures and policies and negotiate agreed positions with early childhood educators on caring for the child. This assists with a satisfactory transition from home to the centre for the parents and the child, informs the educators about the family's lives, and demonstrates to the family that they are valued. Finding out as much as possible about the infant's routines and play behaviours is essential. These routines include feeding, sleeping and toileting patterns, and whether there are any meaningful behaviours that the educators need to be aware of. For example, how does the infant go to sleep? Is it by gentle rocking in a hammock or in an adult's arms; does the child have a comforter of any type to go to sleep with? This information will assist with a smooth transition from home to the early childhood setting. Taking the time to settle a child into a centre is of mutual benefit to all parties.

Not only do relationships between staff and children and staff and families matter, so too do the relationships between staff and staff. The collegiality of an organisation sets the tone of an ECEC setting. This is often referred to as the organisational climate (Bloom, 2014). The way that staff interact with each other sets the *mood* of a workplace. Positive staff relationships are crucial in creating an environment where children and their families can feel emotionally safe, secure and happy. Working with infants especially requires staff to be good communicators, as they work in close quarters and need to communicate well with each other about the children and families. Agreeing to work together for the children and families requires a professional approach to your work. At times you may disagree personally with practices but if they are at the heart of the philosophy then it is your professional duty to enact them, or discuss them with colleagues and management. To enhance relationships with colleagues it is advisable to acknowledge and accept diversity of experiences, ideas, understandings and skills. Caring for infants has many different approaches, and it is essential that the best approaches for the child are discussed and implemented. In interactions with colleagues always remember to express sincere appreciation of individual capacities and contributions, and be professionally courteous. At all times staff emotional wellbeing should be considered, and if an infant is consistently crying then be sure to support the educator who is taking primary responsibility for the child. Cooperative planning and decision-making is important for the best interests of children, families and colleagues. This includes consistent and coherent approaches when guiding children's behaviour.

Educators who work harmoniously, maintaining good communication, benefit the children. Educators can communicate effectively about children and about who will do what, with whom and when. When educators communicate effectively they share decision-making about who will change a child with a soiled nappy, or who will give a child their morning tea, and who will rock a child to sleep. Educators can fill in for each other, children are relaxed with all educators and there is a strong sense of cooperation and shared responsibility.

CONTEMPORARY VIEWS OF LEARNING

Over the past two decades there has been a significant shift in the way that young children are viewed. Raban et al. (2005) point to the shift in the ECEC field from maturationist and developmentalist orientations; for example, developmentally appropriate practice to social-constructivist and ecological orientations (Berk, 2013). The importance of considering children in context is now emphasised, and the influence of the educational approach in Reggio Emilia has been applied to reconstruct young children as capable and competent. This builds on the notion of the Early Years Learning Framework (EYLF) (DEEWR, 2009) that encourages educators to view children as having rights and being capable, and to recognise children's competencies.

Perspectives and practices in teaching and leadership

When planning learning experiences for infants, what do we need to consider? Planning is complex and multi-faceted (Arthur et al., 2015) and requires adults to have a good understanding of the children and their developing competencies. Educators ideally need to have formed secure, respectful and reciprocal relationships that support the child in the early childhood environment for best outcomes in planning for children's learning.

When working with infants it is important to create opportunities for holding infants, sharing their enjoyment in the world, soothing their distress and at all times communicating respect for the child (Lally, 2007). This secure environment gives infants the courage to explore and investigate the world (Lally, 2007). Kolbe (2007) encourages early childhood educators to share a sense of wonder with infants and to engage all of the senses to promote learning; it is essential to stop and stare, touch and listen, to take time to explore and make choices and to take time just to be (p. 11).

Explorative play with responsive educators supports children's learning. As infants develop their independence, and embark on exploring and taking risks in the environment, they learn about their capabilities and interests, and develop theories about the world (Malaguzzi, 1993). Educators engage infants in play opportunities using various teaching strategies that respect young children as holistic learners (DEEWR, 2009):

- *low-interaction teaching strategies,* such as observing, acknowledging, modelling, facilitating, grouping and listening to;
- *mediating teaching strategies,* such as supporting, encouraging, praising, scaffolding, co-constructing, providing feedback and positive reinforcement, questioning and problem solving; and
- *explicit teaching strategies,* such as demonstrating, directing and telling, and instructing (Arthur et al., 2015; MacNaughton & Williams, 2009).

Reflection
Review each of these teaching strategies and consider how you could apply each one to your work with infants.

Quality Area 1 of the NQS (ACECQA, 2011) relates to the educational program and practices. A common response from pre-service teachers when they are told they are to do an infant's practicum is: How will I provide for the children's learning? What experiences would I provide for young children to learn? How can infants experience art, the world around us, mathematics, music and so on? There is no prescribed content for infants to learn; however, the EYLF (DEEWR, 2009) provides five broad learning outcomes for all children, with underpinning indicators that demonstrate ways children can achieve outcomes. Looking at the first of these learning outcomes we may ask how can infants develop a strong sense of identity? Think of the multitude of ways that infants can be supported to develop a strong sense of who they are. For example, a low mirror on the floor placed carefully near a non-crawling child (up to twelve months) provides a child with the opportunity to see themselves in the early childhood setting. They may not recognise the image as themselves; however, observing the infant's response to this mirror provides the educator with an understanding of how the child views his/her reflection. Photos of the child looking at him/herself will further enhance this experience, which continues to build on the child's sense of self.

Inclusive pedagogies

Across all families there will be differing expectations about the pedagogical approach to children's learning. Assumptions that certain families may share values and beliefs needs to be approached sensitively and discussion with each family is essential. For example, many families will view playing as acceptable for an infant but not for a preschooler who will shortly be beginning formal schooling. The experiences adults have had during their own upbringing may reflect particular beliefs about their own family. Families may have varying approaches to maintenance of home languages, such as some families insisting that at the centre only English is spoken to their child as the child is learning his/her first language at home. Discipline approaches often differ, and educators need to articulate their approach about children's behaviour guidance to families and colleagues, and ensure that a consistent approach it taken.

Learning throughout the day's routines

The daily routine for infants provides opportunities for learning and supporting children's sense of security and identity, both within the early childhood setting and within the home. The link between home and the setting can be enhanced when routines are practised consistently by the caregiver with whom the child is familiar. This provides a sense of continuity between the home and the centre. Therefore, strong partnerships forged with the families are essential to consistently support the child's learning and development. Upon enrolment families share with the educator the child's familiar practices, such as sleeping times and habits, eating and drinking times and habits, well-known comforters for the child, nappy change habits, bathing times and behaviours, play times and tummy times. Each of these 'times', or routines, is an opportunity for responsive and nurturing caregiving that supports the child's learning. Consider, for example, changing a child's nappy. You know that the child loves to be sung to, so as you change the child's nappy you sing 'Twinkle Twinkle Little Star'. Later you sing this song when you are playing on the floor with the child, thus deepening the connection between yourself and the child, but also heightening the child's recall of songs. Nappy change provides a wonderful opportunity for one-on-one interaction with the child, and should be a relaxed, enjoyable experience.

All of these routine times need to be practised with attention to the health and safety of the child. For example, when giving a child a warm bottle you need to check the temperature of the milk prior to giving it to them. The way a nappy is changed follows specific procedures to minimise cross-infection; make sure the information on the nappy chart is followed closely, and be familiar with it prior to changing your first nappy.

Reflection

Eloise is 20 months old and loves sucking her dummy when she is feeling uncertain in a situation. She attends child care two days a week. Her mother, Kylie, is trying to reduce the amount of dummy time Eloise has, so as to support her language development. Kylie wants Eloise to only have her dummy when going to sleep. Kylie shares this desire with Eloise's educators, who record this in the Staff Communication Book, which all staff read.

On the first afternoon, when Kylie comes to pick up Eloise she sees that Eloise is sucking her dummy. The educators have changed since the morning drop-off time so Kylie repeats her request to the afternoon educators.

The following day Eloise again has her dummy when Kylie comes to pick her up, and the educator explains that she was crying so staff had given it to her to pacify her. Kylie again explains her request and the educator agrees.

The following week when Kylie comes to pick up Eloise she is again sucking her dummy and again Kylie is told that Eloise had become upset so they gave it to her to pacify her.

Kylie seeks out the centre Director and explains her problem to her. As the Director how would you work to solve this problem to support the child, the family and the educator?

Literacy and musical experiences with infants

The opportunities for infants' learning are vast, and this section provides some key ideas for sharing literacy and musical experiences with them. Story telling, book sharing, and participation in musical experiences can be rich and joyful learning opportunities for infants. The selection of songs and stories needs to consider the language capacities and the concentration span of very young children, as well as their interests. Children love to hear the same songs and stories over and over again, and often you can see them sitting by themselves and 'reading' the story. Stories need to be short, simple, on familiar topics and with repetitive language. Books need clear, realistic pictures showing familiar items or events. Props and stimulus pictures need to be realistic and the educator should use appropriate facial or voice expression to enhance the meaning of the story or song.

Music should be part of every infant's daily routine, as well as part of spontaneous experiences, such as when a child is swinging. Music can be used as play, and in playing it can be a sociable learning experience and teaches children about the elements of music, such as volume, dynamics and pitch (Suthers, 2004). Songs and musical rhymes for babies should take into account their need to express themselves physically as well as verbally, and their preference for body action as a response. Action rhymes are fun and often relate to the child and often require using their body. Some songs are short and repetitive, and accompanied by hand or body actions, and may relate to language the child is learning or understands. Movement to music may use static movements (such

Perspectives and practices in teaching and leadership

as bobbing, swaying, bending and stretching) and simple locomotor movements (such as walking and jumping). Percussion can focus on shaking and tapping actions; for example, using jumbo bells, plastic shakers, tone blocks and strong hand drums. There are numerous resources available to help learn songs to sing with young children.

The physical and human environment

Creating a home-like atmosphere is important to ensure children feel comfortable, safe and secure so that their learning and development is supported. The environment is significant in the early childhood setting as it sets the tone for the centre, and acts as a third teacher (along with other children and adults) for children's learning and development. This environment needs to include the richness of diversity of children's homes, offering more than token learning experiences, such as having one song in one language, and wall displays. It means being thoughtful about all that makes up the environment—the space, materials and resources, use of time, and the way the educators organise these elements.

The physical environment gives infants and adults cues about what can happen in this space; it may raise expectations, stimulate ideas and thinking, and support the building of relationships (Rinaldi, 2006). The environment should invite children to explore, inquire and solve problems, and retain a sense of familiarity, stability and order. Additionally, it should support children to take risks and also provide challenges, support children's health and emotional wellbeing, and be aesthetically attractive.

Reflection

As an early childhood educator, when you first walk into an infants' room consider the impact it has upon you: think about the room's size, shape, lighting and associated mood, the temperature, the furnishings, the equipment and resources, and the beauty of the space. How does it feel to you? Is it noisy, chaotic and crowded? Or intimate, cosy and harmonious? If it feels stressful to an educator then chances are the children will also sense the stress, which in turn raises children's cortisol levels, and impedes opportunities for learning. What about the vegetation in the outside environment,

> the design of the yard/the inside space, and the opportunities for children to engage their senses, such as sounds, smells and textures? Are furnishings soft, durable and easily maintained; that is, can they be washed if soiled?

Health and safety issues are a significant concern when working with infants as their immune system is not fully developed, and educators' health and well-being also needs to be considered as close contact with children is required. The book *Staying Healthy in Child Care* (National Health and Medical Research Council, 2014) provides useful and extensive information on health concerns in child care, especially when working with infants.

Educators need to be knowledgeable about the Education and Care Services National Regulations for children's services (ACECQA, 2014). The regulations outline the minimum standards required for environments for children in early childhood settings. The regulations document the maximum number of children allowed in a group (that is, the group size), the ratio of educators to infants, and the educators' qualifications. They also cover the physical environment. All of these regulations are legal requirements, and impact upon the quality of care and education. They are intended as minimum standards to ensure quality. Requirements related to the physical environment in the Regulations (ACECQA, 2014) include the amount of space per child, both inside and outside; fencing; shade; equipment and resources; furniture; toileting and nappy change facilities; and food preparation facilities.

All early childhood settings have policies and procedures in place regarding the management of the physical environment to guide educators in their practice. This is to ensure optimal safety, health and hygiene for children and adults. As part of this it is likely there will be posters on walls to alert educators to the safety and hygiene procedures. For example, the procedure that needs to be followed for nappy changing to minimise cross-infection and to safely care for the child during nappy change will be posted near the nappy change table. Also, there will be a procedure for checking on infants while sleeping. Infants sleeping require constant checking to minimise the chance of Sudden Infant Death Syndrome (SIDS). Educators need to be well informed about safe preparation procedures of food and beverages for infants.

Perspectives and practices in teaching and leadership

Not only do educators need to be careful about the health and safety of infants but they also need to care for each other and themselves. Such measures may include considering of vaccinations against common immunisable diseases associated with caring for infants; using safe hand-washing procedures; and being mindful of tripping hazards and other occupational workplace hazards.

CONCLUSION

This chapter has provided an introduction to the importance of the first two years of life in the early childhood setting, highlighting the significant role of early years educators in shaping experiences for infants. The enactment of relationships and the choices in the environment available to infants has a significant impact upon each child's learning. Of key importance in working with infants is the establishment of positive relationships with children, forming respectful partnerships with their families and providing a learning environment that is welcoming, safe and stimulating.

FURTHER THINKING

1. What are important qualities of people who work with infants? What personal and professional qualities do you have that will ensure you offer quality education and care for infants?

2. Working with infants often raises the dilemma about the purpose of child care. What do you think the community expects of infant child care? Why?

3. It is important to have a flexible learning environment. What does the environment say about our philosophy of teaching? What does the environment say about our image of children?

REFERENCES

Arthur, L., Beecher, B., Death, E., Dockett, S. & Farmer, S. (2015). *Programming and Planning in Early Childhood Settings*, 6th edn. South Melbourne: Cengage Learning.

Australian Children's Education and Care Quality Authority (ACECQA) (2011). *Guide to the National Quality Standard*. Retrieved 10 September 2014, <http://files. acecqa.gov.au/files/National-Quality-Framework-Resources-Kit/NQF03-Guide-to-NQS-130902.pdf>.

—— (2014). *Education and Care Services National Regulations.* Retrieved 10 September 2014,<www.legislation.nsw.gov.au/maintop/view/inforce/subordleg+653+2011+cd+0+N>.

Berk, L. (2013). *Child Development*, 9th edn. Boston: Pearson.

Bloom, P.J. (2014). *Leadership in Action: How effective directors get things done*, 2nd edn. Illinois: New Horizons.

Department of Education, Employment and Workplace Relations (DEEWR) (2009). Belonging, Being and Becoming: The early years learning framework for Australia. Barton, ACT: Commonwealth of Australia.

Kolbe, U. (2007). *Rapunzel's Supermarket: All about young children and their art*, 2nd edn. Byron Bay: Peppinot Press.

Lally, J.R. (2007). Teaching and caring: Responding to both the vulnerability and competence of infants and toddlers, *Childcare and Children's Health*, 10(3).

MacNaughton, G. & Williams, G. (2009). *Techniques for Teaching Young Children*. 3rd edn. Frenchs Forest: Pearson Education Australia.

Malaguzzi, L. (1993). For an education based on relationships, *Young Children*, November, 9–12.

National Health and Medical Research Council (2014). *Staying Healthy in Child Care.* Retrieved 10 September 2014, <www.nhmrc.gov.au/guidelines/publications/ch43>.

National Scientific Council on the Developing Child (2014). *Excessive Stress Disrupts the Architecture of the Developing Brain.* Retrieved 10 September 2014, <http://developingchild.harvard.edu/activities/council/>.

Raban, B., Nolan, A., Waniganayake, M., Ure, C., Deans, J. & Brown, R. (2005). Empowering practitioners to critically examine their current practice, *Australian Research in Early Childhood Education*, 12(2), 1–16.

Rinaldi, C. (2006). *In Dialogue with Reggio Emilia: Listening, researching and learning.* London: Routledge.

Sanson, A., Hemphill, S. & Smart, D. (2004). Connections between temperament and social development: A review, *Social Development*, 13, 142–70.

Shonkoff, J. & Phillips, D. (2000). *From Neurons to Neighbourhoods.* Retrieved 10 September 2014, <www.nap.edu/openbook.php?record_id=9824>.

Shore, R. (1997). *Rethinking the Brain: New insights into early development.* New York: Families and Work Institute.

Suthers, L. (2004). Music experiences for toddlers in day care centres, *Australian Journal of Early Childhood*, 29(4), 45–9.

Wien, C. & Kirby-Smith, S. (1998). Untiming the curriculum: A case study of removing the clocks from the program, *Young Children*, September, 8–13.

Williams, K. (2014). *Self-regulation from Birth to Age Seven: Associations with maternal mental health, parenting and social, emotional and behavioural outcomes for children.* Retrieved 10 September 2014, <http://eprints.qut.edu.au/71568/1/Kate_Williams_Thesis.pdf>.

Chapter 13

Flexible and sustainable learning environments

Joy Goodfellow

In this chapter you will find:

- environment as a living system
- environment as a reflection of educator philosophy
- children as agentic participants
- environment and the educator's role
- environment and quality of life
- standards and practices within Australia.

This chapter discusses the environment in early childhood education settings both as a place to *be* and a space for teaching, learning and children's development. In considering early childhood environments and educators' roles within them, the chapter focuses on how the environment may be viewed as a living system, how an educator's philosophy may influence what happens within an early childhood environment, and the environmental characteristics that influence children's learning and behaviour. The chapter addresses the nature of sustainability and responsibilities early childhood educators have in working with children to both create and appreciate practices of social and environmental sustainability. Finally, the chapter links the concept of sustainability with examples of key early childhood practice standards found within the Early Years Learning Framework (EYLF) (Department of Education, Employment and Workplace Relations [DEEWR], 2009) and the school-oriented Australian Curriculum (Australian Curriculum, 2015).

Perspectives and practices in teaching and leadership

ENVIRONMENT AS A LIVING SYSTEM

The physical environment in early childhood settings has often been called the third teacher. This concept recognises the environment as a living, changing system, where active and responsive children and adults live in relationships with their social and physical world, and are influenced by the people, structures and resources around them (Torquati & Ernst, 2013). That is, an early childhood environment is a relational space where adults and young children live, play and work. It is a place where curious children learn through their encounters with their social and physical world.

Exposure to the natural environment contributes to what is experienced through the senses. Acting on and responding to the nature and composition of the physical environment means that we are not only influenced by it but also by the dynamic social and cultural composition of that environment. From a social perspective, environments are lived spaces that encompass the embodied experiences of the inhabitants. Through living and being in such spaces, one gives meaning to what is being experienced (van Manen, 1990). Lived spaces are relational, interactional, transitional and pedagogical. They reflect an early childhood education curriculum defined as 'all the interactions, experiences, activities, routines and events, planned and unplanned, that occur in an environment designed to foster children's learning and development' (DEEWR, 2009, p. 45).

This view of the environment as a dynamic system reflects what the philosopher Gregory Bateson (cited by Capra, 1988) recognised as connecting patterns of relationships. Connecting patterns occur where the physical environment supports relationships and learning. Capra challenges us to look not only for patterns but also for the processes occurring behind the more observable actions.

Environment, as a physical place, may be a space where new and different or unexpected connections are made. For example, Sun Kim and Darling (2012) demonstrated how children's investigation of colour blending led to discoveries about the effect of wind and sunshine (that is, nature) on their artwork. Further, a four year old reported in writing by Gandini (2011), 'You can listen to the noise of a place; a tree, for example, tells us about the wind' (p. 317). Children's understanding of connections between natural phenomena and manmade materials often amazes educators who take time to really listen to children. An individual's understanding of what is experienced contributes to the mix

272

Flexible and sustainable learning environments

of the many patterns that connect both within and beyond early childhood environments.

Connecting patterns can be seen in examples of infant–toddler peer interactions highlighted in a recent examination of infants' lives in child care (Harrison & Sumsion, 2014). In particular, one fourteen-month-old infant (who had not yet developed verbal skills) was observed using a 'looking and listening' strategy in his approach to making connections with and entering the play of other infants in a family day care environment. He would first observe what was happening and then, through eye contact and body language, ease himself into the play situation by offering and then retrieving a toy from a peer (Goodfellow, 2014). It was subsequently found that this strategy was one that he used at home as he tried to imitate the play of his older sibling. Indeed, he was transferring his experience in one environment (that is, family and home) to strategies he then adopted in a new and different social/physical environment. The infant's turn taking; capacity to tune in to the other infant; and reciprocity, responsiveness and recognition of the other's capabilities were deemed to all be instrumental in facilitating language development. This example raises questions about an infant's capacity to engage in the dialogic space existing within communicative patterns that connect people, places and things within the physical environment. Educators, whether silent observers or active participants, are most often part of a dialogic and relational space that is lived by those who inhabit that space.

Frederick Fröbel (1895), an early educator, used metaphor to depict the living dynamic of environments. When Fröbel created the first 'Kinder Garten' in Bad Blankenburg (Germany) in 1837 he held a view of a kindergarten being a place where caring relationships provided the context within which the inquisitive child's natural curiosity would unfold. The metaphor of a garden likened the nurturing of young children not only to the physical care and tending of plants but also to the responsibilities held by those in the caring role. There is now research evidence to support the view that children's development occurs not only from within the child but through the child's encounters within their social and physical environment (Nelson, 2007).

Educators are in a powerful position to influence the ways in which young children access, engage with and subsequently learn through their actions and reactions to the relationships they have with adults and peers. When writing about spaces that educate, Ridgway and Hammer (2006) refer to ways in which

273

physical spaces support patterns that connect across respectful relationships. The dynamic, lived and relational spaces within early childhood environments reflect learning communities. Fröbel's metaphor, a sense of interrelated systems conveyed by Capra's 'patterns that connect' and 'learning communities' all reflect a view that learning and development occur through engagement *in situ*. Social, cultural and physical environments are places of encounter. The educator orchestrates places of encounter by choosing what is available to children and how that is organised, attending to the sequence of the day's activities and guiding children in their care. In making such decisions, educators draw from their philosophy of practice as well as their professional expertise and experience.

ENVIRONMENT AS A REFLECTION OF EDUCATOR PHILOSOPHY

What we do reflects our beliefs and values. The ways in which educators work with and respond to children, as well as the spaces they provide for children's learning, are influenced by what individual educators think, feel and value, as well as their professional knowledge and personal practical experience. That is, educators' 'practical wisdom' influences how they think and act within both social and physical environments. Practical wisdom is a way of being, knowing and living that is influenced by values and beliefs. It has reflective, affective and experiential qualities, draws on professional knowledge and involves sound judgement (Goodfellow, 2003).

As adults, if we reflect on the personal choices we make in our everyday lives with respect to such things as clothes and furnishings, we are influenced by colour, texture, style and general functionality. What we do and the choices we make reflect a way of being that supports aspects of our philosophy. In child care, for example, an entrance to a child care centre may be seen as a philosophical statement for it can tell something about what educators value in that place. Entrances suggest something about the people who live there and the extent to which others are welcome. Entrance displays may include local cultural artefacts or comfortable furnishings, such as a soft, cosy couch that invites people to sit together. A children's book or an interesting toy placed on a side table nearby and under a lamp next to the couch may not only capture the child's interest but provide a homelike feeling where adults can comfortably share that book with the child.

Educators' philosophies of practice and professional knowledge will influence the environments they create for children. An educator's philosophy of practice not only reflects their image of the child but the child within their social and physical environment and, by implication, the environment itself. The following reflections provide some insight into how a staff team drew on their philosophies of practice and understandings about both the children and families in the local community when establishing an outdoor environment in a new child care centre.

Reflection

SDN Beranga in Western Sydney is a project developed by SDN Children's Services, a not-for-profit organisation in Sydney. The project has two key components: a long day care 'lighthouse centre' catering for 24 children aged two to six with an autism spectrum disorder, and a partnership arrangement that supports the integration of these children within thirteen satellite (and mainstream) child care centres. The long day care centre is located in a recently developed suburban area of Sydney that experiences hot, dry summers. There are few shade trees, and water conservation is important.

Educators spent some time identifying what they considered to be key elements that underpinned the program and how these should be reflected in the outdoor space. They reviewed the original intention to connect with the land and acknowledge the local Darug people. Beranga is an Aboriginal word from the local Darug language meaning 'we belong'. Educators also identified environmental elements that they considered to be non-negotiable. These included sustainable indigenous plantings and innovative materials to draw heat away and keep areas cool, such as planting mature trees and providing waterways. Elements were selected that resonated with the educators' desire to plan an environment that was for now and the future.

Educators also explored diverse design elements. They researched online, collected design photos and visited local parks to look at the vegetation that thrived there. Creativity was encouraged. Ideas were revisited often and with different groups of individuals until each element resonated with their vision. Individual educators undertook responsibility for searching out information and shared their experiences. They didn't aim for consensus but used the diversity of their perspectives to advocate for the child's voice in the design and implementation of the outdoor spaces. Educators wanted to embed practices recognising culturally authentic and meaningful experiences for children, staff and families to connect with Country.

The collaborative approach to project planning worked well, partly because educators assigned ample time to processes associated with design, review and consultation, as well as opportunities to challenge decision-making. Individual educators recognised an increase in confidence and growth in knowledge about sustainable elements, such as types of materials for paths, types of wood for decking, indigenous plantings, where to plant in the environment, how to plan for water drainage, and how to address the climate of the site using trees and foliage (see Figure 13.1).

In the words of one educator: our values connect us, our practical wisdom supports us, reflection and clarity help us focus our professional knowledge.

Source: Educators at SDN Beranga, Sydney.

CHILDREN AS 'AGENTIC' PARTICIPANTS

Educators' actions also reflect their images of the child. Early childhood educators might reflect on the ways the social and physical environmental patterns connect with an image of the child as:

- being a (potentially) capable social being who may require sensitive adults to assist them in constructing (physical and social) situations associated with their curiosity and learning
- having opportunities to create and test out ideas through sustained engagement or 'sustained shared thinking' (Siraj-Blatchford, 2007)

Flexible and sustainable learning environments

Figure 13.1: A newly created shaded outdoor area at Beranga that uses natural timbers and soft furnishings to create a quiet space to be shared by adults and children
Source: SDN Beranga

- having space to spend time learning through researching with adults and their peers to test out ideas
- being in constant relationship with their surroundings and able to challenge and take from the environment what is meaningful to them
- being entitled to aesthetic environments of beauty and respect
- living in spaces that recognise and honour their presence.

For children, learning occurs from birth. The sensory environment is particularly important for babies because they come to know and understand their world through touch, sound, smell and then vision. If we value such learning during unstructured as well as educator-initiated play, then educators need to take these sensory elements into account when choosing resources and materials for children. They plan the physical environment with attention to sound and

Perspectives and practices in teaching and leadership

Figure 13.2: A shaded outdoor area with designated spaces that offer opportunities for particular kinds of activities
Source: SDN Beranga

light, display items that are visually satisfying and include colour and textures that appeal to the senses.

The child both influences and responds to their social and physical environment. The child's agency or capacity to influence their social and physical environment is important when considering the play choices available to them. For example, a child may creatively use particular materials for purposes other than those they were originally designed for. However, their creative use of materials may inspire other children to explore the potential of those materials. Small and large construction materials, including large cardboard boxes, may offer many different opportunities and have the flexibility for children to develop, arrange and manage spaces for creative play. Coloured paper, cardboard or fabrics with different textures and found objects (such as shells, leaves and bark) may be used creatively in the construction of artwork. There are many opportunities in the outdoor environment where sand, water and 'tools' are available for creative and dramatic play.

With growing competence and independence, children may also choose how to engage with their environment. Engagement is not passive. It refers to the ways in which a child interacts within their environment in developmentally and contextually appropriate ways. Children's engagement is both a necessary condition for learning and a mediator of learning (Aguiar & McWilliam, 2013). For example, the infant referred to earlier who found ways in which to enter play with his peers, appeared to consciously consider ways in which to approach his peers. There was space in his social environment that supported his agentic behaviour. The ways in which educators organise spaces as well as materials and resources within the environment can all contribute to children's engagement.

Researchers who have explored 'lived spaces' of toddlers in child care identified these spaces as being relational, interactional, transitional, curriculum and/or pedagogical spaces (Harrison & Sumsion, 2014). These spaces were places of human encounter within the social, physical and temporal environment of the child care settings in which toddlers were viewed as 'agentic beings' (Press & Mitchell, 2014) who had the capacity to both influence and be influenced by their environment. The complexity of the educator's role in mediating what occurred within those environments highlighted the need for educators to be alert and attuned to the toddler's negotiations both with their peers and across the resources available to them.

ENVIRONMENT AND THE EDUCATOR'S ROLE

In recent years, the schools in Reggio Emilia (Italy) have captured the interest of early childhood educators around the world, partly because of their emphasis on and respect for both the social and physical environments in which educators and children live, learn, work and play. Educators have an important role in planning and organising children's play spaces within a centre's indoor and outdoor environments. The role includes not only careful selection of resources and materials that provide for children's exploration, but also spaces that facilitate children's developing social competency, independence and creativity. From an environmental perspective, competency is about the child's agency and providing a rich environment where the child can interact effectively within both his/her social and physical environments (Maxwell, 2007).

Perspectives and practices in teaching and leadership

The learning environment is everything around the child. While physical places and social spaces include sounds, textures and colour, environmental spaces also need to address accessibility and provision for independence. Educators play a major role in designing, organising and managing children's play spaces and, through intentional teaching, have the power to influence how children live and learn within those spaces.

Overall, educators are instrumental in creating environments for young children with respect to both architecturally designed buildings and the use of naturally occurring physical environments. Well-designed spaces are comfortable, pleasurable places; they invite us to enter and to become involved. Well-designed spaces are also aesthetically appealing.

Aesthetics within child care environments refers to the beauty that permeates both the natural and 'built' or architecturally designed environment. Educators at Reggio Emilia view the power of aesthetics as a connecting principle between pedagogy and architecture (Edwards, Gandini & Forman, 2011). While colour and lighting create a mood (for example, the warmth created by the use of wall lights rather than banks of fluorescent lights), light and shadow can highlight particular areas and alter the ambience of an environment.

Aesthetics also refers to the careful ways in which objects are organised so that they are invitational and pleasing to the eye, inviting one to engage with them. If objects are carefully chosen and displayed then they send messages about care and caring. For example, an arrangement of different kinds of shells placed on a table top scattered with sand and arranged according to their shape, size or colour may invite a child to explore what lives in these shells. Such exploration is facilitated if there is a book on shells lying open nearby. Similarly, building blocks that are sorted on a shelf according to length and shape enable children to make selection choices and exercise judgement when using them in construction.

Competent educators also actively scaffold children's learning within these spaces (Nelson, 2007). They work with the children in establishing clear goals, making meaningful connections across children's expressed ideas and questions, being resourceful and providing feedback. Indeed, educators creatively use a number of strategies to maximise children's learning and minimise children's non-engagement. One strategy is to consider having zoned areas for activities. A zoned area might be a large floor rug where the boundaries of the rug suggest

280

Flexible and sustainable learning environments

Figure 13.3: Children exploring the textures and natural elements within a mud patch
Source: SDN Beranga

a contained space. Other strategies might include the arrangements of furniture, such as shelving or chairs and tables or a sandpit outside that has a seated area around it. Activity centres can be set up in the zones with educators being readily available nearby. Educators are then in a position to be responsive to opportunities for both incidental and intentional teaching (Aguiar & McWilliam, 2013).

Well-defined spaces suggest to children that there is a limit to the type of activity that can occur in such a space (for example, book reading) as well as the number of children and type of play that can occur within that space (for example, a carpeted area where building blocks can be used). Such boundaries serve at least two purposes. One is that of artificial containment so that there is not a spill-over to another activity; second, pathways can be created so avoiding disruption to play activity. Greenman (1988) describes a pathway as 'an empty space on the floor or ground through which people move from one place to another' (p. 68). It is important that there is space for children to move (even meander) through from one area to another without disruption occurring.

Moveable equipment (such as tables, chairs and low storage benches) as well as equipment and construction type resources (for example, building blocks) and natural 'found' objects can all contribute to the flexibility of multipurpose environments.

The physical arrangement of play spaces outdoors, and provisions within the natural environment (such as trees, garden beds and paths), sends messages to children about play possibilities. 'Found' objects (such as rocks, pebbles, bark, sticks and leaves) can be used flexibly in symbolic play and act as prompts for further learning. Natural environments can nurture children's sensory awareness because they have visual, textual, auditory and olfactory elements and provide for active learning.

In summary, there are a number of environmental characteristics that influence children's engagement and agentic behaviour. These include:

- The variety of materials and equipment from which children may choose according to their interests and capabilities as well as the degree of complexity in the materials themselves. Variety may be found in colour, shape and texture as well as number of differing materials. It can also be found in the physical spaces, including lighting, floor covering and displays.
- Planned and scaled spaces (including height and proximity) that support children's independence through enabling them to access play items and materials relevant to their play. Such spaces would include having child-size furniture but also accessible spaces, such as the availability of drinking water within children's easy reach or places where children can independently access snacks.
- Flexible play spaces that children can rearrange in order to personalise the contexts for their autonomous play, such as the opportunity to reconstruct a 'home corner' and make it into a 'shop'.
- Private and restorative spaces where a child can be alone and away from the busyness of a group environment or cubbies where a small group can play together while feeling out of sight of adults. Wilson (1997) describes these as 'habitats' for children (p. 191). Children value making 'secret' places as a form of boundary setting where they can separate themselves from the adult world.
- Group size and amount of space per child are important considerations because they provide a context for connecting socially, emotionally and

physically. For example, a table that has four chairs around it suggests that four children are welcome to sit there.

- Spaces where children's play is not interrupted by others. That is, their learning environment provides for sustained engagement where they can focus their attention on the task at hand without interruption. Sometimes children want to spend some time at a task, such as a piece of artwork or construction, and wish to remain with the task and complete it to their satisfaction rather than leave it partly finished.
- Predictable spaces that have some physical but functional order where children are able to form a view (that is, a cognitive map) of where to find things and how best to move through a space. Therefore, it is important to consider the location of activity areas, such as book corners or construction areas, so that the child knows where to independently access materials and resources.

Reflection

1. What are the key elements that you would include in your philosophy of practice with respect to creating environments for young children?
2. What do you think has influenced your current way of thinking about social/relational and physical environments?
3. If you were in a leadership role, how would you justify this way of thinking?

If the physical and social environment is the third teacher then the question arises: what are the messages that the global environment is sending us and what are the responsibilities of early childhood educators in addressing these messages with young children? Through deliberate, purposeful and thoughtful actions (that is, intentional teaching) educators can build upon children's natural curiosity and explore more complex understandings and accurate knowledge of the environment in which they live.

While learning opportunities are provided through responsive relationships within both the physical and social environments, the last 30 years have seen a surge in interest in how people act on the environment. The issue of

Perspectives and practices in teaching and leadership

Figure 13.4: Children connecting with their community environment by viewing through windows in a fence that screens the noise of passing trains from the play area
Source: SDN Beranga

environmental sustainability has partly come about as a result of more global concerns about population growth and the capacity of planet earth as we know it to support the survival of the growing population. Commentators, scientists and researchers have begun to explore issues around the planet's capacity to sustain population growth, the extent of resource degradation and how people respect and nurture the limits of their physical world.

THE ENVIRONMENT AND QUALITY OF LIFE

Social sustainability encompasses a concern for the quality of life for all without social exclusion (Koning, 2002). Children can be provided with factual information about sustainable practices and be involved in practices through gardening, composting and adopting water use and energy saving. These practices can be supported by pedagogical approaches that are learner-centred and often problem-based and dialogic and provide for active engagement. However, education for sustainability is oriented more towards the adoption of sustainability principles, ethics and values; hence, the notion of stewardship as being caring about (the future) as well as caring for the environment. While educators may plan environments and undertake intentional teaching about the environment, Davis (2009) flagged a concern that there is little recognition of young children being 'agents of change'; that is, education about the environment has surpassed education for the environment (p. 227).

Sustainability is about improving the quality of human life within the capacity of our resources to support the physical, social, cultural and economic systems in which we live. It addresses the basic need to live within our means and meet the needs of the present generation without compromising the needs of future generations. It acknowledges global limitations and the limited capacity of the world to meet the demands that humans are now placing on the planet's ecosystems and focuses extensively on the importance of protecting natural resources and the environment (Brundtland, 1987).

Globally, sustainability crosses boundaries: environmentally (for example, resource management), economically (such as the use of resources and avoidance of wastage) and socially (including standard of living and education). Each one of these three 'pillars' connects with the other. For example, degradation and poverty may occur in overpopulated areas where resources are limited or used inappropriately where people lack the knowledge/skills to manage their environment. However, following Capra's (1988) philosophical and system-oriented perspective, what is very evident are patterns that connect what we do and the way in which we currently live and the potential that this has to affect the lives of future generations (that is, social sustainability) (Koning, 2002).

While global sustainability is a concern within a holistic view of the world, at the local level, educators of young children also have a responsibility to address the sustainable patterns that connect across peer–peer and adult–peer relationships. Attachment theory suggests that when young children develop strong relationships they feel more secure and, in feeling secure, are then able to interact positively and make more of their learning opportunities. One of the strategies employed in early childhood settings in support of attachment growth is that of having key or primary caregiving. Underpinning this model is the belief that having a consistent, dependable, sensitive and responsive adult builds independent children and a trusting relationship with families. The primary caregiving model fosters intimate relationships between educators and children through a curriculum whereby a designated adult is available to individual children through a major part of the child's day and even remaining with a particular group of children over time.

Attention to human needs and wellbeing at a global level is expressed in the Brundtland report to the United Nations (Brundtland, 1987). The report alerted the world to the need to take actions in order to secure resources for the future; otherwise, significant economic, physical, population and human resources will fall into the trap of degradation. The report stated that:

> Sustainability requires views of human needs and well-being that incorporate such non-economic variables as education and health enjoyed for their own sake, clean air and water, and the protection of natural beauty. It must also work to remove disabilities from disadvantaged groups, many of whom live in ecologically vulnerable areas, such as many tribal groups in forests, desert nomads, groups in remote hill areas, and indigenous peoples of the Americas and Australasia. (Brundtland, 1987, paragraph 39)

For early childhood educators, concerns for equity between generations and across cultures, as well as caring for planet earth, require developing a disposition of stewardship. A disposition represents a characteristic way of acting or 'being' that is intentionally oriented towards broad goals (DEEWR, 2009). Katz (1993) suggests that desirable dispositions can be strengthened through appropriate scaffolding, hence the educator's active role in facilitating and supporting learning opportunities. Therefore, educators have an important role in not only organising environments for young children but purposefully guiding children's developing understanding of sustainable practices (Kultti & Pramling Samuelsson, 2014).

Before addressing sustainability issues with children, educators have a responsibility to purposefully gain what Fish (1998) describes as a 'critical appreciation' (p. 102) or honest appraisal of the situation rather than making superficial changes. One of Katz's concerns was that, while children can acquire knowledge and skills, it does not necessarily mean that such learning will be applied in meaningful ways with some kind of critical understanding. Fish (1998) argues that the establishment of standards by external authorities along with the associated inspection and control systems are 'inevitably a façade' (p. 103) unless practitioners take responsibility for and think critically about their work. Ownership of actions and associated decision-making connects with comments made earlier in this chapter about personal professional philosophy of practice.

Early childhood educators in Australia now have standards and curricula to support them in their work. However, as has already been explained, to work from an environmental and ecologically oriented perspective, educators must think carefully about both the present and the future when addressing the 'liveability of our society' (Department of the Environment, Water, Heritage and the Arts, 2010, p. 4).

STANDARDS AND PRACTICES WITHIN AUSTRALIA

At the national level, there are currently three frameworks and standards to guide early childhood educators' work. The Early Years Learning Framework (EYLF) (DEEWR, 2009) and My Time, Our Place (DEEWR, 2011) refer to early years and school-oriented settings, while the standards across all early childhood settings are provided within the National Quality Standard (NQS) (Australian Children's Education and Care Quality Authority [ACECQA], 2011). For educators working with young children in the early years of school, the Australian Curriculum has a particular focus on the interrelationship between physical, human and global sustainability (Australian Curriculum, 2015; Department of Education and Training, 2014).

The EYLF acknowledges children as being 'active participants' in their lives with rights to 'an education that lays the foundation for the rest of their lives' (DEEWR, 2009, p. 5). If children are to develop a respect for the environment then there are a number of outcomes within the document that readily refer to both the disposition to be respectful of each other and the environment and support their stewardship over what happens to the environment in the future. While each of the five outcomes within the EYLF contains elements that are relevant to supporting children's developing understandings within their physical, social and emotional world and the capacity to act on that world, Outcome 2 ('Children are connected with and contribute to their world') directly targets children's responsibilities within their social and physical environment. Educators are challenged to promote children's learning by not only enabling children to have access to natural materials but to 'embed sustainability in daily routines and practices' and 'find ways of enabling children to care for and learn from the land' (p. 29). Educators may also promote learning about social responsibility and respect for the environment by providing/discussing examples of the interdependence between the environment and the life and health of all living things, including plants, animals and humans.

My Time, Our Place: Framework for school age care also takes a holistic and integrated approach to supporting children's capacity to respect their social and natural environments and to become 'world-wise' (DEEWR, 2011, p. 13). The framework emphasises accountability for a sustainable future and the promotion of children's understanding about, and the responsibility they have in, addressing long-term sustainability. Outcome 2 in the document reflects the same Outcome in the EYLF with the expectation that school age children can not only embrace sustainability through daily routines and practices but gain deeper understandings of sustainability within a global context.

Educators who take up the position of sustainability for the environment can look for standards within the Quality Areas in the NQS (ACECQA, 2011) that can be applied to the ways in which they choose to plan, create and organise materials, resources and opportunities for social encounters within the physical environment. For example, Quality Area 3 (Physical Environment: Standards and Elements) identifies that sustainable practices need to be embedded in service operations (Element 3.3.1) but that it is the responsibility of educators to take a holistic approach in fostering 'children's capacity to understand and respect the natural environment and the interdependence between people, plants, animals and the land '(ACECQA, 2011, p. 104). A holistic approach requires that the 'whole of the centre' and the 'whole of the child' must be involved in any environmental education program (Hughes, 2007, p. 11).

Over the past ten years, Early Childhood Australia (ECA), a national advocacy organisation for young children's early education and care, has been proactive in gathering and disseminating information about sustainability. It has included in its professional Code of Ethics the need to 'assist children to understand that they are global citizens with shared responsibilities to the environment and humanity' (ECA, 2006, Section 1, point four). Indeed, ECA provides resources for educators that reflect ways in which education for the environment may be addressed (see also Lee, 2012 as an individual example).

While it is helpful to have educational resources to draw upon for ideas about the creation of child friendly and globally responsible environments, it is more important for educators to take responsible action based on professional understandings and articulated beliefs and values. Some values might include creating connections and a sense of belonging; engaging the senses as well as provoking curiosity and intellectual engagement. Other values around belonging, being and becoming can be found within the EYLF (DEEWR, 2009).

Carter (2007) suggests that if the environment is regarded as a powerful teacher, then there are a number of strategies that can assist in making the connection between personal values, professional understandings and practice:

- involve all educators in identifying what it is that they believe about the educational value of the social and physical environments within which they work with children
- undertake an 'eco-smart audit' or environmental scan of both indoor and outdoor areas to ascertain the extent to which the social and physical spaces (including materials and resources) reflect what educators identified as being their personal and professional understandings about spaces for children's health, wellbeing and learning
- ascertain desirable values that educators hold for children and for themselves and identify how these will be reflected in the environment.

CONCLUSION

Flexible and sustainable environments are relational spaces where children and adults experience and create ways of being that reflect the philosophical understandings of those responsible for establishing such environments. Flexible environments provide opportunities for children's exploration and creative use of resources. Sustainable environments are those that take into account broad social contexts as well as ongoing respect for and conservation of natural resources. It is, therefore, critical that early childhood educators not only consider environmental planning that addresses aesthetics and functionality but work with young children in developing an appreciation of and respect for the environment within which they live.

FURTHER THINKING

1. Early childhood educators have a role in fostering social sustainability in the spaces of peer/peer and adult/peer encounter within early childhood settings. How can educators best be alert to such opportunities?

2. What are some of the key natural resources and activities that all children should have an opportunity to engage with in early childhood environments? What would be different for different age groups?

3. What would be a useful starting point to discuss respect for the environment with young children?

4. How might you set up sustainable practices to encourage the ideas from question 3?

5. To what extent do you think early childhood educators need to begin working through issues regarding sustainability in the hope that they could have a greater influence on the communities within which they live?

ACKNOWLEDGEMENT

Thank you to educators at SDN Beranga who willingly shared their insights into the development of the outdoor space at Beranga. Copyright of all photographs is held by SDN Children's Services, Sydney. Permission has been granted for their use.

REFERENCES

Aguiar, C. & McWilliam, R.A. (2013). Consistency of toddler engagement across two settings, *Early Childhood Research Quarterly*, 28, 102–10.

Australian Children's Education and Care Quality Authority (ACECQA) (2011). *Guide to the National Quality Standard*. Canberra, ACT: Australian Government. Retrieved 5 May 2014, <www.acecqa.gov.au>.

Australian Curriculum (2015). *Sustainability*. Retrieved 2 April 2015, <www.australian curriculum.edu.au/crosscurriculumpriorities/Sustainability>.

Brundtland, G.H. (1987). *Our Common Future: Report of the World Commission on Environment and Development*. United Nations. Retrieved 2 April 2014, <www.un-documents.net/our-common-future.pdf>.

Capra, F. (1988). *Uncommon Wisdom: Conversations with remarkable people*. London: Rider.

Carter, M. (2007). Making your environment 'the third teacher', *Exchange: The early leaders' magazine since 1978*. Retrieved 10 June 2010, <www.ChildCareExchange.com>.

Davis, J. (2009). Revealing the research 'hole' of early childhood education for sustainability: A preliminary survey of the literature, *Environmental Education Research*, 15(2), 227–41.

Department of Education and Training (DET) (2014). *Review of the Australian Curriculum. Final report*. Retrieved 15 March 2015, <https://docs.education.gov.au/documents/review-australian-curriculum-final-report>.

Department of Education, Employment and Workplace Relations (DEEWR) (2009). Belonging, Being and Becoming: The early years learning framework for Australia. Canberra: Commonwealth of Australia. Retrieved 5 May 2014, <www.ag.gov.au/cca>.

—— (2011). *My Time, Our Place: Framework for school age care in Australia*. Canberra: Commonwealth of Australia.

Department of the Environment, Water, Heritage and the Arts (2010). *Sustainability Curriculum Framework: A guide for curriculum developers and policy makers*. Canberra: Australian Government.

Early Childhood Australia (ECA) (2006). *Code of Ethics*. Canberra: ECA. Retrieved 5 May 2014, <www.earlychildhoodaustralia.org.au/code_of_ethics/early_childhood_australias_code_of_ethics.html>.

Edwards, C., Gandini, L. & Forman, G. (eds) (2011). *The Hundred Languages of Children: The Reggio Emilia experience in transformation*, 3rd edn. Santa Barbara: ABC-CLIO.

Fish, D. (1998). *Appreciating Practice in the Caring Professions: Refocusing professional development and practitioner research*. Oxford: Butterworth-Heinemann.

Fröbel, F. (1895). *Friedrich Froebel's Pedagogics of the Kindergarten, or, His ideas concerning the play and playthings of the child* (trans. J. Jarvis). New York: D. Appleton and Company.

Gandini, L. (2011). Connecting through caring and learning spaces. In C. Edwards, L. Gandini, & G. Forman (eds) (2011). *The Hundred Languages of Children: The Reggio Emilia experience in transformation*, 3rd edn.Santa Barbara: ABC-CLIO, pp. 317–41.

Goodfellow, J. (2003). Practical wisdom in professional practice: The person in the process, *Contemporary Issues in Early Childhood*, 4(1), 48–63.

—— (2014). Infants initiating encounters with peers in group care environments. In Harrison, L. & Sumsion, J. (eds) (2014). *Lived Spaces of Infant–Toddler Education and Care: Exploring diverse perspectives on theory, research and practice*. New York: Springer, pp. 201–10.

Greenman, J. (1988). *Caring Spaces, Learning Places: Children's environments that work*. Redmond, WA: Exchange Press.

Harrison, L. & Sumsion, J. (eds) (2014). *Lived Spaces of Infant–Toddler Education and Care: Exploring diverse perspectives on theory, research and practice*. New York: Springer.

Hughes, M. (2007). *Climbing the Little Green Steps: How to promote sustainability within early childhood services in your local area*. Gosford, NSW: Gosford and Wyong City Councils.

Katz, L.G. (1993). *Dispositions and Implications for Early Childhood Practices*. ED360 104. Urbana, IL: ERIC Clearinghouse on Elementary and Early Childhood Education.

Koning, J. (2002). Social sustainability in a globalizing world: Context, theory and methodology explored. In *More on MOST: Proceedings of an expert meeting*. The Hague: UNESCO.

Kultti, A. & Pramling Samuelsson, I. (2014). Guided participation and communication practices in multilingual toddler groups. In L. Harrison & J. Sumsion (eds), *Lived Spaces of Infant–Toddler Education and Care: Exploring diverse perspectives on theory, research and practice*. New York: Springer, pp. 147–59.

Lee, C. (2012). *'Stories from the heart': Connecting children and families with our earth*. Research in Practice Series. Deakin West, ACT: Early Childhood Australia.

Maxwell, L. (2007). Competency in child care settings: The role of the physical environment, *Environment and Behavior*, 39(2), 229–45.

Nelson, K. (2007). *Young Minds in Social Worlds: Experience, meaning, and memory*. Cambridge: Harvard University Press.

Press, F. & Mitchell, L. (2014). Lived spaces of infant–toddler education and care: Implications for policy? In L. Harrison & J. Sumsion (eds), *Lived spaces of Infant–Toddler Education and Care: Exploring diverse perspectives on theory, research and practice*. New York: Springer, pp. 225–40.

Ridgway, A. & Hammer, M. (2006). Spaces that educate. In M. Fleer, S. Edwards, M. Hammer, A. Kennedy, A. Ridgway et al., *Early Childhood Learning Communities: Sociocultural research in practice*. Frenchs Forest, NSW: Pearson, pp. 95–117.

Siraj-Blatchford, I. (2007). Creativity, communication and collaboration: The identification of pedagogic progression in sustained shared thinking, *Asia-Pacific Journal of Research in Early Childhood Education*, 1(2), 3–23.

Sun Kim, B. & Darling, L.F. (2012). Shades of pink: Preschoolers make meaning in a Reggio-inspired classroom, *Young Children*, 2(3), 44–50.

Torquati, J. & Ernst, J.A. (2013). Beyond the walls: Conceptualizing natural environments as 'third educators', *Journal of Early Childhood Teacher Education*, 34, 191–208.

van Manen, M. (1990). *Researching Lived Experience: Human science for an action sensitive pedagogy*. London, Ontario, Canada: State University of New York Press.

Wilson, R. (1997). Environmental education: A sense of place, *Early Childhood Education Journal*, 24(3), 191–4.

Chapter 14

Professionalism for early childhood educators

Louise Mary Thomas

In this chapter you will find:
- an outline of two key professional expectations in ECEC—the educator's expertise and relationship building
- professional relationships—parents, colleagues and authorities
- ethics.

What makes the biggest difference to educational outcomes for children? Is it the teacher to student ratio? Is it the quality and quantity of resources in the classroom? Is it the appropriateness and authenticity of the curriculum frameworks? While each of these, and many other factors, do have a significant impact on children's learning, widespread research claims that the most significant factor in learning outcomes for children is the quality of the educators supporting the learning process (Hargreaves, 2013). How early childhood educators identify as professional—understandings applied to roles, responsibilities, advocacy and leadership in the work of being and becoming an early childhood professional—has significant influence on how they negotiate professional practices and ultimately the quality of their support to children's learning. This chapter examines key elements in the work of early childhood educators that contribute to their identification as professional.

KEY DISCOURSES OF PROFESSIONALISM IN EDUCATION

The work of early childhood education and care (ECEC) professionals is anchored to a combination of two key expectations. First, it is expected that, as a professional, an early childhood educator will have a particular level of expertise and will draw on this expert knowledge to inform their practice and guide the practices of others. Second, it is expected that as an early childhood professional, practice will be embedded within respectful and authentic relationships with a range of key groups—children, families, colleagues, authorities and communities. It is argued that these expectations are at times competing and it is the continual work to hold these expectations together that represents what it means to be and become an ethical professional (Thomas, 2012).

The way in which these expectations are put to work in the everyday practices of early childhood educators can be considered through various ways of thinking about professionalisation. Two key ways to think about professionalism used in this chapter are a traditional understanding of being professional and a managerial understanding of being professional. Each of these views creates a particular understanding of what it means to be professional and this influences ways in which early childhood educators identify and are identified in terms of professionalism. If we look at each of these representations separately we can consider how these may position early childhood educators in their roles and responsibilities, how this then positions them in society, and the expectations placed on them in regard to leadership and advocacy.

Traditional understandings of professionalism draw on a number of key elements to represent the practices of teachers: teacher autonomy of practice; specialised, expert knowledge; internal control mechanisms (for example, teacher registration or required membership of professional associations); expectations of behaviour, monitored through an expectation that individuals adhere to a code of ethics. (At times throughout this chapter the term 'teacher' is specifically used to indicate early childhood educators who have a university-based teacher education qualification.) *Managerial professionalism* presents a different set of elements that can be seen to influence teacher practice. This representation of what it is to be professional is driven by a move towards centralised control of education agendas and decentralised management of education administration. Within this framework of professionalism individual practices are dominated by an acceptance of and compliance with the expectations of authorities external to the professional group. This allows for claims of professional status via demonstrations of accountable and effective practices that meet expectations of authorities (Ball, 2012). Representing professionalism as managerial reduces the focus on autonomy and emphasises compliance with state-driven expectations. In this way professional identity is shaped within a shifting education climate in which a culture of efficient performance of predetermined practices dominates, presented as educational performativity (Ball, 2012). To identify as professional within a culture driven by performativity reduces links to teacher autonomy and expert knowledge, which are predominant expectations of traditional professionalism. There is an erosion of teachers' sense of professionalism that is linked to autonomous, contextualised curriculum and pedagogic decision-making in favour of a professionalism that is the enactment of corporate, state-driven education agendas. The view of professionalism that dominates at any particular point is shaped by the social, cultural and political context of the place and time.

The early childhood education sector has not been immune to social, economic and political changes that have contributed to a shifting representation of what it means to be professional (Woodrow, 2011). Professionalisation of the early childhood sector, in the name of status raising and 'quality improvement', has seen a shift away from emphasis on traditional representation of professionalism driven by qualification requirements monitored by the profession, autonomy and adherence to codes of ethics. This shift has seen a move towards an emphasis on managerial professionalism involving professional judgement based on performance of externally controlled practices and outcomes, what Ball (2012) referred to as 'performativity'. A culture of performativity within the early childhood sector is evident through a greater emphasis on predetermined outcomes and performance indicators set by the state to measure 'quality' (Osgood, 2011). In this way professional autonomy competes with a need to demonstrate accountability by means of effective and efficient performance of corporate measures.

The above descriptors have presented two competing ways of thinking about early childhood professionals. Presenting professionalism in this way puts a focus on binary thinking, the notion of good/bad, right/wrong professionalism in early childhood education and care, where what it means to be and become an early childhood professional requires 'either/or' choices. An alternative path is the opportunity to think and act in terms of 'both/and' ways of being. That is, holding together *both* traditional *and* managerial ways of being and becoming professional. This approach requires problematising a reliance on the certainty and security that comes with privileging one way over another, and accepting the uncertainty and complexity of holding together what may seem to be opposites. For early childhood educators this holding together of seeming opposites is evident as they work to respond to expectations that they draw on their expert knowledge *and* they engage in authentic and responsive relationships with other groups with whom they work.

PROFESSIONAL RELATIONSHIPS

The professionalism of the early childhood education and care sector is characterised through a dominance of nurturing and collaborative relationships and through an increasing emphasis on mandated relationships. These relationships are enacted through engagement with children and parents/carers, colleagues (for example, teaching partners) and authorities (for example, employers and regulatory systems). How these relationships contribute to understanding of professional and ethical practice can be viewed from multiple perspectives. The following sections will present different perspectives on professional relationships with parents, colleagues and authorities. This is done with the intention of presenting variously argued ways of identifying what it means to be and become professional by way of the relational work of early childhood education and care. This chapter should be read not to identify the right or best way to engage in relationships but to appreciate the importance of challenging any taken-for-granted assumptions or ways of thinking about such relationships; to ask why particular ways of thinking and acting in these relationships dominate at particular times and in particular contexts. It is only when taken-for-granted thinking is questioned that possibilities for 'both/and' thinking can emerge. It should be noted that although relationships with children contribute significantly to professional practice of ECEC educators, this element is dealt with specifically in other sections of this book and so is not addressed in this discussion of professional identity construction.

Perspectives and practices in teaching and leadership

Relationships with parents

There are particular understandings of accepted practices for both early childhood educators and parents when engaging in relationships in early childhood settings. Engagement in caring and nurturing relationships (with families, children and colleagues) is a normative expectation of being a 'good' early childhood teacher (Feeney et al., 2012; Langford, 2010). At the same time rational, scientific expertise (for example, developmental psychology and brain research) is recognised in the enactment of professional relationships between early childhood educators and parents (MacNaughton, 2004; Weems, 2004). This presents a normative expectation that to claim professional status early childhood teachers must have, and exercise, expertise in the field of ECEC. There is an embedded rhetoric of 'partnership' as the key way to engage relationships between early childhood educators and parents. This representation has been interpreted variously and it can be argued that particular interpretations of partnership have become taken-for-granted practice for educators in the ECEC sector. The notion of partnership can be presented as parent participation and parent education. In both these representations of partnership there is a particular positioning of early childhood educator and a particular positioning of parent and it is these representations that contribute to how it is possible and acceptable for early childhood educators to identify as professional.

Parent participation

The conceptualisation of partnership comes with the premise that when parents are involved in care and education settings children will benefit, with enhanced learning, greater correlation between home and early childhood setting, and more effective family functioning (Arthur et al., 2015; Rodd, 2013). Of course it is a 'taken-for-granted' assumption that every 'good' parent would wish to maximise benefits for their child. An understanding of the good parent as a participating parent creates a binary opposite between the 'good' parent and 'non-participating' parent. Such a binary can be read as: the 'good' parent participates appropriately in order to maximise the benefit for their child; the parent that does not participate does not act in the best interests of their child. Creating a judgemental binary like this does not particularly represent true partnership interactions.

While it can be argued that parent participation is beneficial, it is often claimed that to effectively action these beneficial practices there are conditions that need to be placed on this participation (Thomas, 2012). These conditions include parents accepting information from ECEC educators about what the service will (and will not) provide and accepting their obligations in this service provision. Such conditions of involvement establish and maintain teachers as the partner in 'the know', and parents as required to conform in order to partake of the services on offer. This enables early childhood teachers to be positioned as experts and parents to be assigned the role of client/consumer in the partnership. The 'good' or responsible parent actively engages in partnerships with teachers that involve conforming or complying with the expectations of education and care settings (MacNaughton, 2003). It is a discourse of conforming parent that allows for children and the state to benefit from education and care provision. A parent–teacher partnership represented in this way does not involve equality between partners.

Parent education

Parent education, in its many guises, is presented as a key component of the teacher–parent relationship, and as such a contributing factor to ways in which professional identity is constructed for and by early childhood teachers. Positioning teachers as experts and parents as needing this expert knowledge is accepted to the extent that it is a normalised or taken-for-granted way of representing the exchange between early childhood teachers and parents. Such normalisations of teachers as the expert and parents as needing this expertise create a link to the participatory relationship discussed previously—parents need to learn (via the teacher's expertise) to do things the way they are done at the centre or school; and parents can learn to be 'better' parents from teachers' expertise. This reinforces hierarchical categorisations of teachers and parents, such that teachers are able to maintain a more powerful stance in the parent–teacher relationship through their claim to hold the expertise neces- sary to meet the responsibility to help parents 'fit the system'. The concept of parent education can be seen to present 'partnership' as a form of governance. This form of governance acts on both parents and teachers through normal- isations of what it is to be a good parent or good teacher. Access to and use of expert knowledge presents one norm of what it is to be a good early childhood teacher. So again what can be seen as an element of professionalism is the capacity to both accept and challenge such normative practices and expectations.

These representations of partnership that operate through parent participation and parent education require expertise as an essential element of what it is to be an early childhood professional. This way of representing professionalism is dependent on a level of certainty on the part of early childhood educators, certainty that comes from claims to be the holder of expert knowledge. But what happens when teachers challenge such a hierarchical relationship and accept that parents also bring expertise to the relationship—particular expertise about their own children? When parents are seen as having expert knowledge this can introduce a challenge to a key concept of what has been taken for granted in terms of what it means to claim to be a professional educator; that is, having sole claim to expertise. Challenging hierarchical relationships between parents and teachers (Grieshaber & Ryan, 2006) has a flow-on effect for teachers' reliance on expertise as the basis for claims of professionalism and how teachers are able to speak of their identity constructions. One flow-on effect can be the need to accept a level of uncertainty that comes when there can no longer be a reliance on hierarchical relationships and educators have to construct their professionalism within the uncertainty of partnership with parents where they cannot claim that their expertise is privileged over that of parents.

It is not my intention to make claims about which perspectives of parent/teacher relationships are true, best or even most appropriate. The intention is to question what Tobin (1995) presented as 'unquestionable assumptions', as to leave such assumptions unchallenged is to limit the multiple possibilities of what it could be to identify as an early childhood professional and to present a too simplified response to what is a complex undertaking; that is, being and becoming an ethical professional.

There are other relationships that inform professionalism of early childhood teachers that similarly are driven by taken-for-granted assumptions of expected practice. The ways in which relationships with colleagues and relationships with authorities are incorporated into the professionalisation of the early childhood sector will be discussed next. As with relationships between parents and early childhood teachers, this is done to challenge reliance on normalising elements of what it means to be professional. This again opens the possibility of thinking

Professionalism for early childhood educators

otherwise (beyond normative, unchallenged ways of thinking) as we consider what it means to be an early childhood professional.

Relationships with colleagues

Early childhood teaching is a task most often undertaken as a member of a group (Rodd, 2013). The work of early childhood education involves some level of interaction between early childhood teachers and their colleagues. A further key aspect of the early childhood sector is an expectation that individuals will actively locate themselves as members of a united professional group (Rodd, 2013). As with relationships with parents, there are taken-for-granted expectations of professional relationships with work colleagues and expectations of behaviours as a member of the early childhood profession. There is an expectation that early childhood teachers will work as members of a united team (Rodd, 2013). This approach to collegial interactions is identified as 'best' for children. Over twenty years ago, Almy (1988) wrote of 'being a team, working together for the good of the children' as an 'early childhood education tradition' (p. 51). Such an emphasis on collaborative team work maintains its privileged position as a key element of current early childhood mantra of what it means to be an early childhood professional (Arthur et al., 2015; Feeney et al., 2012; Rodd, 2013). It is suggested that to be a good early childhood professional requires a commitment to practices that are collaborative and supportive in relationships with colleagues.

Within collegial relationships early childhood teachers are expected to use 'expert' knowledge to both challenge and support as a 'team member'. These expectations generate particular, and at times competing, norms of behaviour. This presents a particular representation of professionalism that requires the early childhood teacher to engage in collaborative teamwork, and enact leadership of the team that both supports and challenges the practices of team members. Claims of expertise afford teacher-qualified early childhood educators the opportunity to identify as both collaborative, supportive team members and as challenging, supportive leaders, while maintaining positions of expert in their relationships with differently qualified colleagues.

As the holders of expertise, early childhood teachers are afforded the opportunity to locate themselves as supportive when they provide access to this knowledge to less qualified team members. In this way qualified early childhood

301

teachers are positioned as both supportive and expert. Early childhood teachers are able to locate themselves more powerfully in their supportive relationships with colleagues by drawing on their expected use of expert knowledge. One way in which this is enacted is when teachers use their expertise to influence or supportively challenge perspectives of less qualified staff members with the intention of building their expert knowledge. This expertise is used to both support and challenge within an early childhood team and, through either process, maintain a position of power in the relationship.

The promotion of an expected level and type of expertise for early childhood teachers, informed by scientific and rational ways of knowing (for example, developmental psychology and, more recently, brain research) has been entrenched as a dominant discourse in moves to professionalise the sector (Dahlberg & Moss, 2005; Thomas, 2009). What is required to 'perform' as an early childhood professional is to draw on such expertise when engaging with colleagues. This form of relationship represents a norm of being an early childhood professional (Osgood, 2006a). Early childhood teachers are placed in the more powerful position in their relationships with differently qualified colleagues because of their claims to expertise. Therefore, expertise becomes a means of demonstrating their professionalism. As such the expectation of expertise becomes a form of governance (self-regulation or external control) in relation to collegial interactions. In this way expertise is a mechanism by which qualified early childhood teachers are positioned both powerfully within early childhood teams and are also controlled in how they interact in these teams, as expertise both enables and constrains what it is to be an early childhood professional. Questioning assumptions about a privileged positioning of early childhood teachers' expertise does not require a denial of the importance of expertise but rather offers opportunities to think otherwise about expertise and to acknowledge the varying forms of expertise without an imposed hierarchy.

The current focus on unity in early childhood education goes beyond centre-based collegial teams. An expectation of unity exists across the early childhood profession as a whole. Such unity represents a means by which status as a profession is claimed for and by members of the early childhood sector. Unity in the guise of standards, set curricula, policies and regulations is presented as a means of responding to and ensuring community expectations of high quality. In this way standards become mechanisms by which particular values and practices of early childhood teachers are normalised (Osgood, 2006a, 2006b); and expectations of unity for the sector become a means by which to manage and control early childhood teachers' practices and values. So, expectations of demonstrated expertise and collaborative promotion of a unified profession create a particular identifiable norm of what it is to be an early childhood professional.

To construct and maintain status as knowledge experts and as members of a professional body, early childhood teachers are expected to make visible their expert knowledge within the communities in which they work and within society as a whole. As members of the early childhood profession, early childhood teachers are expected to draw on their expertise as they engage in the relational aspects of their work. This use of expertise requires early childhood teachers to position themselves not only as leaders in team-based relational groups, but also as leaders who advocate and as activists within the early childhood sector as a whole.

When hierarchy is used to privilege some ways of knowing this can represent one claim to professionalism. However, a continual challenging of a fixed, taken-for-granted way of engaging in relationships with colleagues represents an alternative way to claim professionalism. Such an alternative is professionalism that is based on authentic relationships that require acceptance and valuing of diverse ways of knowing rather than favouring one form of expertise. As with parent–educator relationships, this way of constructing professionalism requires the capacity to hold together an acceptance of certainty that comes with early childhood expertise and the uncertainty that comes when this expertise is constantly questioned and challenged because it has to work with equally acknowledged other forms of expertise.

Relationships with authorities

A third element of the work of early childhood teachers that demonstrates professionalism involves relationships with authorities. Viewing early childhood teachers as members of a professional group is connected to interactions between the early childhood teacher and authorities. Three key factors that represent authority in the early childhood sector are employers, legislation and the agencies that implement legislative requirements, and professional standards. For early childhood teachers their professional practices are driven by what is considered expected behaviours (or normalised behaviours) of a professional group.

Perspectives and practices in teaching and leadership

The relationship between teachers and the first form of authority, employers, has significant influence on the way in which early childhood teachers identify as professional. A key component of the relationship between teachers and employers is that of appraisal of work practices and work outcomes (Ball, 2013). How such appraisal processes are enacted is significantly dependent on the perspectives afforded professionalism. Traditional professionalism would position appraisal as recognition of the work of individual teachers and would allow the opportunity for the quality of this work to be assessed and rewarded according to the profession itself. Managerial professionalism would present appraisal as a means of monitoring performance to ensure accountability and the effective delivery of the needs of the organisation and ultimately the needs of the consumer. In this context the required outcomes and the assessment of these outcomes will be determined not by an autonomous professional or professional group but by the employing body managing the provision of the service on behalf of the client or consumer. Performance management or appraisal undertaken in such a context shifts the monitoring of teachers from the profession itself to the bureaucracy of the employing authority (Ball, 2013; Day, Flores, & Viana, 2007). When the professionalisation of the sector is driven by a managerial lens, early childhood teachers are expected to demonstrate their true professionalism by making a commitment to be a good employee (Feeney et al., 2012). A professional is thus identified as an employee who works hard to meet outcomes determined by others, namely the client consumer. It is the ability to be effective and accountable in the delivery of organisational needs that forms the basis of a teacher's appraisal and his/her ensuing identity as professional.

The second form of authority significant within the work of teachers is that of legislation. Increased demands of a regulatory culture have added complexity to the work of early childhood teachers (Fenech & Sumsion, 2007). Over the past decade in Australia this regulatory culture has been driven by an agenda emerging from the National Quality Framework (NQF) for Early Childhood Education and Care and School Aged Care (Council of Australian Governments [COAG], 2009). The key focus of this agenda has been to increase the quality of service provision and the achievement of this has emphasised the requirement to enhance the qualifications of staff. This has also been labelled as a mechanism for enabling the professional status of those employed in the sector. With professional status linked to regulatory requirements it can be argued that this professionalisation is framed by a managerial lens, where individuals' practices and their professional accountability are mandated rather than autonomously driven. In this way legislation, as a mechanism of accountability, affords society an opportunity to exercise control of the provision of education (Fenech & Sumsion, 2007). In the name of 'public accountability' (p. 109), Fenech and Sumsion (2007) suggest that there is a danger that early childhood teachers can be denied opportunities to engage in their work autonomously. However, they also argue that through their engagement with regulatory requirements early childhood teachers are able to use regulations to support their autonomous professional decisions. As a result, early childhood teachers' experiences of regulative impositions can be conceptualised as a 'double-edged sword' (Fenech, Sumsion, & Goodfellow, 2006, p. 49). Such a situation establishes an expectation that early childhood educators engage in both a managerial professionalism of being accountable and implementing expected practices, and being autonomous. This presented an additional layer of complexity to the professional identity of early childhood teachers.

Professional teacher standards represent a third educational authority that impacts on teachers' identification as professional. In Australia professional standards or criteria have been associated with both accreditation of teacher qualifications and the practice of teaching (Australian Institute for Teaching and School Leadership [AITSL]; Australian Children's Education and Care Quality Authority [ACECQA]). Such standards represent a means by which the quality of teachers' qualifications and the quality of teachers' work can be assessed against a set of performative criteria. The implementation of professional teacher standards represents both external controls and internal claims to professional status. However, this control is often disguised as a mechanism by which the status of teachers is enhanced. Society is able to exercise such controls via bureaucratic mechanisms because teachers are willing participants in the process. This represents societal control through demands of bureaucratic accountability, which are masked in claims of enhanced professional status (Thomas, 2009; Woodrow, 2011). In this way, the introduction and implementation of professional standards can be seen as a means of professionalising the sector with a focus on the concept of professionalism as the achievement of community approval for teachers' professional practices. For early childhood teachers, whether they are making claim to status as professional through AITSL or ACECQA recognition of their qualifications and their practices, there is an expectation of adherence to socially accepted measures of what it is to be a 'good' early childhood teacher.

Relationships between early childhood teachers and authorities manifest variously within both traditional and managerial discourses of professionalism. Autonomy and expectations of effectiveness and accountability are the discursive practices at work within these two discourses (Day et al., 2007). The expectations that early childhood teachers will at once be autonomous in their practices and demonstrate effective and accountable compliance with the expectations of an education system adds to the complexity and uncertainty of what it is to be and to become professional.

In addition to the ways in which professional relationships demonstrate professionalisation of the early childhood sector, a further element of this process has been the development and implementation of a Code of Ethics as a component of early childhood teachers' work. Such a process is presented as a means of both status enhancement and control. How this is identified in early childhood contexts is addressed in the following section.

ETHICS: AN ELEMENT OF PROFESSIONALISM

Ethics and engagement in ethical practice are formed from, and inform, different representations of professionalism. Professionalism can be framed within a modernist perspective, where there is a truth to be adhered to by members of the group. Professionalism represented in this way is shaped partly by adherence to codes of ethical practice (Roberts, 2005); that is, membership of the group is determined through acceptance and agreement in regard to commonly held ways of thinking and behaving, represented through a Code of Ethics. Professionalism can also be framed within a postmodern perspective, where there are many truths to be debated and considered in relation to different contexts. In this instance, professionalism is evident through an individual engaging in relationships based on 'respect for otherness' and limitations of knowing this 'otherness' (Dahlberg & Moss, 2005, p. 83). Within such a representation, membership of a professional group is not dependent on a set of fixed values. While ethical engagement is important, it is not formulated through a universal code. Paramount to this process is the individual's willingness and ability to engage in dissensus, disagreement and uncertainty about ways of thinking and behaving; that is, a challenge to the modernist notion of an established truth or universal notions about professionalism. This presents early childhood professional identity not as a fixed construct dependent on fixed normative representations of professionalism (either traditional or managerial) but as a multiple, fluid construct emerging from multiple and fluid relations between self and other. To present ethics as relational affords the possibilities of multiple, and never fully coherent, identity constructions born from multiple, and never certain, engagements in relations between self and other. Instead of one relationship being central to the formation of early childhood professional identity (for example, membership of a professional group, articulated in part through normative expectations of relationships with others and adherence to a Code of Ethics), such professional identity is constructed through multiple and constantly changing relationships and ethical engagements that are neither fixed nor certain (Thomas, 2009).

The constructions of professional identities of early childhood teachers are constant processes of 'becoming' and these 'becomings' are located within relational encounters and this context provides a key component of what it means to engage as an ethical professional. To present a particular identity requires engagement in a process of locating self and other in relation to the available or taken-for-granted norms (Butler, 2005); for example the norms of what is expected to be an early childhood professional. Certainty, in relation to self-identity, professional identity requires a positioning of self and other in relation to the available norms and expectations. This presupposes the capacity for a coherent identification of self and of other at any fixed point in time. Difference between 'self' and 'other' creates a risk to the construction of coherent self-identities (Butler, 2005). Acceptance of difference between self and other, where there is no attempt to make other like self as part of the process of identifying self, is often difficult if individuals are reliant on a sense of certainty in their identity. To resist such certainty what is asked of an individual is an acceptance of the limitations of fully knowing both 'self' and 'other' by resisting the expected norms of relational engagement, and challenging an acceptance of a necessity to know self and other in relation to these norms (Butler, 2005). Acknowledgement of the limits of self-knowability enables and constrains ethical relations between the knowable and unknowable self and the knowable and unknowable other. Three key ethical and social relations for early childhood teachers that were identified through the chapter were professional relationships with parents,

Perspectives and practices in teaching and leadership

colleagues and authorities. Ways in which early childhood teachers are able to speak of themselves as professional and ethical are made available through their engagement in these relationships. Considering new and multiple ways of 'doing relationships' allows for possibilities of new and multiple ways of constructing professional identities. Such constructions create new spaces for 'doing ethics' in ECEC.

CONCLUSION

Significant components of the professionalisation of the early childhood sector addressed in this chapter are engagement in relationships with key stakeholders and engagement with ethics. In an increasingly corporatised early childhood sector, teachers are presented with specific (and, at times, contradictory) expectations of how to enact these elements of professionalism. Claims of professionalisation of the sector have created particular expectations of how early childhood teachers engage in professional relationships: they are expected to be partners and the providers of a service to parents. They are expected to work with colleagues as a unified team and engage with differences. When relating to authorities, early childhood teachers are expected to work autonomously and to be accountable to these authorities. Competing understandings of ethics are also presented as components of a professionalised early childhood sector. Ethics is offered as a structured and unifying guide based on shared values and beliefs, usually presented in the form of a Code of Ethics. It is also presented as a relational exchange based on interaction between self and other, where understandings of both self and other are never fixed or fully knowable.

This chapter has presented professionalism of early childhood educators as both requiring adherence to ethical codes and embedded within the context of authentic and uncertain relationships with others. To be professional involves an expectation of being expert, and with this comes expectations of certainty in practices and behaviours. To engage in the work of being an early childhood educator involves relationships, which, due to their contextual nature, at times involve uncertainty. One way to respond to this is to not rely on a binary of either certainty or uncertainty in identifying as professional, but to look for other possibilities of being professional by making spaces for both certainty and uncertainty where being professional is embedded within complex and multiple relationships. What is made available in this process is the possibility of a space for 'new' ways early childhood educators can construct professional identities and new ways of doing ethics. This space privileges rather than denies the complexities and uncertainties of professional identity in ECEC. Such new possibilities for identity constructions and ethics are embedded within uncertainty and dissensus in the form of resistance to expected norms, and within an acceptance of the role of certainty or consensus in conformity to the norms of professionalism.

FURTHER THINKING

1. In what ways does autonomy both enable and constrain professionalism in ECEC?

2. How do professional relationships impact on the daily work of early childhood educators?

3. In what ways do mandated professional standards and regulatory requirements influence professional practice?

4. What does it mean to claim to be an ethical professional in ECEC?

REFERENCES

Almy, M. (1988). The early childhood educator revisited. In B. Spodek, O.N. Saracho & M.A. Peters (eds), *Professionalism and the Early Childhood Practitioner*. New York: Teachers College Press, pp. 48–55.

Arthur, L., Beecher, B., Death, E., Dockett, S. & Farmer, S. (2015). *Programming and Planning in Early Childhood Settings*, 6th edn. Southbank: Thomson.

Ball, S. (2012). *Global Education Inc.: New policy networks and the neo-liberal imaginary*. London: RoutledgeFalmer.

—— (2013). *The Education Debate*. University of Bristol: Policy Press.

Butler, J. (2005). *Giving an Account of Oneself*. New York: Fordham University Press.

Council of Australian Governments (COAG) (2009). *National Quality Framework for Early Childhood Education and Care*. Canberra, ACT, Australia: COAG.

Dahlberg, G. & Moss, P. (2005). *Ethics and Politics in Early Childhood Education*. London: RoutledgeFalmer.

Perspectives and practices in teaching and leadership

Day, C., Flores, M.A. & Viana, I. (2007). Effects of national policies on teachers' sense of professionalism: Findings from an empirical study in Portugal and England, *European Journal of Teacher Education*, 30(3), 249–65.

Feeney, S., Christensen, D. & Moravcik, E. (2012). *Who am I in the Lives of Children? An introduction to early childhood education*, 7th edn. Upper Saddle River, NJ: Pearson Education.

Fenech, M. & Sumsion, J. (2007). Early childhood teachers and regulation: Complicating power relations using a Foucauldian lens, *Contemporary Issues in Early Childhood*, 8(2), 109–22.

Fenech, M., Sumsion, J. & Goodfellow, J. (2006). The regulatory environment in long day care: A 'double-edged sword' for early childhood professional practice, *Australian Journal of Early Childhood*, 31(3), 49–58.

Grieshaber, S. & Ryan, S. (2006). Beyond certainties: Postmodern perspectives, research, and the education of young children. In B. Spodek & O.N. Saracho (eds), *Handbook of Research on the Education of Young Children*. Mahwah, NJ: Lawrence Erlbaum Associates, pp. 533–54.

Hargreaves, A. (2013). Professional capital and the future of teaching. In T. Seddon & J.S. Levin (eds), *Educators, Professionalism and Politics: Global transitions, national spaces and professional projects*. London: Routledge, pp. 290–310.

Langford, R. (2010). Theorizing an early childhood educator's authority for the advancement of social goods, *The Alberta Journal of Educational Research*, 56(3), 291–303.

MacNaughton, G. (2003). *Shaping Early Childhood: Learners, curriculum and context*. Maidenhead, Berkshire: Open University Press.

—— (2004). Children, staff and parents: Building respectful relationships in New Zealand and Australian early childhood contexts—The Australian context, *Australian Journal of Early Childhood*, 29(1), 1–7.

Osgood, J. (2006a). Deconstructing professionalism in early childhood education: Resisting the regulatory gaze, *Contemporary Issues in Early Childhood*, 7(1), 5–14.

—— (2006b). Professionalism and performativity: The feminist challenge facing early years practitioners, *Early Years*, 26(2), 187–99.

—— (2011). Contested constructions of professionalism within the nursery. In L. Miller & C. Cable, *Professionalization, Leadership and Management in the Early Years*. London: SAGE Publications.

Roberts, L.M. (2005). Changing faces: Professional image construction in diverse organizational settings, *The Academy of Management: Review*, 30(4), 685–711.

Rodd, J. (2013). *Leadership in Early Childhood*, 3rd edn. Sydney: Allen & Unwin.

Thomas, L.M. (2009). Certainties and Uncertainties: Ethics and professional identities of early childhood educators. Unpublished doctoral thesis, Brisbane: Queensland University of Technology.

—— (2012). New possibilities in early childhood teachers' professional identity constructions and ethics, *Australasian Journal of Early Childhood*, 37(3), 87–95.

Tobin, J. (1995). Post-structural research in early childhood education. In J.A. Hatch (ed.), *Qualitative Research in Early Childhood Settings*. Westport: Praeger Publishers, pp. 223–43.

Weems, L. (2004). Troubling professionalism: Narratives of family, race and nation in educational reform. In B.M. Baker & K.E. Heyning (eds), *Dangerous Coagulations? The use of Foucault in the study of education*. New York: Peter Lang Publishing, pp. 225–60.

Woodrow, C. (2011). Challenging identities: A case for leadership. In L. Miller & C. Cable, *Professionalization, Leadership and Management in the Early Years*. London: SAGE Publications.

Acknowledgements

Joanne, Wendy and Maryanne wish to thank all the contributing authors for the richness of their work and collegial willingness to respond to our inquiries and requests throughout the process. We also wish to thank Nicole Baker at the University of Newcastle who read and provided feedback on the whole book. Thanks also to the various early childhood teachers, communities, families and children for their contributions to so many of the chapters. And finally, thanks to the team at Allen & Unwin who supported us through the editing and production process.

Index

Abecedarian Project 224
Aboriginal and Torres Strait Islander children
    Aboriginal Playgroups and Enrichment Program
        146
    'Big Buddies' program 147
    Children and Family Centres 134
    Commissioner for Aboriginal Children and
        Young People (Vic) 60
    connecting with families of 152
    crèches 28–9, 145
    cultural safety 149–61
    developmentally vulnerable 144
    diverse cultural needs 156
    ECEC services 145–6
    education history 14–15, 18–19
    educational challenges 146–9
    Eight Aboriginal Ways of Learning framework
        153, 154
    Footprints in Time longitudinal study 100, 156
    Forest Schools 81
    formal education 15, 18–19
    importance of education for 144
    independence and autonomy 157–8
    Indigenous Readers are Achievers program 147
    inequality of educational achievement 148, 156,
        168
    marginalisation and cultural displacement 156,
        168
    Multifunctional Aboriginal Children's Services
        (MACS) 28–9, 124, 126–7, 133, 145–6, 149
    NAPLAN results 148–9
    National Partnership Agreement on Indigenous
        Early Childhood Development 134
    'Native' schools 15
    playgroups 145, 146
    positive community relations 150–1
    preschool attendance 144, 152
    reading statistics 147
    rights 59–60
    school attendance rates 145, 152, 158
    schools not meeting needs of 156
    social inclusion 159–60, 168
    social, physical and educational needs 156–8
    Stolen Generations 38–42, 168

    Taylor's longitudinal study 152, 156, 158
    ways of learning 153–5
    'What Works' website 147, 160
Aboriginal and Torres Strait Islander Children and
    Family Centres 134
Aboriginal and Torres Strait Islander culture 168
    cross-curriculum priorities 218, 219
    embedding Aboriginal perspectives 173–6
Aboriginal and Torres Strait Islander peoples
    assimilation 15, 19, 38, 168
    Bringing Them Home report 38–40
    children see Aboriginal and Torres Strait Islander
        children
    'Closing the Gap' report 144
    collective local names 142
    diversity among 142
    elders participating in schools 156, 157
    embedding Aboriginal perspectives 173–6
    identification as 141
    inclusion 159–60, 168, 173–6
    intercultural priorities 168
    knowing particular histories 151
    languages 155
    learning about 173–6, 218, 219
    learning from 159
    National Sorry Day Committee 40
    population statistics 142–4
    positive community relations 150–1
    poverty 152
    recognition as First Australians 168
    relationships 152
    right to a distinct status and culture 59
    right to land 60
    right to self-determination 60
    school visits by elders, artists etc 156, 157
    staff exchanges 175
    Stolen Generations 38–42, 168
    terminology 141–2
    UN Convention on Rights of Indigenous Peoples
        169
Aboriginal English 155
Aboriginal languages 155
Aboriginal pedagogy 153–5
Aboriginal perspectives 168, 173–6

313

Index

Aboriginal Playgroups and Enrichment Program 146
access to education 62, 102, 168
accreditation 29–30, 305
Albrechtsen, Janet 176, 177
Anderson, Maybanke 20
anti-racist pedagogy 158, 161
Ariès, Philippe 34–5
Asia, learning about 218, 219
assessment 211–12, 226–8
    authentic 226, 228
    definition 213
    formative 227
    National Quality Standard 227
    summative 227
Atkinson, Dr Sue Lopez 69
attachment 257–61, 285
Australian Association for Pre-School Child
    Development (AAPSCD) 23–4
    Lady Gowrie Child Centres *18*, 22–5
Australian Bureau of Statistics Childhood Education
    and Child Care Survey 123
Australian Children's Education and Care Quality
    Authority (ACECQA) 29, 190
    accreditation by 305
    Code of Ethics 191, 192, 237–8
Australian Curriculum 96, 111, 133, 134, 168, 214,
    217–20
Australian Curriculum Assessment and Reporting
    Authority (ACARA) 96, 111, 134, 218
Australian Early Development Census (AEDC) 100,
    144
Australian Institute for Teaching and School
    Leadership (AITSL)
    accreditation by 305
    Professional Standards for Teachers 111, 191, 192,
        193, 305
Australian Pre-School Association (APA) 26
Australian Professional Standards for Teachers 111,
    191, 192, 193
Australian Raising Children Network 178
Australian Research Alliance for Children and
    Youth (ARACY) 100
authentic assessment 226, 228

babies *see* infants
Barad, Karen 64
Bateson, Gregory 272
Beach Kindergartens 83
belonging 216, 257
Belonging, Being and Becoming: The early years
    learning framework (EYLF) for Australia 81, 100,
    133, 134, 213–16
    assessment 226
    Australian Curriculum and 220

concepts of becoming, being, belonging 216
curriculum 123, 133, 213–16
ethics 193–4
holistic approach 215
inclusion 159, 168
intentional teaching 224
learning outcomes 214, 217, 219, 235
NQS and 217
pedagogical principles and practices 222
play-based learning 96
practice 217
principles 217
range of theories recognised 72
relationships with families 237
secure attachment 235
sustainability principles 287–9
view of children 261, 287
Beranga 275–6, *277, 278, 281, 284*
Blaise, Mindy 46, 66
boarding schools 15
bottom-up theories 51, 52, 68
Bourdieu, Pierre 55, 57
Bowlby, John 27
Braidotti, Rosi 64
brain development 253–6
British Association for Early Childhood Education
    (UK)
    Code of Ethics 192
British Index for Inclusion 171
Brooker, Liz 56
Brown, Dr Vera Scantlebury 26
Brundtland Report 286
Buckey, Ridie Lee 21
Burman, Erica 54
Bush Kindergartens 83, 115

Capra, F 272, 274, 285
centre-based child care 122, 123–5
    see also child care/day care
Child Care Act 1972 27, 28
child care/day care
    accreditation 29–30
    centre-based 122, 123–5
    curriculum 123, 133, 134
    family day care 122, 124, 126, 133
    fee subsidies 29
    for-profit/private centres 129
    government support 27–8
    history 21–2, 27
    home-based 124, 133
    increased participation in 27, 123, 125
    Indigenous children, for 145–6
    integrated child and family centres 124, 127, 133
    kindergartens and 21–2, 25

long day care centres (LDCs) 29–30, 123–5
National Quality Framework (NQF) 112, 123, 133, 135
not-for-profit/community-based centres 129
policies 133, 134
privatisation 29–30
regulation 123
regulatory authorities 133
terminology 125
wartime children's centres 25
Child Migrants Trust 40–1
childhood
constructions of 114–15, 261
historical constructions 34–47
regulating 44
social construction 35, 37, 57, 261
studies 43, 45–7, 57–8, 100
children
capability and competence 225, 256, 261–2
constructing own lives 57, 233
historically 34–47
participation in society 46, 57, 135
relationships with *see* relationships with children
rights of *see* children's rights
study of 23–4, 43, 45–7, 57
children's rights 58–9, 196, 233
Aboriginal children 59–60
EYLF view 261
movement 58
play 97
questioning 59
UN Convention (UNCRC) 46, 58, 98
Clark, Mamie Phipps 54
clock watching 258
collaboration 245, 246, 301
collegiality 245–7, 260, 301
communication
children, with 234–5
families, with 108, 109, 240, 259, 263
infants 256
staff 261
community 80, 102–3
Aboriginal, positive relations 150–1
building sense of 243
environment, connecting with 284
involvement 243
community-based child care 129
compulsory schooling 124, 127–8
age of 20, 36–7, 128
history 15, 18, 20, 35, 45
contexts 121–8, 137
continuity of care 257
corporal punishment 15
cortisol 253

Creative Curriculum 223–4
creativity and environment 278, 279
Crèche and Kindergarten (C & K) Association (Qld) *17*, 26, 43–4, 132, 133
critical theory 65–8
Crombie, Tracy 179
cultural capital 55
cultural competence 45, 149, 168, 216, 225, 240–1
cultural diversity 54, 101, 259
see also diversity
cultural historical approach 75–8, 98
cultural reproduction theories 55
cultural safety *see* Indigenous cultural safety
curriculum 211–22, 228
aims of 214
Australian Curriculum 45, 96, 111, 127, 133, 134, 168, 214, 217–20
child care centres 123, 133
connecting to child's interests 242
critical thinking about 220–2
definition 212
educator's knowledge of content 224–5
enacted curriculum 221
hidden curriculum 221
history 14–15, 19
intended curriculum 221
international comparisons 213–14
kindergarten/preschool 126, 133, 134
lived curriculum 212, 221
national 45, 133
null curriculum 221
play-based 37, 95, 96–7, 103–8, 112
professional accountability 111–14
push down phenomenon 104
school 133, 134

Dame schools 15
day care *see* child care/day care
Deleuze, Gilles 64
Department of Education and Early Childhood Development (Vic) 191
developmental psychology 52–5, 233
devices, use of 114
Dewey, John 74, 223, 227
disability 166, 259
community agencies and services 181
Education Adjustment Profile 179
hearing impaired children 170
historical approaches 167
inclusion 164–73, 179–81
Individualised Education Plan 179
mainstream schools 166
professional development re 180–1
special schools 166

Index

disability (*cont.*)
    UN Convention on Rights of Persons with
        Disabilities 169
discipline
    communicating approach to families 263
    corporal punishment 15
diversity 164–5
    Aboriginal peoples 142, 156
    Australian population 165
    cultural 54, 101, 259
    educational responses 167–9
    environment of centre 266
    families 108–11, 239
    historical approaches 167, 182
    inclusion 164–82 *see also* inclusion
    labels and categories 164–5
    shifts in understanding of 167
    staff, among 261
documentation 81, 107, 113–14
    including families in 242

Early Childhood Australia (ECA) 189
    Code of Ethics 191, 192, 193, 288
early childhood education and care (ECEC)
    benefits of investment in 101, 130
    considerations and challenges 103–15
    contexts 121–8, 137
    government interest in 95, 101, 130
    history 20–6
    importance of 95, 130
    integrated 128–9
    international models 98–9
    models 129–30
    policy 130–7
    practical approaches and theories 72–88
    prior-to-school contexts 122–7, 133, 134
    recent influences on 98–103
    school contexts 123, 124, 127–8, 133
    terminology 122
Early Childhood Environmental Rating Scale
    (ECERS) 136
Early Childhood Reform Agenda 26
Early Years Learning Framework *see* Belonging,
    Being and Becoming: The early years learning
    framework (EYLF) for Australia
Early Years Reform Agenda (EYRA) 126, 132–7
*Early Years Workforce Strategy: The early childhood
    education and care workforce strategy for Australia*
    135
ecoliteracy 83
economic research 101
Education Acts *17*
Education and Care Services National Law/
    Regulations 135

Guide to 193
    minimum requirements for environment 267
educational programs 103–8, 262–3
educators 7
    curriculum content knowledge 224–5
    philosophy *see* philosophy of educator/centre
    professional accountabilities and expectations
        111–14
    professionalism *see* professionalism for educators
    relationships *see* relationships
    role 86, 97, 110
Eight Aboriginal Ways of Learning framework 153,
    154
environment 266–8, 271–89
    aesthetics 277, 280
    children as 'agentic' participants 276–9, 282
    collaborative project planning 276
    community 284
    connecting patterns 272–3
    connections between natural and manmade 272
    creativity and 278, 279
    design 275–6
    diversity 266
    Education and Care Services National
        Regulations 267
    educator philosophy, reflecting 274–6
    educator's role and 279–84
    engagement with 115, 272, 279
    entrance to centre 274
    family's orientation to 260
    flexible play spaces 282, 289
    health and safety issues 267–8
    home-like 266
    infants 257–61, 266–8
    'lived spaces' 279
    living system 272–4
    moveable equipment 282
    natural 81–4, 115, 272, *281*
    outdoor areas *277, 278,* 282
    physical 266–7, 272–84
    planned and scaled spaces 282
    predictable spaces 283
    private and restorative spaces 282
    Reggio Emilia view 279, 280
    scaffolding children's learning 280, 282
    secure 262
    sensory 277
    social *237,* 272, 283
    sustainability 275, 284–9
    'third teacher' 7, 266, 272, 283
    zoned areas 280–1
equal opportunities 61
equity pedagogy 61
essentialist feminism 62–3

316

ethics 187–201, 306–8
  acceptance of difference 307
  Codes of 190–4, 306
  definition 188
  ethical responsibilities 187–201
  ethical symmetry 197
  EYLF 193–4
  National Quality Framework (NQF) 193
  National Quality Standard (NQS) 190, 193, 199
  overview 188
  participation 194–6
  partnership 199–200
  power 196–9
  professional ethics in ECEC 190–201
  professionalism and 306–8
  research ethics 188–90
explicit teaching strategies 262
explorative play 262
EYLF see Belonging, Being and Becoming: The early
  years learning framework (EYLF) for Australia

families
  Aboriginal, connecting with 152–3
  communication with 108, 109, 240, 259, 263
  diversity of 108–11, 239
  education of 299–301
  expectations of 104, 106, 242, 263
  framing of family practices 172
  hierarchical relationship with teacher 299, 300
  inclusion based on 170
  orientation to centre 260
  participation 298–9
  relationships with see relationships with families
  values and beliefs 263
family day care 122, 124, 126, 133, 135
family-grouping children 258
fee subsidies 29
fees 15, 18, 29
feminism 22, 60–5
  block play examples 62, 63, 65
  essentialist 62–3
  gender equality and equity 61
  key ideas 61
  liberal 62
  'new' material 64–5
  poststructural 63–4, 233
Ferguson, Jean 23
Finnish school system 36–7
food preparation 267
forced migration 40–1
formative assessments 227
foundation year 127, 133
Footprints in Time: Longitudinal Study of
  Indigenous Children 100, 156

Forest Schools 81–4, 115
Forgotten children 38–42
Foucault, Michel 63
Frankfurt School 65
Free Kindergartens 21
Freire, Paulo 66
Fröbel, Frederick 273, 274
Fröebelian kindergarten methods 20–1, 273
funding, history of 15, 18, 22, 28–9
  fees 15, 18, 29
  Prices and Incomes Accord 28–9
  state-funded schools 16, 20

Gardner's theory of Multiple Intelligences 87–8
gender equality 61
gender equity 61
gender identities 66
Gesell, Arnold 53
Giugni, Miriam 69
Goodenough, Florence L 53
government
  ECEC policy 130–7
  interest in ECEC 26, 95, 101, 130
  reform agenda 126, 132–7
  support for child care 27–8
government schools
  history 14–15
  mass schooling 35, 42–5
Gowrie, Lady Zara 23
Guattari, Félix 64
Guide to the Education and Care Services National
  Law and Regulations 193

habitus 55, 56
Haraway, Donna 64
Hawke, Robert 29
health and safety issues 267–8
HighScope approach 73–5, 223
holistic practices 215, 253, 262
home-based care 124, 133
home schooling 124, 128
Howard, John 176, 177, 178

imitation and repetition 86
immigration and diversity 165–6
inclusion 164–82
  Aboriginal children 159–60, 168
  Aboriginal perspectives 168, 173–6
  adequate resourcing 170
  barriers to 172
  belonging 216, 257
  British Index for Inclusion 171
  disability 166, 179–81
  diversity and 164–82

Index

inclusion (*cont.*)
  embedded practices 167
  embedding Indigenous perspectives 173–7
  engagement 170
  environmental constraints 172
  family-centred approach 170
  framing of family practices 172
  hearing impaired children 170
  historical approaches 167
  in-class strategies 179
  inclusive educational practices 169–71
  Indigenous children 159–60, 168
  intercultural priorities 168
  labels and categories 164–5
  minimum standards 181
  one-off approaches 167, 173
  pedagogical adaptations 170
  policy 167–9, 181
  professional education 171, 180
  same-sex parents 176–8
  socio-economic disadvantage 166
  special education 179–81
  teacher education 172
  theoretical barriers to 172
  whole centre approach 173
Indigenous children *see* Aboriginal and Torres Strait Islander children
Indigenous cultural safety 149–61
  connecting closely 152–3
  knowing particular histories 151
  positive community relations 150–1
  recognising social dynamics 158–9
  social inclusion 159–60
  social, physical and educational needs 156–8
  strategies 149–61
Indigenous Employment Strategy 175
Indigenous peoples *see* Aboriginal and Torres Strait Islander peoples
Indigenous Readers are Achievers program 147
Infant/Toddler Environment Rating Scale (ITERS) 136
infants 252–68
  attachment 257–61, 285
  brain development 253–6
  continuity of care 257
  cultural diversity 259
  daily routine 259, 263–5
  definition 252
  educator's impact on development of 252–5
  educator's view of 255–7
  environment 257–61, 266–8
  explorative play 262
  families, relationship with 252, 255, 259–60
  inclusive pedagogies 263
  knowing habits and routines of 255, 260, 264

  literacy experiences 265
  musical experiences 265–6
  nappy changing 264, 267
  'primary caregiver' approach 258
  relationships 252–61
  responsive care helping development 253–5
  secure environment 262
  self-regulation, learning 254
  sense of belonging 257
  sense of identity 263
  sleep routine 254, 255, 259, 260, 264
  staff relationships and 260–1
  staffing arrangements 257
  teaching strategies 262
  temperament 254
  vulnerability 255
informal care 122
integrated child and family centres 124, 127, 133
integrated ECEC 128–9
intelligence theories 87
intelligence types 87
intentional teaching 223–4
intercultural priorities 168
interest-based learning 223
international approaches to curriculum 213–14
international comparisons 131, 213
international models of ECEC 98–9
investigations 105, 106

Kant, Immanuel 188
Kindergarten of the Air 24
kindergarten/preschool 20–6, 124
  curriculum 126, 133, 134
  day nursery split 22, 25, 28
  demonstration preschools 23
  foundation year 127, 133
  funding 28
  history of 20–6
  Indigenous children's attendance 144, 152
  integrated child and family centres 124, 127, 133
  National Quality Framework (NQF) 112, 123, 133, 135
  operation 124
  policies 133, 134
  regulatory authorities 133
  state government interest 26
  terminology 122, 125
Kindergarten Teacher Colleges 22
Kindergarten Unions 20–6
Kohlberg, Lawrence 53
Kura Yerlo Children's Centre 147

Lady Gowrie Child Centres *18*, 22–5
Landon, Carolyn 151

318

Index

learning
contemporary views of 261–8
daily routine, through 263–5
infants 261–8
interest-based 223
literacy experiences 265
musical experiences 265–6
play-based 37, 95, 96–7, 103–8, 112, 157, 195, 262
relationships supporting 225, 231, 253–5
liberal feminism 62
listening pedagogy 233–5
literacy experiences 265
long day care centres (LDCs) 29–30, 123–5, 133, 135
see also child care/day care
Longitudinal Study of Australian Children (LSAC) 100
low-interaction teaching strategies 262
Lynch, Phillip 27

Malaguzzi, Loris 79, 99
managerial professionalism 295–6
material feminism 64–5
mediating teaching strategies 262
Melbourne Declaration on Educational Goals for Young Australians 101, 214
mobile children's services 124, 133
models of ECEC 129–30
international 98–9
Montessori, Maria 21, 85
Montessori Method of Education 21, 84–6
multiculturalism 167
Multifunctional Aboriginal Children's Services (MACS) 28–9, 124, 126–7, 133, 145–6, 149
Multiple Intelligences theory 86–8
Mundine, Kerry 69
Murdoch Children's Research Institute 100
Murphy, Lois Barclay 53
music and movement 265–6
My Early Childhood Education (NZ)
Code of Ethical Conduct 192
MySchools website 134
My Time, Our Place: Framework for School Age Care 215, 217
Australian Curriculum and 220
learning outcomes 217
outside school hours care 127, 215
practice 217
principles 217
sustainability principles 287, 288

nappy changing 264, 267
National Assessment Program (NAP) 134
National Assessment Program—Literacy and Numeracy (NAPLAN) 134
Indigenous students 148–9

National Association for the Education of Young Children (US)
Code of Ethical Conduct 192
National Childcare Accreditation Council (NCAC) 29
National Partnership Agreement on Indigenous Early Childhood Development 134
National Quality Framework (NQF) 112, 123, 133, 135, 216–17
child care regulation 123, 133, 135
quality rating 136
regulatory culture 304
relationships with families 199
National Quality Standard (NQS) 111, 131, 132–6, 217
assessment 227
child care regulation 123, 133, 135
collaborative partnerships 199, 238
educational program and practices 262, 263
ethics 190, 193
EYLF and 217
infants, caring for 256
quality rating 126, 136, 217
relationships among staff 244
relationships with families 152, 199, 259
sustainability 288
National Statement on Ethical Conduct in Human Research 18
national studies of young children 100–1
'Native' schools 15
natural environment *see* environment
neuroscience research 99–100, 130–1
non-compulsory schooling 124
Nordic countries
ECEC programs 98–9
Finland school system 36–7
Forest Schools 81–4, 115
not-for-profit/community-based child care 129
Nursery School Teachers' College 22
nutrition 23–4, 132

occasional care 124, 133
OECD *Starting Strong* reports 128, 130, 213
'Orphan' schools 15
orphans, forced migration 40–1
outdoor activity 115
outdoor play areas *277, 278,* 282
outside school hours care (OSHC) 124, 127, 133, 135

parent education 24, 299–301
parental expectations 104, 106, 242, 263
parents *see* families
participation
Aboriginal elders 156, 157

Index

participation (*cont.*)
  children 194–6
  ethics of 194–6
  parents 241, 298–9
partnership *see also* relationships
  collaborative 199, 238, 241
  embedded rhetoric of 298
  ethics of 199–200
  families, with 107–11, 170 199, 225, 237, 264, 298
  involvement distinguished 238–9
  parent education 299–301
  parent participation 241, 298–9
pedagogical leadership 112
pedagogical relationships 225
pedagogy 19–21, 211–13, 222–5, 228
  Aboriginal 153–5
  anti-racist 158, 161
  definition 212–13
  EYLF, principles in 222, 224
  inclusive 263
Percival, Thomas 188
performativity 296
Perry Preschool Project 224
philosophy of educator/centre
  environment reflecting 274–6
  ethical 190, 193
  image of infants 255–7
  involving families in developing 241–2
  relationship building 248
  service's philosophy statement 193
  staff collaboration 245, 247
physical environment 266–7, 272–84
Piaget, Jean 53, 74
play 44, 45, 96–7, 104
  children's right to 97
  definition of 96, 97
  explorative 262
  participation and 195
  relationship building and 236–7
play-based learning 37, 95, 96–7, 103–8, 112, 157, 195, 262
playgroups 124, 133
  Indigenous children 145, 146
Plowden Committee Report, UK 26
policy 130–7
  Australian 130–2
  Early Years Reform Agenda (EYRA) 126, 132–7
  key part of ECEC 131
  layers of 132
  quality 136–7
  shifts 135
positivism 52
poststructural feminism 63–4, 233

poverty 152, 166–7
power 196–9
  asymmetrical use of 197
  child participation 198
  ethics of 196–9
prejudice 54, 69, 158–9
Prejudice No Way website 160
preparatory schools 15
preschool *see* kindergarten/preschool
Prices and Incomes Accord 28–9
prior-to-school contexts 122–7, 133, 134
private/for-profit child care centres 129
private schools 15
professional accountabilities and expectations 111–14
professional education re inclusion 171, 180
professionalism for educators 294–309
  ethics 306–8
  expertise 295, 299, 300, 302
  key expectations 295
  managerial 295–7, 304
  performativity 296
  public accountability 305
  quality improvement 296
  relationships 295, 297–306, 308
  relationships with authorities 303–6
  relationships with colleagues 301–3
  relationships with parents 298–301
  shifting view of 296
  traditional 295, 296, 297, 304
Project Approach and Emergent Curriculum 223
Project Headstart, USA 23
public accountability 305
public education, history of 14–20, 35–6
  Aboriginal children 15, 18–19
  age appropriate 19–21
  compulsory attendance 15–16, 18, 20, 45
  free 18
  secular 16, 18
  state-funded 16
push down phenomenon 104

quality 136–7
  concept of 137
  interactions with children 235–7
  measures of 136
  Montessori approach 85
  professionalism and 296
  rating system 126, 136, 217
Quality Improvement and Accreditation System (QIAS) 136
Quality Improvement Plan (QIP) 136, 247
Queensland College of Teachers (QCT) 191

Index

racial identification study 54
racial inclusion
   embedding Aboriginal perspectives 173–6
   Indigenous children 159–60, 168
   promoting 54, 69, 158–9
racialising practices 175–6
reception *see* kindergarten/preschool
Reggio Emilia Educational Research Project 78–81,
   99, 113, 261, 279
   'community' and 'dialogue', notions of 80
   documentation 81, 113
   environment 279, 280
   view of childhood 80, 261
regulatory authorities 133
   relationships with 305–6
regulatory culture 304
Reid, Sir George Houston 20
relationships 231–48
   building 241–4, 248
   connecting patterns of 272–3
   pedagogical 225
   professionalism and 295, 297–306, 308
   supporting children's learning 225, 231
relationships with authorities 303–6
   appraisal of work practices and outcomes 304
   employers 304
   legislation 304
   professionalism 303–6
   public accountability 305
relationships with children 225, 232–7
   affecting learning and development 253–5
   basis of ECEC work 232
   educator's view of children 232
   infants 252–5
   listening pedagogy 233–5
   modelling pro-social behaviour 236
   play and 236–7
   quality interactions 235–7
   reciprocal 236
   responsiveness 253–5
   social environment 237
   temperament and 254
relationships with colleagues 244–7, 260, 301–3
   collaboration 245, 246, 301
   collegiality 245–7, 260, 301
   communication 261
   cooperative planning 261
   diversity, accepting 261
   hierarchy 303
   infants, caring for 260–1
   mood of workplace 260
   National Quality Standard 244
   para professionals 244
   professionalism 301–3

   respect 244, 245
   teamwork 245, 246–7, 301
   unity 302
relationships with families 107–11, 170, 199, 225,
   231, 237–44, 298
   Aboriginal families 152–3
   building sense of community 243
   collaborative partnerships 199, 238, 241
   communication 108, 109, 240, 259
   connecting curriculum to interests 242
   cultural competence 225, 240–1
   different ways of participation 241
   documentation, involvement in 242
   exchange of information 243
   family diversity 239
   hierarchical relationship 299, 300
   infants' families 252, 255, 259–60, 264
   linking with community organisations 244
   National Quality Standard 152, 199, 259
   parent education 299–301
   parent participation 298–9
   partnership 107–11, 170, 199, 225, 238, 264, 298
   partnership and involvement distinguished
     238–9
   professionalism 298–301
   strategies for building 241–4
   supporting children's learning 225, 231
   transformative relationships 240
   working parents 241
religious schools 15
   opposition to public schooling 16
research ethics 188–90
Researching Effective Pedagogies in the Early Years
   (REPEY) study 223, 224
responsiveness 253–5, 273
Revolutionary Planning Group 67–8
Rinaldi, Carlina 99

safety and hygiene 267
same-sex parents 176–8, 239
Scandinavia *see* Nordic countries
school
   Aboriginal content 156
   compulsory 15, 18, 20, 35, 45, 124, 127–8
   constitutional responsibility for 44
   curriculum 133, 134
   ECEC context 123, 124, 127–8, 133
   history 14–15
   Indigenous children *see* Aboriginal and Torres
     Strait Islander children
   mass schooling 35, 42–5
   policies 133
   regulatory authority 133
   starting age 20, 36–7, 128

321

Index

school inspectors 18, 19
school performance data 111, 134
SDN Beranga 275–6, *277*, *278*, *281*, *284*
self-regulation, developing 254
shared sustained thinking 234, 276
SIDS 267
situated knowledges 52
sleep
  checking infants 267
  infant's routine 254, 255, 259, 260, 264
  SIDS 267
social class and education 55, 56
social construction of childhood 35, 37, 57, 261
social inclusion *see* inclusion
social justice principles 101–3, 200
socialisation 43, 56
socio-economic disadvantage and vulnerability 100,
  166
  Indigenous children 144, 146, 152
sociology 55–60, 233
  childhood studies 57
  cultural capital and habitus 55–6
  key ideas 56
  research 56
Special Integrated Community Engagement (SpICE)
  model 150
special schools 166
staff relationships *see* relationships with colleagues
staffing arrangements 257
Stephanie Alexander Gardens 115
Stolen Generations 38–42, 168
stories 265
stress, effect of 253
summative assessments 227
sustainability 284–9
  adoption of principles of 285
  Brundtland Report 286
  ECA Code of Ethics 288
  environment of centre 275, 284–7
  EYLF 287–9
  global 285
  learning about 218, 219, 284–7
  My Time, Our Place Framework 287, 288
  National Quality Standard 288
  social 284, 285
sustained cognitive engagements 234
sustained shared thinking 234, 276
Sydney Day Nursery (SDN) Association (NSW) *16*,
  17, 22, 43, 132, 133
  Beranga 275–6, *277*, *278*, *281*, *284*

Taylor, Affrica 66
teachers *see also* educators
  assessment 19

Finland 37
salary 19
terminology 7
training 19, 23, 37
teachers' associations and unions 19
teachers' colleges *17*, 19, 22
teamwork 245, 246–7, 301
technology, effect of 114
Telethon Kids Institute 100
temperament 254
theories 51–2
  bottom-up 51, 52, 68
  critical theory 65–8
  developmental psychology 52–5
  early childhood education approaches applying
    72–88
  feminism 60–5
  modification of 51
  sociology 55–60
  top-down 51, 52, 68
Tonkin, Daryl 151
'Too Much Too Soon' campaign 104
top-down theories 51, 52, 68
transformational teaching 66–7
transformative relationships 240
transitions 107–8

unhurried time 258
United Nations Convention on the Rights of
  Indigenous Peoples 169
United Nations Convention on the Rights of Persons
  with Disabilities 169
United Nations Convention on the Rights of the
  Child (UNCRC) 46, 58, 98
  African Charter 46
  children's rights movement 58
  concept of childhood 35, 46
  Euro- and US-centric view 46
universal access to ECEC 102

vaccinations 268
Vygotsky, Lev 53, 76–7, 98

Walkerdine, Valerie 54
ways of learning 96–7
  Aboriginal children 153–5
'What Works' website 147, 160
Whitebread, David 104
Wirt, Rev Loyal Lincoln 44
wise practice 131
working mothers/parents
  attitudes to 21–2, 25, 27–8, 45, 260
  purpose of ECEC for infants 260
  relationship with 241